PRAISE FOR *LEAP*

"A truly remarkable book that addresses the fundamental challenge facing managers who seek to sustain growth. Powerful case examples illustrate important concepts drawn from science and sociology as well as business."

—JOSEPH L. BOWER, Donald Kirk David Professor, emeritus, Harvard Business School

"Howard Yu's excellent new book answers the most fundamental question in business—how do we survive over the long term through thoughtful adaptation? *Leap* shows you how to go about deliberately thinking about adapting your business, and investigates the forces of technology and today's global market realities that companies must either adapt to thrive, or ignore at their peril. Every leader can benefit from the wisdom found in this book."

—JØRGEN VIG KNUDSTORP, Executive Chairman, LEGO brand group

"In a world driven by global competition and constant change, businesses increasingly struggle to achieve long-term success. This book is a unique source of strategic ideas that will enable complex organizations to reinvent themselves and drive sustainable growth."

—URS ROHNER, Chairman, Credit Suisse Group

"Howard Yu argues that, even in a future age of machine intelligence, the human ability to innovate will be the primary factor enabling companies to thrive. His advice will be invaluable to managers and CEO's worldwide."

—V. G. GOVINDARAJAN, Coxe Distinguished Professor of Management at the Tuck School of Business, Dartmouth University, and author of *New York Times* bestseller *Reverse Innovation*

"At a time when big business is challenged by start-ups, when 100 year old business models have run out of steam, and when you next competitor can come from a totally unrelated industry, Howard Yu offers important guidance on how to reinvent corporations and the need for top leaders to show compassion, pride, solidarity and vulnerability as organizations embark on the process. The marriage of big data and humanity can fundamentally change business. I can't recommend this book highly enough."

—POUL WEIHRAUCH, Global President Petcare, Mars Inc.

"As technology's tectonic shifts reshape how companies win, Howard Yu shows the criticality of good management today. In *Leap*, he's written a valuable guide to help managers prepare their companies for long and successful lives."

—KEITH FERRAZZI, Chairman of Ferrazzi Greenlight
and author of *New York Times* bestsellers
Never Eat Alone and *Who's Got Your Back*

"A deeply thoughtful journey on why human curiosity and creativity matter more, not less, than ever in the new brave world of ubiquitous connectivity and smart machines. And why and how we as leaders need to learn to leap—and not just incrementally extrapolate what we already know."

—JOUKO KARVINEN, Chairman of Finnair

"This book provides great frameworks to help you rethink the role innovation plays in your business. A terrific and inspiring read, very accessible and deceptively easy to absorb. It challenges readers to think differently and act differently to generate new growth from products and services."

—CHENG HSING YAO, managing director of GuocoLand Singapore

"Professor Yu believes pioneering companies can in fact thrive if they are prepared to rethink the way they do business."   —*Financial Times*

"Yu is a fluent and imaginative storyteller. He has a knack for the pithy phrase. The substantive, detailed accounts he offers really hit home. That may be in part because the products he describes—pianos, cotton, soap— play an active role in family life. But it's also because Yu makes an eloquent plea for the primacy of human judgment and influence."

—*Strategy+Business*

"This deeply researched mix of strategy guide and business history is a strike against complacency."   —*Inc. Magazine*

"A live-wire personality with a boyish look that makes him appear younger than his 38 years, Prof Yu is an expert on corporate disruption— why it happens, what it means, and how companies can prevent it from happening to them."   —*Straits Times*

LEAP

LEAP

*How to Thrive in a World
Where Everything
Can Be Copied*

HOWARD YU

PUBLICAFFAIRS

NEW YORK

PublicAffairs
Hachette Book Group
1290 Avenue of the Americas, New York, NY 10104
www.publicaffairsbooks.com
@Public_Affairs

Printed in the United States of America

First Edition: June 2018

Published by PublicAffairs, an imprint of Perseus Books, LLC, a subsidiary of Hachette Book Group, Inc. The PublicAffairs name and logo is a trademark of the Hachette Book Group.

The Hachette Speakers Bureau provides a wide range of authors for speaking events. To find out more, go to www.hachettespeakersbureau.com or call (866) 376-6591.

The publisher is not responsible for websites (or their content) that are not owned by the publisher.

Print book interior design by Linda Mark

Library of Congress Cataloging-in-Publication Data
Names: Yu, Howard, author.
Title: How to thrive in a world where everything can be copied / Howard Yu.
Description: New York: PublicAffairs, [2018] | Includes bibliographical references and index.
Identifiers: LCCN 2018009025| ISBN 9781610398817 (hardcover) | ISBN 9781610398800 (ebook)
Subjects: LCSH: Strategic planning. | Competition. | Organizational change. | Technological innovations—Management.
Classification: LCC HD30.28 Y7995 2018 | DDC 658.4/012—dc23
LC record available at https://lccn.loc.gov/2018009025

ISBNs: 978-1-61039-881-7 (hardcover); 978-1-61039-880-0 (ebook)

LSC-C

10 9 8 7 6 5 4 3 2

To the memory of my father, Jimmy

CONTENTS

PART III
WHAT NEEDS TO HAPPEN NEXT

Introduction

HOW COMPETITION WORKS

The opening up of new markets, foreign or domestic . . . illustrates the same process of industrial mutation that incessantly revolutionizes the economic structure from within, incessantly destroying the old one, incessantly creating a new one. This process of Creative Destruction is the essential fact about capitalism.

—Joseph Schumpeter,
American-Austrian economist (1883–1950)

O UTLASTING COMPETITION IS DIFFICULT. DOING SO OVER decades or a century often seems impossible. Since the great Industrial Revolution, every country that has become rich started by copying others: the French copied the British, the Americans copied the Germans, and the Japanese pretty much copied everybody else.

In the midst of this competition, countless players fell. Yet some pioneering companies have managed to endure and even prosper over the course of centuries. How is that possible?

WHEN EVERYONE'S A GENIUS: A RACE TO THE BOTTOM

Greenville, South Carolina, 1872

Henry P. Hammett—who was the mayor of Greenville, South Carolina, a century and a half ago—was a happy man. He was also a man of considerable size. He rode in a buggy specially made to hold his magnificent plumpness. Bald-headed and clean-shaven with heavy jowls and pasty skin, Hammett was no stranger to the Carolina elite. Addressing a gathering at the City Club, the Greenville native pronounced the arrival of the Richmond and Danville Railroad.[1] "The section of [the Piedmont] along its entire line possesses all the natural advantages of all the elements necessary to make a county rich, prosperous, and great," bellowed Hammett at the audience. "The traveler passing through it cannot fail to be impressed with its beauty and advantages, and the capitalist must see that it is one of the very best fields for investment."[2] To the mayor, the newly launched railroad was the Piedmont's best chance at reforming its economic outlook. It offered an opportunity to shed the Piedmont's former reputation as a poor white enclave burdened by indebted farmers and mountain dwellers—remote, aloof, and primitive.

During the golden age of American railroading between the late 1870s and 1890, some 73,000 new miles of track were built. That translated into about 7,000 miles a year. Much of that went into the Deep South and western areas.[3] The vision of a national rail network that traversed the Piedmont, linking it to Charlotte and Atlanta, extending up to New York and down to New Orleans, and cutting through the shortest possible route in a straight line was so arresting that the Piedmont railroad advertised itself as an "Air-Line"—a term that predated commercial aviation.[4] It was also a vision so compelling that Mayor Hammett took up his own advice given at the business gathering and set up the Piedmont Manufacturing Company (PMC), taking advantage of the newfound connectivity. On March 15, 1876, PMC began exporting cotton sheeting rolled onto cylinders with diameters of up to 36 inches, using the most modern textile machinery available for manufacturing, to a fast-growing market overseas: China.

The project was a huge success. By 1883, after acquiring some $80,000 worth of machinery, PMC had become the largest textile producer in South Carolina, with 25,796 spindles and 554 looms. Five years later, Hammett opened a second factory, Piedmont Number Two. Then he opened a third, Piedmont Number Three, the following year.

The Chinese loved the cheap, coarse, durable cloth. Consumers started to sidestep the more expensive British imports, and the Piedmont's low wages and large factories became known worldwide. It turned out the demand for textile goods, like that of many other commodities—coal, petroleum, iron, and steel—was highly elastic. Consumers bought more cloth if the price was lower; they stopped buying in the face of a price increase. A traveler wandering through China reported, "There was not a hole in the East in which I did not find a Piedmont brand."[5]

Despite this breakneck expansion, others quickly came to dwarf PMC. Bigger names—Holt, Cannon, Gray, Springs, Love, Duke, Hanes—swept through the region as the international market took off. Collectively, they ended the tight grip British manufacturers had over the Asian market since the Industrial Revolution. And by the 1930s, southern spindles accounted for 75 percent of the US total. Local news routinely attributed the stunning success to the salesmanship and ingenuity of the hardworking southerners, who had pretty much put everyone else out of business.

Then the one-dollar blouse from Japan arrived.[6]

Shortly after World War II, it was the Japanese who acquired the same knack for ingenuity and low wages. These hardworking foreigners produced textiles even more cheaply than the Piedmontese. But over the course of the following decade, apparel production in Japan would also slip to even cheaper labor in Hong Kong, Taiwan, and South Korea. And when the wages rose in those places, the textile plants moved farther out to China, India, and Bangladesh in an epic race to the bottom. Textile workers in China and Indonesia in 2000 were paid less than $1 an hour; in the United States, workers earned around $14.

By the end of the twentieth century, large, populous US mill towns had all but dwindled to mere shadows of their former selves. Industrial buildings were boarded up and abandoned, painfully repurposed, or reopened as museums. In October 1983, a fire destroyed much of Piedmont Number One—which had been designated a National Historic Landmark in recognition of the company's importance to the South's textile industry. No one was hurt. Weeds had long sprouted through the cracks of the company parking lots. There wasn't anyone around. Piedmont Number One had, in fact, stopped manufacturing textile in 1977. The remaining ruins were dismantled and quietly hauled away and the name was removed from the National Register of Historic Places.[7] Today, the Greenville Textile Heritage Society continues to record the living memories of its aging inhabitants, using a method that some historians would readily agree with: oral history.[8]

One might therefore conclude that textile manufacturing is just exceptionally transient, and no one can prosper for long. Yet it's not the only one. Take the personal computer, for instance.

Consider for a moment the engineering marvel of the hard disk drive (HDD). With conventional tape storage, if a user needed to access data located at the end, the drive had to read through the entire tape before it could look up the relevant information. HDD sped things up by storing and retrieving blocks of data, not sequentially as was the case with cassette tapes, but in a random-access manner. To do so, a hard drive made up of rotating disks spins some seven thousand times per minute while magnetic heads arranged on moving arms read and write data onto the disks. The technological feat is equivalent to a pilot flying a fighter jet at over 600 miles per hour at an altitude of around 3,000 meters (about 9,850 feet) and dropping tennis balls into buckets six hundred times without making a single mistake. This was the kind of engineering marvel that only IBM's San Jose laboratories could ordain in the 1950s. Launched in 1956, the first workable model drew much inspiration from Thomas Edison's early phonograph cylinders.[9] Since then, HDD technology has substantially improved—the physical size of the hard drive has been shrunk while the storage capacity has multiplied. But the center of innovation slipped elsewhere. Today, competitors sprawl across the globe. Toshiba in Japan, followed by several Taiwanese companies, has come to aggressively compete in the sector with brutally efficient manufacturing processes. So fierce has been the pricing pressure that the industry has been driven to a zero-profit-margin subsistence.

The renewable energy sector is another example. Wind turbines, the business of which General Electric (GE), Siemens, and Vestas pioneered, were once almost entirely made by Western companies. In less than two decades, Chinese manufacturers, such as Goldwind and Sinovel, have become major suppliers in the global market, grabbing much market share from the earlier players. Then there is solar panel manufacturing, which offers yet another example, with China's Yingli achieving the leading position as the world's largest manufacturer in 2013. In fact, seven of the top ten panel makers—all latecomers to the sector—are now based in China.

From textiles to computer storage to renewable energy, one question applies: Is the displacement of early pioneering companies an inescapable fate in the modern economy? Or is it possible to prevent being buried by the competition?

THE MIRACLE DRUG

Basel, Switzerland, 2014

A five-minute drive away from downtown Basel, in northwestern Switzerland, is a sprawling web of integrated office complexes. They constitute the global headquarters of the world's third-largest pharmaceutical firm, Novartis. Fanning out from the main courtyard, each building features elements associated with the contemporary architecture: stainless-steel structures with floor-to-ceiling glass walls; minimalist gravel gardens occasionally met with larger-than-life, ultra-modern sculptures. If not for the hordes of black-suited managers and white-coated technicians, this place could be mistaken for a museum of modern art.

British architect Sir David Alan Chipperfield designed one of the buildings, the Fabrikstrasse 22. Its open spatial structure is aesthetically striking, as noticeable as the interdisciplinary collaboration demanded of the scientists working inside. Inside these buildings, biology, chemistry, computational science, and medicine all come together; experts run cellular experiments and data-heavy analyses to uncover the main culprits behind cancers. Such efforts are part of a larger endeavor to treat the untreatable. And the sleek, modern headquarters reflect the level of prosperity Novartis has come to enjoy.

Although the buildings are new, its location is not. The company's two predecessors, CIBA-Geigy and Sandoz, which merged to form Novartis in 1996, had long settled along the banks of the mighty Rhine and their histories ran deep in Basel. CIBA had begun producing its first fever-reducing drug—antipyrine—in 1887. In 1895, the competing firm, Sandoz, manufactured and marketed synthetic saccharine and plant-based codeine. Roche, another Swiss rival established in 1896, expanded abroad: first to Milan in 1897, then to Paris in 1903, and to New York in 1905. More than a century later, in early 2014, the combined market capitalization of the two giants, Novartis and Roche, was still on the upswing, exceeding $400 billion. Novartis alone in 2014 spent $9.9 billion on research and development, a staggering sum that Roche closely matched.[10]

Unlike other industrial-heartland-turned-rust-belt cities, Basel's standard of living remains one of the highest in Western Europe. Across the Rhine is an eclectic collection of city center buildings: impeccable old town houses surrounded by narrow stone streets, exemplary industrial structures, and contemporary residential estates—all vastly different in style, but coexisting in perfect harmony. Unlike the Piedmont's short-lived fortunes, Basel's bounty seems limitless.

So, why were the economic prospects of the textile companies so brutally transient while those along the Rhine are so graciously stable? When they face the onslaught of new competition, what causes some pioneers to escape relatively unscathed while latecomers sweep others away?

A PEARL SHINES NO MORE

When they come face-to-face with a puzzle, academics read, observe, interview, debate, and write about it. This book is the direct result of research efforts that began when I joined the IMD business school in Switzerland as a full-time faculty member back in 2011. The executive education programs have served as my primary laboratory, allowing me to explore the core idea regarding how businesses thrive in a world where everything can be copied. The program participants, many of them seasoned international business leaders from different industries, have been my intellectual guides, taking me through their firsthand accounts about the rise and fall of even lesser-known companies. From this vantage point, I have enjoyed a view of the collective experience and the privilege of arriving at an overall synthesis.

Still, my fascination—or perhaps, obsession—with industry dynamics and the constant displacement of early pioneers goes back much further to a time before I thought of joining academia. Born and raised in Hong Kong, I watched the inevitable migration of knowledge and capital. I remember my elementary school teachers describing the economy of Hong Kong as an "entrepôt," a term the British applied to my city when it served as the only window between China and the rest of the world. Virtually all merchandise and goods—cheese, chocolate, automobiles, raw cotton, and rice—had to pass through Hong Kong on their way in and out of China.

With its low labor costs, Hong Kong rose as a major manufacturing hub for labor-intensive industries. The once-sleepy fishing village became "the Pearl of the East," a shining example of economic development. By 1972, Hong Kong had replaced Japan as the world's largest toy exporter, with garment and apparel manufacturing forming the backbone of our economy. Li Ka-shing, one of the richest men in Asia with an estimated net worth of $30 billion, started out as a factory man, a supplier of hand-knit plastic flowers, before he moved into property development, container port operation, mass transportation, retailing, telecommunications, and much else.

But in the early 1980s, Hong Kong's manufacturing cluster imploded. Factories moved to mainland China and, with them, manufacturing jobs. They first moved across the border to Shenzhen, then to Guangdong Province, and then to the rest of China. Unemployment in Hong Kong soared, crushing the optimism that had characterized residents for so many years. In the year of my graduation from college, my classmates were speaking of the need to acquire new skills to remain self-sufficient. That was before we had landed our first jobs. To survive, we told ourselves, we had to reinvent.

And Hong Kong did just that. It cast aside its former manufacturing and colonial identity and reinvented itself as a financial and logistics hub for the region. That reinvention of Hong Kong was where I grew up. It happened at the time when policy makers throughout the world were singularly praising outsourcing as "efficient." It all happened before any free-market economist became alarmed that emerging market firms might one day catch up with established ones in the West. It was an era of unbridled trust in globalization. But for us Hong Kongers, including myself, it was the age of distrust. Everyone I spoke to yearned for stability and continuity. I wanted to find out how to achieve just that.

STABILITY, AN IMPOSSIBLE QUEST?

Why is it that knowledge and expertise mercilessly fled across the border from the Piedmont and Hong Kong, while Switzerland's homegrown industries continue to remain solid, intact, and prosperous?

When I pose this question to senior executives, they often look quizzically at me, then flatly state, "Pharmaceuticals are more high-tech than textiles and toys," or "Big Pharma owns a lot of patents," or some variants of such answers. The reasoning is based on the observation that complex drug discovery and commercialization have so far protected the Swiss giants, whereas the absence of a requirement for special skills and knowledge in garment and toy manufacturing offers no protection to anyone in the sector.

This explanation sounds compelling, even self-evident. But it fails to account for the fact that numerous industries with mind-boggling technologies have also failed to resist competitive encroachment, and lower-cost competitors have displaced them over time. If complex knowledge and technology were the deciding factor in deterring competition, economists would have been able to show a survival chart plotting the typical life span of a company against the industry's technological complexity. The more complex the technology in a sector, the longer the average life span of a typical incumbent.

This would make a simple, elegant, and noteworthy model worth hammering into the minds of business school students all around the world.

Alas, no such graph can be plotted. Foreign rivals arriving late on the scene have outcompeted the established pioneers behind products as diverse as hard disks, automobiles, wind turbines, and mobile phones. Suddenly, even the term *high-tech* seems to require additional explaining. Weren't the textile manufacturers in the Piedmont once cutting edge, too? All these counterarguments prove that the high-tech explanation is insufficient to account for the disparity between the fates of those from the Piedmont and the fates of those from Basel.

A second common explanation for the disparity concerns the nature of knowledge itself. Some executives rightly point out that pharmaceutical discovery remains highly uncertain and risky. This is evident from Novartis's astronomical research and development costs, which it incurs with no guarantee that a drug will succeed in clinical trials and eventually make it to the marketplace. Today, commercializing a single new drug can average some $2.6 billion, with the amount projected to double every five years. By comparison, the innovation efforts in such sectors as textiles, electronics, wind turbines, and solar panels are far less costly and more predictable. From this perspective, as long as a company operates within a sector in which product development remains highly uncertain, the window of opportunity remains closed to latecomers looking to threaten existing incumbents. Rich experience, deep knowledge, and subject expertise are needed to tackle complex problems inherently unpredictable; the barriers to entry are simply too high for inexperienced latecomers to overcome. Or so the explanation goes.

While it may sometimes be true, history is replete with examples of latecomers who successfully eliminated uncertainties previously thought insurmountable. Consider automobile production. For a long while, quality variance was accepted as a fact of life. Managers at Ford, General Motors, and Chrysler believed that no amount of engineering ingenuity could overcome fundamental human error. So, when Toyota and Honda started to introduce lean manufacturing and just-in-time inventory management, Western experts and consultants and academics were taken completely by surprise. They failed to imagine how a host of quality-control toolkits could bring a formerly unruly chaotic industry swiftly into order and discipline. Before long, Tokyo relegated the former automotive capital—Detroit—to its current rust-belt status.

So, foreign latecomers can indeed succeed in industries in which product innovation and manufacturing were previously considered inherently unpredictable, and we'll see yet another example in the next chapter. But why hasn't this scenario played out in the pharmaceutical industry or, at least, to as great an extent as it has in other industries? Yes, patents and regulations may bar copycats from selling the exact same formulations. But nothing forbids a latecomer from learning how to discover drugs in the first place and to develop that capability. Why hasn't anyone done so? Conversely, what can pioneering companies do to successfully prevent displacement and stagnation?

A ROADMAP AHEAD

"History doesn't repeat itself, but it does rhyme," goes the saying. The expression captures the spirit in which this book was written. Throughout this book, I will compare the industry histories and the actions that different companies have undertaken. Contrasting their diverging outcomes, I will distill five fundamental principles at work. These principles both explain and predict how companies can prosper when labor, information, and money move easily, cheaply, and almost instantaneously.

In the simplest terms, the search for unique positioning that guarantees sustainable advantages is illusory. Intellectual property, market positioning, brand recognition, manufacturing scale, and even distribution networks can never withstand competition for long. No value proposition, no matter how unique, remains unchallenged. Good designs and great ideas get copied regardless of patent laws and trade secrets. The only way to prosper under such conditions over long periods is to *leap*: Pioneers must move across knowledge disciplines, to leverage or create new knowledge on how a product is made or service is delivered. Absent such efforts, latecomers will always catch up.

Why, then, don't pioneering companies leap more often? Complicating this matter often is the fact that executives are under tremendous pressure to meet the ongoing demands of their current businesses. What is good in the long run hurts in the near term. To be ready to leap would therefore require a different way of thinking about and leading the business.

Principle 1: Understand your firm's foundational knowledge and its trajectory.

We first look at the question of why incumbents find it so difficult to preempt new competition. Even in the absence of any technological disruption or shift in consumer preferences, latecomers often mount formidable challenges against early pioneers. We look at how Yamaha's music business crippled Steinway & Sons as part of this investigation. There had been no fundamental change in piano making, but Steinway was almost destined to struggle. This counterintuitive and disturbing observation exposes why and how copycats can often encroach on and then overtake industry pioneers. To avert this dangerous trajectory would require executives to, first and foremost, reassess a firm's foundational or core knowledge and its maturity. Circumventing the danger must begin by knowing where we are.

Principle 2: Acquire and cultivate new knowledge disciplines.

What we will learn from the history of modern medicine is that knowledge uncovered in one area often leads to new discoveries elsewhere. And it is this ongoing discovery process that ultimately opens new paths for growth. In this light, competitive advantage depends most critically on the assimilation of new knowledge and the timely creation of new markets and new businesses. Only by forging ahead, rather than refining what has already been, can a pioneer avoid being caught by copycats. Such is how the once little-known Basel-based pharmaceutical firms have managed to stay ahead for nearly a century and a half.

The role of managerial choices cannot be overstated here. Granted, some firms are born lucky in their industries: new discoveries by the scientific community render the matter of where to leap a no-brainer. Other sectors are less lucky; there may be no obvious answer. Still, time and time again, I have come across companies whose prospects should have been doomed, yet they consistently came out in the lead. For instance, Procter & Gamble has maintained its leading position in household consumer goods by leaping toward new knowledge disciplines. We shall explore this in greater detail.

Principle 3: Leverage seismic shifts.

If history is a tool that enables us to understand the past—helping us establish the concept of leaping into new knowledge disciplines—we must project our understanding of history into the future. Where should we look for opportunities to leap?

Although important variances exist between industries, certain seismic shifts to the global economy will be felt by everyone regardless of who you are and where you live. Like the invention of the steam engine in the eighteenth century or the harnessing of electricity in the nineteenth century, two intertwining forces will propel all companies into the second half of the twenty-first century: the inexorable rise of intelligent machines and the emergence of ubiquitous connectivity.

All winners must leverage the seismic shifts around them and leap accordingly. So, whether one is a technology creator, traditional manufacturer, startup entrepreneur, or nonprofit organization, we must identify those forces that matter the most in the coming decades and reconfigure our competencies ahead of others.

Principle 4: Experiment to gain evidence.

The aforementioned principles notwithstanding, concrete choices must be made. A bold decision always looks good—until it is proved wrong. To borrow Donald Rumsfeld's phrase of "unknown unknowns," executives may not even be aware that they don't possess a critical piece of information. To facilitate evidence-based decision making, managers must carry out frequent experimentation to reduce the dark space of ignorance and to arrive at conclusions with the required level of familiarity.

Here is another way of looking at it. The biggest risk that threatens the survival of a large and complex organization lies in political infighting and collective inaction. Arguments that play out in the boardroom may resemble empty rhetoric and amount to nothing more than personal beliefs. Experimentation is the window of truth to let light in from outside. We will therefore look at how critical assumptions can be identified and then proved right through rigorous experiments.

Principle 5: Dive deep into execution.

Awareness is not the same as commitment, so insights alone never suffice. Because strategy and execution are inextricably linked, unless ideas are translated into everyday actions and operational tactics, a pioneer is still at risk of being displaced by copycats. Thinking doesn't equate to doing.

The fundamental advantage of well-weathered pioneers is their prior knowledge; when it is combined with a new knowledge discipline, they can alter the existing trajectory of product development. What makes it so hard for pioneering companies to leap, however, is that game-changing ideas can easily be filtered out as business proposals move up the corporate ladder. That's why committed executives at the very top must be ready to intervene and implement a new directive when necessary. I call the instances in which top executives personally intervene at critical junctures, wielding the power to overcome specific barriers, the CEO "deep dive." Deep dives are different from micromanagement because they rely on knowledge power rather than position power. This last principle removes the final hurdles that may stand in the way of an established company's efforts to reconfigure and rewire itself.

❖ ❖ ❖

Now that you've got this roadmap in hand, we'll begin by investigating precisely why some pioneers thrive while others die. These stories will inform our guiding principles for responding to an ever-changing, often confusing world.

PART I

WHAT HAPPENED

1

THE PIANO WAR: WHEN STRENGTH
BECOMES A WEAKNESS

> Those who cannot remember the past are condemned to repeat it.
> — GEORGE SANTAYANA,
> PHILOSOPHER (1863–1952)

THE FINEST PIANO OF ALL TIME

STRETCHING ALONG STEINWAY STREET BETWEEN ASTORIA BOU-
levard and Twenty-Eighth Avenue in Queens, New York City, is an
area commonly known as Little Egypt. Along the street, the Al-Iman
mosque faces a throbbing nightclub. A hookah bar shares the same
block with a mirror-lined bakery from which waft the smells of bak-
lava and Turkish delight. Continuing to walk north a little farther, one
would eventually come to the venerable Steinway & Sons factory.

The place looks like any old-fashioned plant, with red brick walls
and closely spaced windows lining two long wings. Inside, many of the
machines are older than the workers who operate them. Bare fluorescent
lights hang from the ceiling. Smooth jazz drifts out of a radio sitting in one
corner. A mile east of the plant, airplanes can be seen taxiing into position,
nose to tail, at La Guardia Airport, on land that Steinway once owned.

Steinway used to own a lot more. A tract of over 400 acres of land, including the entire Little Egypt, was once part of the Steinway Village. Surrounding the factory were a lumberyard, a cast-iron foundry, and workers' housing, as well as a post office, a library, a park, a public bath, and a fire department. There was a fire engine—Steinway Hose Company No. 7—which now sits immortalized in the New York City Fire Museum.[1] All this grandeur began in 1853, when a German immigrant named Henry Engelhard Steinway launched his piano-making firm with a plan to "build the best piano possible" by "treating each and every piano better than many doctors treat their patients."[2]

As far as piano making is concerned, little has changed over time. Steinway's insistence on handcrafting with minimal automation is still evident. To manufacture a U-shaped rim, the chassis of a grand piano, eighteen sheets of hard maple veneers, measuring 22 feet each in length, are manually coated with glue and stacked together. A team of workers, who once mostly included Italians but are now from many different countries of origin, wrestles the structured plank through the twisting confines of the factory floor, hauling it over to a bending press that shapes it like a grand piano. Starting from the straight edge, six men push hard, forcing the single piece around the curves in a synchronized, almost choreographed motion. Dripping sweat, they secure the bent plank in position and tighten it with some 65-pound giant clamps, twisting spindles, turning knobs, and hammering oversize wrenches as clanging sounds echo over the concrete floor. The newly pressed rim is then dated with white chalk and is sent to a dim conditioning room for ten to sixteen weeks to "relax" under controlled temperature and humidity before assembly can begin.[3]

To an outsider, a piano is bewilderingly complicated. Each piano is made up of nearly twelve thousand tightly fitting parts; tight fits are considered paramount to tonal quality. Even with the modern computer-controlled system, every single part, from the soundboard to the bass to the treble bridges, is deliberately cut such that it is slightly bigger than required. This allows experienced craftsmen to manually shave off the extra bulk by hand. "If the tool were to cut the wood to a standard size," general manager Sanford G. Woodard explained in

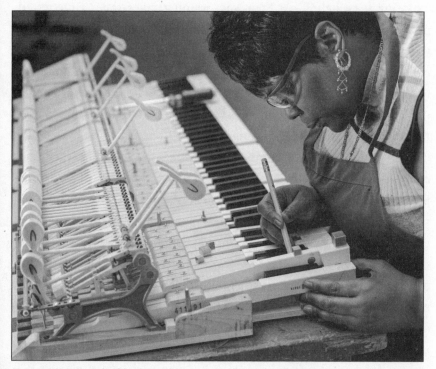

Steinway & Sons builds their pianos one at a time, applying skills that have been handed down from master to apprentice, generation after generation. After a century, their pianos are still made by hand in Queens, New York. *Photo*: Christopher Payne.

1991, "it would fit with others but not perfectly; the only way to do that is by hand."[4] It takes two years to manufacture a grand piano, and no two Steinways sound the same. Each has a distinct coloration of sound, and varying nuances of strength and delicacy. Every Steinway possesses its own "personality."

In this regard, a tone regulator is vital, whose guiding hands are to harness all of a piano's subtleness, getting the most out of each creation by amplifying its unique appeal. "Sometimes you have a piano that is nice and even and mellow . . . and you will disturb it too much if you try to make it brilliant," one tone regulator told the *Atlantic Monthly*. "Say, I would like to take a picture of something, a person, and I would like to have a lot of light in there—full light. And I don't have it. Yet with a subdued light, the object shows certain qualities, certain mysteries. . . . And you don't want to disturb that, risk it, by exposing it to light."[5] At Steinway, training takes time. Time-tested processes are honored. A tone regulator spends one to three arduous years as an apprentice before working independently.[6] "We believe in nepotism, supremely," Horace Comstock, working as a tour guide at the factory, told the *New York Times*. Visitors, who are shown photos of Steinway workers since the World War I era, are also reminded that the only noticeable change is their clothing.[7]

For more than 90 percent of concert artists, including such legendary virtuosos as Vladimir Horowitz, Van Cliburn, and Lang Lang, Steinway grand pianos are the instrument of choice. Arthur Rubinstein, whom many consider to be the greatest pianist of the twentieth century, once declared, "A Steinway is a Steinway and there is nothing like it in the world."[8] The pianos grace homes as stately as the White House, and museums as monumental as the Smithsonian Institution. They dominate the nation's concert stages, major symphony orchestras, and recording studios. They are known for their extreme longevity. The wood used to make a Steinway never rots, and the metal parts never rust. The idea of planned obsolescence, which has powered market growth for refrigerators, computers, and mobile phones, is not applied to pianos. And, unlike automobiles, Steinways don't have annual model changes. Former CEO Peter Perez reportedly said that the most serious competition he faced came from vintage Steinway grands, which sometimes command four times more than their original retail prices.[9]

Despite these remarkable achievements, Steinway's financial results over the past five decades have been anything but stellar. One crisis to another has been what management traversed in a prolonged downward spiral. In 1926, Steinway sold 6,294 pianos, its all-time record; in 2012, it sold just over 2,000.[10] The company changed ownership three times between 1972 and 1996, passing from Columbia Broadcasting System (CBS) to a group of private investors led by the brothers John and Robert Birmingham, and then to Selmer Industries—the number-one band instrument maker in the United States. All these changes had already happened before Steinway went public in 1996 to be listed on the New York Stock Exchange, only then to go private when the hedge-fund firm Paulson & Co. bought Steinway for $512 million in 2013. That sale in 2013 stirred up much apprehension among piano lovers, who decried the transaction and called it an opportunistic land grab. "The wolves have won again," denounced one person at Piano World, a large online forum.[11]

How can we explain the downward spiral that even the best piano maker in the world failed to avoid?

DYNASTY AT RISK

In midtown Manhattan, just steps away from Carnegie Hall on West Fifty-Seventh Street, stands what was once Steinway's flagship building. Close to its entrance was an octagonal space that executives called the rotunda, a two-story, 35-foot-high space with lavish paintings by N. C. Wyeth and Rockwell Kent. Under the painting of vibrant skies and billowing clouds, which were capped by a domed ceiling, allegorical scenes of lions, elephants, goddesses, and nymphs told the story of the influence of music on the human race.[12]

In February 1968, Henry Z. Steinway, the fourth-generation president who would also be the last president to bear the family name, was in a discussion with his executives. They had recognized that "the future principle competition would be Yamaha, the first time Steinway has been challenged on a worldwide basis." At six foot two, Henry was taller than anyone else in the family, and his Brooks Brothers suits accentuated his commanding presence appropriately. He urged his executives to do "what [was] necessary to meet this challenge" and laid out an action plan for circulation among the members of the management team:

1. Part of Yamaha's success in the US is due to availability of the product—their dealers can deliver at once and ours cannot. We must intensify our efforts to produce more grands.
2. We can never meet Yamaha on price, so our promotion, publicity, etc. must give the reasons why one should buy Steinway more intensively.

3. Our piano must be made to look better in detail—what we talked of as the "nit-picking" kind of complaints. I will arrange to bring in a Yamaha grand and a European Steinway for side-by-side comparison with ours.

4. Our policy of not permitting our product to be placed on sales floors with Yamaha by our dealers must be continued.

5. We shall try to assemble as much information as possible on Yamaha. I will undertake to put this together. Would like you all to search your files and send me copies of anything you have.[13]

What had seemed particularly striking to Henry was the rapid ascendancy of the new competition. Yamaha, once an obscure manufacturer, had been focusing on upright pianos to cater to the space-conscious Japanese, producing small home-use pianos infinitely different from any concert grand seen in the palatial showroom on West Fifty-Seventh Street. But somehow this competitor from Japan, from a country where almost nobody played a piano until a decade after World War II, had become a formidable challenger to the preeminent Steinway & Sons. What happened?

THE INCONVENIENT STRANGER

In 1960, Yamaha opened its first office in Los Angeles and hired Jimmy Jingu, an American of Japanese origin, to manage sales in the United States. But Jingu's efforts failed for the most part. Local dealers and retailers were reluctant to buy from an unknown company. "I'm sorry, we only deal with well-known brand names and companies of substance." "We won't buy Japanese." "Your company doesn't have staying power." Such were the comments Jingu kept hearing. Only one retailer, Sam Zimmering, was impressed by the piano's quality and value. Even so, he didn't think the Yamaha brand had the right appeal; he wanted to sell the pianos under some other names.

Fortunately, one of Zimmering's sales managers, Ev Rowan, was more enthusiastic. He thought Yamaha was crazy not to go it alone. "Put the Yamaha name on these pianos and I can sell them nationally,"

Rowan insisted.[14] With his fifteen years of retail and wholesale music experience and deep insights into the US market, Rowan was exactly the kind of person Yamaha needed. So, Yamaha hired him.

Gruff, temperamental, and self-important, Rowan was never a popular executive. But he was a man possessed by an idea. Working in a modest office in Pershing Square in downtown Los Angeles, he managed to persuade the Los Angeles Unified School District to buy a few dozen Yamaha pianos, lending the manufacturer much-needed credibility. To overcome the general perception in the United States that Japanese products were poorly made, Rowan also solicited independent piano tuners and technicians to share their opinions and organized workshops to demonstrate the piano's reliable quality. This unprecedented outreach program became the longest-running technician training course in history and was fondly called the "Little Red School House." Still, memory often plays strange tricks, discarding things that happened at an earlier time and ignoring details that were then so vivid. The rise of Yamaha pianos, as it turns out, goes back way further than these seminal events in the United States.[15]

Back in 1887, a young man in Japan named Torakusu encountered a Mason & Hamlin reed organ in the village of Hamamatsu. The imperial government had just begun to sponsor Western music. Scores of foreign manufacturers, including W. W. Kimball Co., Story & Clark, Estey Organ, and Mason & Hamlin, were exporting reed organs to Japan. Family lore has it that Torakusu decided to build one himself. Without access to the standard components, he made use of parts available locally and improvised the construction: He made the organ's keys of buffed tortoise shells rather than ivory, and made the reeds using a stoneware chisel to hand-cut each brass plate. The bellows consisted of black paper weather strips, and bovine bones constituted the vocal tabs.[16] No one knows how it was that the young Torakusu was so talented with tools that he could replicate what he had only previously seen. Yet his organ performed remarkably well.

Shortly afterward, Torakusu traveled across Hamamatsu, where his company's headquarters would soon be located. In the pursuit of new investors, Torakusu managed to raise ¥30,000 (about $10,000 in to-day's money) and christened the musical instrument company with his family name: Yamaha.

Yamaha popularized harmonicas during World War I. During World War II, like many companies in the private sector, Yamaha was drafted into the war effort. It produced boats, machinery, and other plastic products. The firm survived the defeat and returned to music shortly afterward. In 1947, with the Allied powers approving civil-ian trade, Yamaha began to export the famous harmonicas again. In 1950, Genichi Kawakami, the fourth-generation president, took over the firm, and almost immediately, Kawakami went on a three-month world tour.

The newly installed CEO was at first refused a plant tour at the C. G. Conn Company in Elkhart, Indiana, because no one wanted to entertain an unfamiliar Japanese stranger. But he got to visit the Kimball and Gulbransen piano factories in Chicago, the King band instrument factory in Cleveland, and the Baldwin piano factory in Cincinnati. In Europe, he toured Steinway's Hamburg plant and those of several other German piano makers. These visits must have been eye-openers. "We were so primitive in comparison. Until I had gone abroad, I did not realize that we had so much to learn. Our products were not good enough to export,"[17] said Kawakami. For the next three decades, Kawakami resolved to bring Yamaha in line with its Western counterparts and eventually surpassed every one of them. He installed automated woodworking machinery in the timber yard to process materials and had conveyor belts set up throughout the factory to transport the pianos along assembly lines.

In 1956, Yamaha commissioned Japan's first fully automatic dry-ing kiln, which became the largest capital outlay for the company to date. The kiln was designed to bake moisture out of freshly cut lum-ber and had an extraordinary capacity, able to hold enough wood for fifty thousand pianos—at a time when Yamaha was only making fif-teen thousand pianos a year. The project was harshly condemned as profligate and excessive and became a lightning rod for criticism. Still,

Kawakami was undeterred. Countering the assertions of all critics, the CEO insisted that Yamaha would soon fill all the unused space with new pianos. And he was right.

The Japanese had always embraced music. Mastering a musical instrument and owning a piano had long been seen as signs of success, education, and worldliness. The buoyant postwar economic growth and the country's strong interest in Western music turned it into an enormous domestic market for Yamaha. Piano sales swelled to an all-time high in the 1960s, when just about anyone in Japan with enough income would buy one. Piano production increased by 400 percent, from 25,000 in 1960 to 100,000 units in 1966. This made Yamaha the largest manufacturer in the world, with about seventeen times the volume of Steinway.

To spur demand further still, Kawakami established the Yamaha Music Foundation in 1966 as an independent nonprofit. It offered piano lessons for a modest fee, and the franchise spread to other countries. By the 1980s, the foundation was running nine thousand music schools in Japan with 680,000 enrollees and reaching nearly 1 million music students worldwide.

Meanwhile, inside Yamaha's factory, many manufacturing processes were automated, stamping out as much human interference as possible. A computerized system would identify pieces of veneer and direct them through overhead Y-shaped carriers to seven different rim presses, which corresponded to the different sizes of grand piano that Yamaha made. Just two employees were needed to guide the veneer to the correct position before a hydraulic cylinder came down with a pneumatic hiss and shaped it into the press. The rim adhesive would then dry in fifteen minutes, thanks to the high-frequency curing method.[18] The entire process was designed with minimal variations in production, a system that couldn't be more different from that of the heartbreakingly labor-intensive craftsmanship at Steinway.

Even so, most US-based musical instrument manufacturing companies did not consider Yamaha a competitor as late as the mid-1960s. When Story & Clark's vice president, Robert P. Bull, visited Yamaha in

1964, he reported being astounded that hardly anyone in the United States was aware of the firm's size and scope. "I was amazed," he said, upon seeing Yamaha's manufacturing prowess.

In 1966, Yamaha announced, "We have now succeeded in manufacturing a test model of what we believe to be the world's finest concert grand piano." This prototype was the Yamaha Conservatory CF, manufactured using traditional handcraft procedures, and was launched in 1967 at the Chicago Trade Fair.

It was common knowledge that Yamaha engineers routinely bought and dismantled Steinway grand pianos to emulate their methods. "If a quiz on Steinway pianos were given to Yamaha and Steinway engineers, I am not sure who would score better," a senior Steinway manager observed. Although many would challenge whether Yamaha's CF could be benchmarked directly against Steinway, the piano did receive some positive reviews and Yamaha did not hide its ambition. "We are chasing hard, we want to catch up with Steinway," stated one Yamaha manager, even though another executive conceded that it was "unfair to compare the two, it's like comparing Rolls-Royce with Toyotas." But they all agreed that the competition "makes us nervous, Steinway too, no doubt."[19]

To promote its concert grand pianos, Yamaha launched an "artist program" in 1987 that was almost identical to Steinway's Concert and Artist Program. It, too, sought to woo famous artists to choose its pianos for public performance. The biggest blow to Steinway came during a nationally televised concert by André Watts with the New York Philharmonic to commemorate his first concert at Carnegie Hall twenty-five years earlier. Watts had been on the roster of "Steinway artists"—among hundreds of other concert pianists who received complimentary Steinway pianos, whenever necessary, in return for public endorsements. These preeminent pianists had access to a three-hundred-unit-strong cache of pianos, available in over 160 cities throughout the United States. A pianist only needed to visit a Steinway dealer in the city, try out the grand pianos on offer (which could be as few as one piano in rural areas or more than forty in New York City), and ask that the chosen piano be delivered on a given day. Steinway would pick up the tab for all arrangements with the exception of a small charge levied for hauling the piano to the concert hall.

When the cameras zoomed in during Watts's concert, the television audience gasped at the name "Yamaha," which was emblazoned on the side of the piano in big gold letters. Watts was purported to be among the Steinway-approved pianists who had become disillusioned by what he deemed to be Steinway's poor service. The company's regional dealers lacked adequate facilities to maintain grand pianos at the required and expected level of perfection. Despite Steinway's assertions it was improving, progress had been slow and effort not obvious. Watts became the first defector to Yamaha's artist program. Other budding concert performers were also courted by Yamaha at major universities, such as Stanford and Michigan, and at music societies and conservatories, which often acquired dozens of pianos at a time. All this simply signified that a foreign player had finally invaded the concert arena, in the words of a Steinway official, the "lifeblood" of the company. Yamaha had become the largest piano builder in the world, with a production volume of 200,000 musical instruments a year, vastly overshadowing Steinway's 6,000.

IT'S GOOD TO BE LATE

When we study the history of piano making in my executive seminars, seasoned managers usually attribute Yamaha's success to the following factors: (1) Ev Rowan, the entrepreneurial sales manager who relentlessly pursued the American market; (2) the piano market boom in Japan, which allowed Yamaha to achieve economies of scale in its home base; (3) the automation of the manufacturing process, which drove down the cost of production even further; (4) Yamaha's voracious desire to produce concert grands, entering an ever-more-profitable segment of the market; and (5) a visionary leader who persisted with his expansion strategy over the course of three decades.

These are all true, yet they are merely proximate causes. They provide the immediate explanations for Yamaha's success but do not

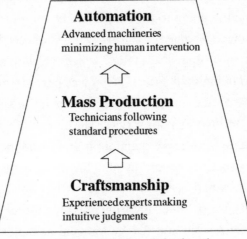

Figure 1.1 The knowledge funnel

articulate the ultimate cause. What is useful is to go deeper and see what ultimately enabled Yamaha to do everything listed above and to triumph over Steinway.

Consider this: Why do I drink water? The immediate answer is, "I am thirsty," which, of course, is only the proximate cause. The real reason is that water dissolves nutrients and minerals, and it helps to move them around our body. Water regulates body temperature and protects internal organs. Deprived of water, the human body rapidly falls apart. The conclusion? We need water to stay alive. This is what I call the ultimate cause in that the explanation goes back further along the chain of causation, referring to the fundamental condition that sets in motion the unfolding of fortuitous events.

Figure 1.1, which I call the knowledge funnel, depicts a process that we observe in piano making as well as in the textile industry.[20] The very same model, as we shall see, can also explain other industry dynamics, including those in the pharmaceutical industry and a host of sectors in our modern economy, which we examine in the next chapters.

At Steinway, where the production approach was rudimentary and traditional, it was the adept craftsmen, guided by deep expertise and human hands, who produced the unparalleled high-end musical instruments that concert pianists hankered for. Such are the defining characteristics of supreme craftsmanship. Human intuition and expert judgment rule the day. This is unavoidable in any nascent industry. Knowledge, at this early point, has yet to be translated into written rules. Know-how remains exclusive to a small group of leading experts.

But knowledge evolves. As experience accumulates, people's understanding improves. Industry know-how, which once resided solely in the mind of a few masters, is then increasingly documented for posterity. Business academics, who have the unfortunate tendency to overcomplicate things, call this process—knowledge codification—during which unspoken know-how is made explicit. But it really just means writing down what you know so that you can share it with colleagues. A consequence of this development is that lesser-skilled workers begin to replace the pioneering experts. Any workers can follow standard procedures, rulebooks, and guidelines. After all, when everything that an expert knows has been handed down as a rule book, there is little need for additional meddling. In other words, when expert knowledge is codified, more people can master the fundamentals. Human intuition becomes less important as rule-based decision making is replacing it. And perhaps more ominously, codified knowledge can be easily disseminated through borrowing, copying, imitation, or stealing. As history has proved, what begins as an act of human creativity by a world-class expert usually ends in machine automation.

NOT SMARTER, JUST FASTER AND BETTER

By automating many of the production steps, Yamaha led in the areas of standardization and precision manufacturing. Its conveyor belt system and the rapid drying kilns of enormous size meant the time required for Yamaha to produce a piano went from two years down to three months. During the initial phase of automation, standardized products always appear less sophisticated than those traditionally handcrafted. Machines are not capable of reproducing the kinds of intricate nuances found among handcrafted goods, and thus, products built using the newly automated processes are only suitable for the mass market or the low-end segment. But that low-end segment is precisely the foothold market that offers engineers the time, the money (however meager), and the opportunity to improve and do further work.

As technology and quality improve, this affordable version of the product attracts new customers, which in turn spurs demand further. Following this trajectory, the company that has mastered automation early on will naturally become the big winner, taking advantage of a growing industry. This is how Yamaha's meteoric rise began. This is how Steinway & Sons spiraled into decline, in large part due to its myopic obsession with craftsmanship at the expense of technological advancement and automation.

By the time Yamaha entered the concert grand segment, it was a global contender. With a far bigger balance sheet, a diverse set of technologies, and many advanced production techniques, Yamaha could marshal many more resources in marketing, distribution, recruitment, and production. The money it gained from the low-end segment had become the wellspring that allowed it to enter the high end.

The most remarkable part of this outcome is perhaps the fact that all these changes occurred while the underlying product stayed constant, which only makes Steinway's predicament all too painful to watch. Simply put, a piano involves hammers striking strings to make sound, as it has always been. The function and form of the finished goods and the requirements of leading artists had barely changed. Unlike Kodak and Polaroid that were decimated by digital photography, Steinway & Sons was nestled in a world of constancy. Still, as industry knowledge matures—from early-stage craftsmanship to late-stage automation—fortunes tilt, favoring early pioneers less and latecomers more. To compete successfully at different stages of the knowledge life cycle demands very different organizational capabilities. And they vary, not in degree, but in kind. When left unchecked, latecomers always crowd out early pioneers. It's nice to be late.

This is not to say that Yamaha never exerted creativity. Quite the contrary—as Yamaha strived to exploit the full potential of advanced manufacturing, it needed to introduce new processes and systems. Every time the company further automated its production, an act of innovation was involved. But creative talent shifts from building a higher-quality *product* through craftsmanship to devising a better manufacturing *process* based on automation to reduce costs and improve production yields. Thus, Yamaha ended up with ever-cheaper approaches to manufacturing pianos more efficiently and meeting the insatiable demand.

But couldn't a pioneer protect its know-how by filing patents and trademarks, thereby nipping latecomers' efforts in the bud? Couldn't Steinway & Sons have staved off Yamaha by guarding its trade secrets better?

Textile manufacturing in the early nineteenth century tells us otherwise.

THERE IS NOTHING IN THE WORLD THAT CAN'T BE LEARNED

In 1810, a thirty-five-year-old Harvard College graduate, Francis Cabot Lowell, traveled with his wife and young sons to England to engage in what many regarded as the first and most consequential episode of commercial espionage in modern history.

Textile manufacturing was regarded by many as the high-tech industry of its day. As imperial Britain knew all too well, its supremacy in global trade depended upon the tremendous mechanized textile machines. Between 1851 and 1857, exports of cotton products from England more than quadrupled, from 6 million to 27 million pieces annually.[21] By the end of the 1850s, cotton goods comprised nearly half of British exports. At its peak, Britain's textile industry manufactured almost half of the world's cotton cloth. A vast network of cotton mills flourished in the industrial basin of the Midlands, stretching through Glasgow, Lancashire, and Manchester.

To protect this all-important industry, the British government forbade any export of textile machinery and related factory diagrams and plans. Fearing that the skilled labor might carry ideas abroad, Britain prohibited textile workers from leaving the country. Offenders could be arrested on the spot, jailed for a year, and fined up to £200. Such rulings make modern-day patent laws and nondisclosure agreements look meek. Companies also went to great lengths to avoid information leakage. They closed mills to visitors, swore employees to secrecy, and cloaked their factories "with the defensive features of a medieval castle," embellishing machinery to make it appear more complex than it really was.[22]

Lowell, a blue-blooded Bostonian from an elite shipping family, presented himself as a "well-connected, mild-mannered American merchant traveling in Europe . . . for reasons of health."[23] He gained access to several large-scale British mills initially by connecting with his mercantile friends. During the two-year sojourn in Scotland and England, he must have strolled through dozens of plants while feigning inattention as he clandestinely piled up countless trade secrets.[24] A mathematics major at Harvard, Lowell possessed just the kind of aptitude to memorize the critical details of "cotton manufacturing"—the process flows, the details of gearing, and the inner working of a power loom. Before returning home to Massachusetts, he smuggled copious copies of machine drawings through customs. And Lowell turned out to be just one of many.

Countless others also evaded Britain's emigration laws and left for the United States with complementary technologies, sought-after skill sets and industrial know-how. By 1812, just about all textile mills in Massachusetts had mastered everything they needed to know about mechanized textile manufacturing.[25] And here lies the advantage of the latecomer: in the past, water-powered machinery was only used for spinning. Independent laborers working at home with their own equipment, commonly referred to as the cottage industry, carried out weaving. They constituted a network of small off-site facilities, located close to cities, where deep labor pools were readily available.[26] But Lowell's Boston Manufacturing Company reconfigured the manufacturing process by deploying water power for spinning as well as weaving, bringing both steps of the operation under one roof. Unlike its British counterparts, Lowell's firm had no legacy of existing infrastructure. He didn't have to worry about the depreciation of existing assets. By setting up a huge mill town, Lowell not only reaped the benefits of greater economies of scale, but also rid the company of its dependency on the local labor market. Turning rural areas into residential communities would, of course, require lots of capital investment. But that was exactly the sort of major up-front investment that would make British manufacturers—being profit-conscious and return-seeking—hesitate.[27]

British novelist Charles Dickens during his first tour to the United States in 1842 visited the new town of Lowell. He was profoundly moved by the material comfort offered to workers at the large facility, despite his reputation as the harshest critic against modernity of his time:

> I happened to arrive at the first factory just as the dinner hour was over, and the girls were returning to work; indeed, the stairs were thronged with them. . . . [They] were all well-dressed; and that phrase necessarily includes extreme cleanliness. . . .
>
> They were healthy in appearance, many of them remarkably so, and had the manners and deportment of young women: not of degraded beasts of burden. . . .
>
> The rooms in which they worked were as well ordered as themselves. . . . In all, there was much fresh air, cleanliness, and comfort as the nature of the occupation would possibly admit of. . . .
>
> I solemnly declare, that from all the crowd I saw in the different factories that day, I cannot recall or separate one young face that gave me a painful impression; not one young girl whom. . . . I would have removed from those works if I had had the power.[28]

Mill town after mill town sprung up across New England. The biggest of them all, the Amoskeag Mills on the Merrimack River, with 650,000 spindles and seventeen thousand employees, produced 500 miles of cotton cloth per day.[29] With their size and scale, the New England mills took the growing American mass market away from the British exporters, leaving the Brits just the niche market of fancy hats and goods, where greater "artisanal" expertise still mattered.

Artisanal or not, Britain's dominance over international trade was over, marking the beginning of an inexorable decline. During the

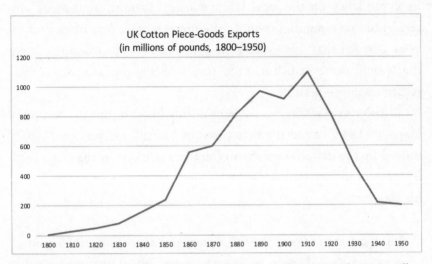

Figure 1.2 *Source:* R. Robson, *The Cotton Industry in Britain* (London: Macmillan, 1957), 332–333. Data reported for the initial year of each decade. Cited in Pietra Rivoli's *The Travels of a T-Shirt in the Global Economy: An Economist Examines the Markets, Power, and Politics of World Trade,* 2009.

steepest plunge in the early twentieth century, as shown in Figure 1.2, mills across Lancashire in the northwest of England closed at a rate of almost one a week. Scores of empty factories were the only legacy left of an industry that had once been Britain's pride.

THE RICHER YOU ARE, THE LESS YOU SPEND

As if history is destined to repeat itself, trade secrets and patents couldn't shelter Steinway, either. As early as the 1960s, CEO Henry Z. Steinway noticed the rising threats from Yamaha and was reportedly "scared to death of them."[30] Such intense fear and hatred had since characterized the relationship between the nemeses, but no significant reform occurred at Steinway. Over the next five decades, Steinway helplessly auctioned off, one after another, many of its buildings that had historically been part of the Steinway Village in northern Astoria, Queens. The original 400-acre campus was slowly chipped away, and eventually reduced to the gritty complex of a few red-brick factory buildings at the tip of the Steinway Street that we know today. During the course of half a century, sales declined from six thousand pianos a year to less than two thousand in 2012.

In a (frankly, too late) effort to fight back, Henry Steinway's successor, Peter Perez, reluctantly approved the launch of the Model K. It was an upright, slightly more affordable piano, made to compete against Yamaha. In a private conversation, nevertheless, CEO Perez confronted one of the members of staff, who had spent nearly two years on the project. "I still wonder if this is the best way to spend our limited time and resources," he asked. "Aren't we diverting our attention from grand pianos, where we're strongest? And won't a new product introduction at this time merely create delays and confusion? Maybe we should sit down and rethink our plans for the future." The Model K was finally launched after a long and gruesome internal debate. Predictably, it neither made an impact on Yamaha nor restored Steinway's dwindling fortunes.[31]

What prevented Steinway from responding more radically when time was still on its side? Why couldn't Steinway invest in automation and follow the same expansive strategy as Yamaha?

At the height of the rapid ascendancy of Japan's economy in the 1980s, Harvard professors Robert Hayes and William Abernathy published an influential article in the *Harvard Business Review* titled "Managing Our Way to Economic Decline." The authors accused American managers of relying too heavily on short-term financial measurements, such as return on investment (ROI), to guide investment decisions instead of taking a long-term view of product and technological development. American managers, in their view, were collectively suffering from "competitive myopia." Profits had gone into shareholders' pockets instead of updated machinery.

At about the same time, another colleague, Carliss Baldwin, together with the former dean of Harvard Business School, Kim Clark, argued that the unwillingness of American companies to invest in new technology was rooted in corporate aversion to cannibalizing existing products or processes. Managers feared most the eventuality that a company's new products and services with lower profit margins would cut directly into the sales of existing ones.[32] The authors offered a simple explanation for the seemingly irrational managerial behaviors. To evaluate investment opportunities, managers would often run the numbers through financial analytical tools, such as discounted cash flow (DCF) or net present value (NPV) calculations. The crux of such an exercise is comparing the investment proposals with the alternative scenario of not investing or doing nothing. To project the future cash flows or returns of different options, one has to extrapolate historical data. And by extrapolation, managers often assume that the present health of the company will continue indefinitely as long as the existing production system is adequately maintained.

But this is a dangerous premise. It's an unrealistic assumption that causes too many companies to hesitate to launch a new product with a lower margin than the existing one. It only drives managers to offer more high-end products in an attempt to differentiate oneself when responding to competitive pressure. And for Steinway, there was simply no more headroom for growth when the firm was already sitting at the top end. The inevitable result was the loss of market share.

Complicating the matter further is the extent to which the apparent benefits are deceptive when one becomes obsessed with marginal cost. Under the watchful eyes of the financial controller, upgrading an existing production process always appears more attractive than creating a completely new process. When reusing existing technologies or expanding the current production setup, only a relatively minor capital investment is required to increase production volumes. Or when an old factory adds another shift, the increased labor costs appear minimal because of the continued use of fully depreciated equipment assets. By contrast, creating something completely new—a fully automated assembly line, for example—involves up-front investment that may take many years to amortize, so it negatively impacts profitability in the near term.

For Steinway to fulfill some incremental demand, it didn't need to spend millions of dollars on automated factories. In the short term, it could simply hire another team of craftsmen to work an additional shift in the existing plant. This is classic marginal thinking. In their evaluation of the two alternatives—build something new or leverage existing infrastructure—managers ignored the sunk and fixed costs and based their decisions on the marginal costs and revenues that each alternative involved. This doctrine, as taught in every fundamental course in finance and economics, biases companies to leverage what they have put in place to succeed in the past instead of guiding them to create the capabilities they'll need in the future. The argument against building an automated factory is especially compelling when the quality of pianos rolling out from the assembly line could hardly meet the expectations of concert artists—the most powerful constituent of Steinway & Sons. So, from the perspective of a rational manager whose year-end bonus depends a lot on the business performance of the next quarter, why bother?

These two forces—the unwillingness to cannibalize current sales and the tendency to leverage what we have today—deprive many investment projects that pioneering incumbents desperately need to stay ahead in the long run.

TRAPPED IN THE GILDED CAGE

The calculation for Yamaha, by contrast, was considerably simpler. It did not have any legacy systems rooted in century-old refined craftsmanship. So, every dollar it invested in advanced production systems promised better-quality products that would generate ever-higher margins.

What's more, Yamaha was starting from the bottom of the heap, and its investors were accustomed to a much lower level of profitability than Steinway's. Ironically, their dimmed expectations had enabled Yamaha to invest in new capabilities and take on new markets. Investment at Yamaha wasn't an option, it was oxygen. At Steinway, it was always agonizing. What you see depends on where you stand.

In the face of increasing competition, as all struggling business leaders would, Henry Steinway turned to Washington for help. He lobbied the Nixon administration to extend the piano tariff on Japanese imports.[33] In the enormous hearing room, members of the Tariff Commission sat at the front, while the American piano manufacturers and

Japanese representatives sat on either side, facing each other. After the murmuring and rustling of the courtroom fell away, Henry Steinway proclaimed in his opening plea that his company was not itself affected by imports but was concerned for the other seventeen domestic manufacturers.

At one point, the cross-examiner representing the Japanese couldn't help but probe Henry why he would ask for more tariffs, even though he supposedly had more ordered than he could deal with. The CEO delivered a stock response, saying that his pianos were sold out because only Steinway manufactured the best piano in the world. The short supply was due to the painstaking training required to develop fine craftsmen. But it was clear to everyone in the room that Steinway was trapped in a gilded cage.[34]

As for Yamaha, it soon decided to sidestep future political wrangling and came up with a better strategy. It set up its own American piano factory in Georgia[35] and began to preach the "made in America" gospel.

WHEN STRENGTH BECOMES A WEAKNESS

The problem that Steinway faced was not uniquely American, nor was it specific to piano making. The problem was a pattern of thinking that had led to serious trouble for companies in all industries globally. The unwillingness to cannibalize existing sales and the obsession over marginal cost also explains why British cotton producers were slow to invest in new production methods, while Francis Lowell and his compatriots raced ahead. The same forces explain how the southern mills in the Piedmont region displaced the northern mills two decades later by building even larger-scale cotton mills; how the Asian manufacturers, in turn, supplanted the southerners by introducing the one-dollar blouse; and so on.

Before we go any further, let's pause and reflect on the implications of the knowledge funnel we mentioned earlier in the chapter. The knowledge funnel implies that any competitive advantage is transient. What made companies succeed as early pioneers won't keep them in the leading position as industry knowledge matures. Steinway & Sons relied on the same advantage for too long. Eventually, knowledge that resided in the form of craftsmanship and was embodied in the minds of experienced staff became all too limiting. In other words, core competencies turned into core rigidities, preventing the firm from responding appropriately to the strategic threat that Yamaha posed.

Steinway's difficulties might be mourned only by piano lovers, but there is a lesson in it for all of us. Managers must ask themselves what knowledge discipline is the most fundamental to their company. What is the core knowledge of their business? And how mature or widely available is it? And the kind of historic problem that Steinway faced has only escalated with time because of recent developments. Thanks to our increasingly connected world, powered by the Internet and modern communication methods, the duration of any advantage is shrinking. Written documents, digital records, people, and capital all migrate across geographical boundaries at speeds unimaginable just decades ago. Intellectual property, trade secrets, and even human expertise can only marginally defer the onslaught of latecomers. Soon enough, some latecomers will be armed with equal understanding and perhaps newer and more potent approaches that will topple the incumbents.

With this in mind, let's return to the Basel-based pharmaceutical companies that settled along the Rhine almost a century and a half ago and explore what enabled them to become the pioneers of the field and to maintain their leading positions so many decades later. What is so special about these drugmakers? How have they remained dominant when most pioneers in other equally high-tech industries—say, those associated with personal computers or wind turbines—have pretty much been dispossessed by others? How have they managed, at least so far, to circumvent the problems that have plagued everyone else?

2

THE FIRST ADVANTAGE OF A PIONEER: WHEN COMPETITION WORKS LIKE A MUDSLIDE

Just because something doesn't do what you planned it to do doesn't mean it's useless.

—THOMAS EDISON,
AMERICAN INVENTOR (1847–1931)

IN THE BEGINNING, THERE WAS CHEMISTRY

THERE HAD BEEN DYE MAKERS BEFORE THE DRUG PRODUCERS. The modern-day pharmaceutical industry—advanced and sophisticated—can be traced back to its lowly cousin: the textile industry. St. Gallen, now a tranquil city just south of the turquoise Lake Constance, was a busy manufacturing hub in the fifteenth century. Its quality textiles, best known for their intricate embroidery and exquisite lace, were sold throughout France, Britain, and Germany. The meandering rivers and magnificent lakes of Switzerland offered the otherwise hopelessly landlocked nation a convenient export route. The history of pharmaceuticals here was as much about science as reinvention. Born in the same era as this textile industry, the foundational knowledge began with organic chemistry. But it was the shift to other disciplines—time and time again—that enabled an industry where pioneers could thrive and escape the exact predicament that Steinway found inescapable.

Traditionally, textile-printing craftsmen obtained dyes directly from vegetable extracts.[1] Coloring was so precious that it was reserved for kings, nobles, and high priests. Madder roots, for instance, cost 90 German marks per kilogram in 1870, and one kilogram of madder would yield about 140 grams of dried red dye. Geigy, a chemist's shop in Basel that had been trading in "Materials, Chemicals, Dyes and Drugs of all kinds" for over one hundred years,[2] saw in 1868 that real opportunities lay, not so much in dyeing cloth itself, but in developing and manufacturing dyestuffs as input materials.[3] Geigy went on to retrofit a factory[4] to manufacture aniline fuchsine—a cheap "marvelous red"[5] on a "grand scale."[6] Geigy's chemical equivalent cost merely 8 marks per kilogram.[7] So, before long, the company was selling fuchsine as quickly as it could make it. Chemical dyes became a big moneymaker.

A few blocks east of Geigy's new factory was another bellwether chemical firm, which a silk dyer had founded in 1839.[8] When chemist Robert Bindschedler took over the business, he added many new dyestuff products and built up distribution outside Switzerland. The original workforce of thirty had doubled within a year,[9] and, by 1881, there were 250 workers and twenty chemists. Bindschedler renamed his company in 1884 the Society of Chemical Industry in Basel, or CIBA for short.[10] Five years later, manager Edouard Sandoz resigned from CIBA and founded his own firm, the Sandoz corporation.[11] With ten workmen and a 15-horsepower steam engine,[12] the first dyes Sandoz produced were alizarin blue and auramine.[13] By 1913, Geigy, CIBA, and Sandoz were exporting a total of 9,000 tons of dye around the world annually. The hardy mountain folk had turned Basel into a chemical powerhouse and themselves into dye magnates.

Despite all the commercial success, the deleterious side of the business was obvious. Dye manufacturing gave rise to dangerous pollution. Factory workers toiled in poorly ventilated facilities, holding only thin cloths over their nose. Washing after work was never enforced, and, in the evenings, workers would walk home with their arms, neck, and face smeared with brilliant streaks of iridescent sheen.[14] The toxins caused skin discoloration, blood in the urine, and convulsions. Bladder cancer, known as aniline tumor, was so common that local doctors described it as "the most noticeable occupational disease."[15] The life of a laboratory technician was hardly any better. Chemistry was poorly understood, and the search for better and brighter colors was left to trial and error among the brave. To extract uric acid, for example, lab technicians would boil barrels of animal fats, dissect boa constrictors, and grind bat feces.[16] They spent their days handling mixtures of hydrochloric and sulfuric acids, mixing caustic alkalis, and concocting poisons, including arsenic. The alchemy work was practically medieval, and explosions and fires happened often.

None of these challenges slowed down the Basel industry. During the heady gold rush, chemists, managers, entrepreneurs, and investors jostled to make a profit at every turn. The twentieth century would dawn before anyone paid attention to workers' welfare and the industry's environmental impact. Paradoxically, the deadly poisonous dyes that the Swiss pioneers so relentlessly pursued would one day yield a lifesaving enterprise.

THE WORLD'S FIRST BLOCKBUSTER

In 1883, a German chemistry professor named Ludwig Knorr successfully synthesized antipyrine, the first fever- and pain-reducing compound for treating influenza.[17] Until then, painkillers were derived from the botanical world. Cocaine was extracted from coca leaves, salicylic acid from willow bark, and morphine, the most potent of all, from opium poppies. The basic drug manufacturing technique was distillation, which involves boiling and steaming plant leaves that are then left to condense the vapor to obtain the active ingredients.

Born to a wealthy merchant family, Dr. Knorr wrote his dissertation on a series of experiments of phenylhydrazine, a compound commonly used as a dye intermediate.[18] His experiments led him to the creation of antipyrine, one of the first synthetic drugs ever made, starting with coal tar—a by-product of the coal industry discovered in the wake of the Industrial Revolution. Encouraged by his supervisor, Knorr filed a patent for his invention and worked with a small dye factory called Hoechst, located in a Frankfurt suburb, to manufacture the drug.[19] Antipyrine proved itself highly effective in reducing fever and treating influenza symptoms, at a time when epidemics repeatedly ravaged Europe. Sales took off.

Across the Atlantic, a doctor in the United States reported in 1885 that antipyrine "acted like magic" and cured his five most severely ill patients, who had previously suffered from migraines and on whom even morphine had had no effect.[20] Another physician from Rhode Island claimed that the effect of antipyrine was "almost immediate . . . and, within an hour or two, there [was] complete relief."[21] So popular was the new drug in the United States that the *New York Times* declared on January 1, 1886, that "among the many remedies that have been discovered to alleviate the ills of suffering humanity, none is more important than Antipyrine."[22] The only worry concerned "the manufacturers in Germany not being able to supply the demand" worldwide.[23] Antipyrine had become the world's first blockbuster drug.[24]

To the chagrin of Hoechst, CIBA began to produce the same compound in 1887. No patent protection existed yet in Switzerland for chemical products. In *le pays de contrefacteurs* (the land of counterfeiters),[25] Swiss chemists were free, and even encouraged, to imitate foreign inventions. The Swiss imitation was so successful that CIBA was awarded a grand prize at the 1900 World's Fair in Paris.[26]

Out of desperation, Hoechst promptly signed a price-fixing agreement that guaranteed CIBA and Sandoz a fixed portion of the worldwide business.[27] It was meant to prevent any one company from undercutting the other manufacturers. But, by then, the importance of this nascent pharmaceutical business was all too clear. CIBA would emulate the German model, from this point onward, to systematically invest in extensive research and development. Over the years, CIBA also deepened its external relationships with many universities and research institutes, and this early university-industry collaboration helped produce numerous technical papers, with research outcomes that served as guidance for technology development and contributed to the company's long-term performance.

Meanwhile, Sandoz established the first in-house pharmaceutical laboratory in 1915 and later appointed Swiss chemist Arthur Stoll head of research. Stoll went on to isolate an active ingredient, named ergotamine, from ergot, that was used to induce abortions and to stanch bleeding after childbirth. Under the name Gynergen, the drug was launched in 1921.[28] By the turn of the century, the three Basel companies—CIBA, Geigy, and Sandoz—had all established a solid foundation in organic chemistry and, consequently, had shifted their product focus from commoditized dyestuffs to the highly profitable pharmaceuticals. Making poisonous chemicals was less financially attractive than pursuing the elixir of life. But here lies the critical question: Why didn't the pharmaceutical industry become commoditized in the following decades, much as the traditional textile industry had? Recall the knowledge funnel mentioned in the last chapter. Had there been no other breakthrough discovery in drug making, the focus of the industry would have inevitably marched toward cost cutting. Dominating such a world would have depended as much on mass production techniques as it would have on automation by advanced machinery. As the piano war between Steinway and Yamaha had demonstrated, latecomers could have easily triumphed over the pioneers in this scenario.

Fortunately for CIBA, Geigy, and Sandoz, that was not the world in which they found themselves in Basel. Pharmaceuticals would soon move away from organic chemistry and jump into a whole new field. Starting from synthetic chemical compounds, a new wave of discovery in microbiology was about to push the industry in another direction. It was this new knowledge discipline—the study of microorganisms—that opened up headroom for growth in the subsequent decades.

THE MICROBE HUNTER

In February 1941, a British policeman fell desperately ill from a life-threatening infection of streptococcal and staphylococcal bacteria after a rose thorn scratched his face.[29] The infection was so menacing that his scalp oozed pus, and one of his eyes had to be removed.[30] Penicillin had already been discovered a decade earlier by Alexander Fleming. He had been among the first to notice that the "mold juice" from a certain fungus could dissolve bacteria. Even though no one had yet perfected the drug dosage and much was left to trial and error, the policeman's condition gradually improved through a series of experimental treatments.

Then, the supply of penicillin ran out. Surface culture fermentation in the laboratory—the only process available at the time—could not possibly produce an adequate quantity fast enough; scientists had to wait for new mold to grow. Desperate attempts were made to create more, including the retrieval of penicillin from the patient's own urine. But without enough medication, the infection returned. The policeman relapsed and died.[31] It wasn't until the outbreak of World War II that the pharmaceutical industry would master the mass production of antibiotics.

As World War II wore on, the Allied powers saw that the loss of military lives was due as much to unsanitary conditions as it was to bullets and bombs. It became clear that only through submerged fermentation in big tanks and large boilers, the same technique used in breweries, could doctors cease small-volume surface cultivation on isolated petri dishes. By 1943, Merck in the United States created just such a production process using *Penicillium chrysogenum* and cornstarch liquor. In less than two years,[32] 6.2 trillion units were being produced, a speed unimaginable when surface cultivation had been done in shallow trays. Pfizer, another US competitor, began its mass production in 1944, two years after being listed on the stock exchange. At a time when its annual revenue barely exceeded $7 million,[33] Pfizer boldly invested $3 million in converting an empty ice plant in Brooklyn, New York, with the goal of repurposing all of the 10,000-gallon tanks for deep-tank fermentation.[34]

To call Pfizer's investment an audacious undertaking would be an understatement. "The mold is as temperamental as an opera singer, the yields are low, the isolation is difficult, the extraction is murder, the purification invites disaster, and the assay is unsatisfactory," Pfizer president John L. Smith later remembered.[35] But as happened with so many wartime endeavors, Pfizer conquered the engineering challenge and saw the production volume of penicillin rise and costs drop. In June 1944, the wonder drug was made available to all Allied forces operating in Normandy. And, largely due to the successful production of huge quantities of the first modern pharmaceutical-grade medicine, the market valuation of Merck and Pfizer took off, putting both companies firmly on the Dow Jones Industrial Average Index ever since.[36]

Sensing that microbiology was becoming a key discipline for drug development, the Swiss were determined not to be left behind.

❖ ❖ ❖

In 1957, Sandoz formalized its own soil-screening program.[37] The approach was based on the emerging theory that bacteria-fighting fungi mostly lived in the soil.[38] The earthy, pleasant smell of springtime that we recognize from walking through the woods is, in fact, the smell of humus—the organic, broken-down material in the soil. Clearly, soil must contain a self-purifying property that gives it the capacity to recover its original composition, even when dead plants and diseased animals fall onto it year after year. The disease-suppressing capacity of humus led scientists to hypothesize that antibiotics made by microbes should be available for harvest and could be effective at killing fatal pathogens.[39] Like its American counterparts, Sandoz sent out scientists on expeditions and hired people to collect samples. The company enlisted ad hoc travelers, missionaries, airline pilots, and overseas students. The company got soil from cemeteries and sent up balloons into the air to collect windblown particles. Field workers went down to the bottoms of mine shafts, and up to the tops of mountains, and everywhere in between. Employees were told to keep an eye out for promising molds when cleaning out their refrigerator.[40] It was a rush to hit the next pay dirt.

And so in the summer of 1969, microbiologist Jean-François Borel brought home to Sandoz samples from the desolate Hardangervidda highland in southern Norway,[41] and, in them, the research team found the fungus *Tolypocladium inflatum*.[42] Although Borel's sample showed little antibacterial effect, it did show an amazing ability to halt the growth of other fungi.[43]

In medical research, discoveries come slowly and take twists and turns that no one can anticipate. Borel proceeded to isolate the active ingredient. It turned out that it could act as an immunosuppressant—a crucial substance for organ transplants that prevents the patient's own immune system from attacking the newly transplanted organ. Importantly, Borel's immunosuppressant inhibited only a specific chain of chemical reactions that was responsible for organ rejection[44] without destroying any white T-cells that fight infection. Such selectivity and reversibility offered a more nuanced, gentle approach to existing treatments, which were nonselective and often destroyed the patient's overall immune system.

But Borel needed a lot more of the fungus to continue his line of research; much of the initial stock had been depleted by 1973. High-level executives at Sandoz meanwhile grew skeptical regarding the compound's commercial prospects.[45] By one calculation, Sandoz would have to invest at least $250 million in clinical trials and manufacturing facilities,[46] and, in 1976, sales projections for 1989 did not exceed $25 million.[47] In other words, the market for a drug dedicated to organ transplants looked too limited. Borel's pathbreaking discovery was about to get shelved.

As with most events in the history of research, what followed was a combination of personal tenacity, political savvy, and a stroke of good luck. Borel used his last remaining stock to demonstrate the compound's effectiveness in treating other autoimmune diseases, including rheumatoid arthritis and nephrotic syndrome in the kidneys. Suddenly, this tilted the economic calculation in the compound's favor: Inflammatory diseases had long been regarded as a priority at Sandoz; they were associated with a far bigger market than organ transplants alone.[48] Based on the revised estimation, management gave Borel the blessing.

The compound unfortunately dissolved poorly in water. Solubility is paramount in medicine for achieving the desired dosage in blood circulation.[49] Only one option was left, and that was to follow the example of a long line of medical researchers who had experimented on themselves with preapproved substances. Borel dissolved some of the compound in alcohol and drank the mixture himself, to see whether the compound would reappear in the bloodstream. Miraculously, it did. That removed the final hurdle to commercialization.[50] He christened the invention *cyclosporine*. In November 1983, the US Food and Drug Administration (FDA) approved cyclosporine for treating several autoimmune diseases as well as preventing organ transplant rejection, just as Borel had envisioned thirteen years earlier.[51] In 1986, he received the prestigious Gairdner Award,[52] which many consider a precursor to winning the Nobel Prize in Medicine.[53]

GOOD LUCK OR SELF-DETERMINATION?

By the mid-twentieth century, the research focus of the pharmaceutical industry had decidedly switched from organic chemistry to microbiology. So complete was the transition that, in 1967, Switzerland's Roche founded the Institute of Molecular Biology in the United States. Almost immediately after, CIBA also commissioned the Friedrich Miescher Institute (FMI), naming it after the Basel-based physician and physiologist who had discovered nucleic acids inside the nucleus of a cell.[54] Thus, conceptually, CIBA and Sandoz were leaping from organic chemistry to microbiology in drug making. The pharmaceutical firms no longer competed solely on cost and volume based only on the first knowledge discipline, namely organic chemistry. Such a strategy would have limited them to only a few products; that is, antipyrine or other painkillers. But instead, as illustrated in Figure 2.1, the pharmaceutical industry was heavily influenced by the discoveries of the external scientific communities. The second knowledge discipline of microbiology gave the Basel incumbents a new lease on life.

Importantly, every time a shift in discipline occurs, industry knowledge rolls back to an earlier stage in its maturity. When Pfizer first industrialized the production of penicillin—with the development of deep-tank fermentation—the manufacturing process was unpredictable

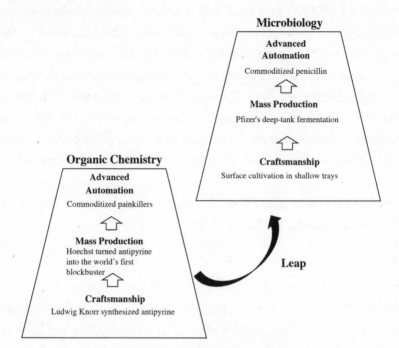

Figure 2.1 The knowledge funnel

and subject to a number of difficult variables. Pfizer had to draw upon the internal expertise of a handful of food chemists, who knew how to mass-produce citric acid by fermenting sugar.[55] This marked a return to the early transition from craftsmanship to mass production. So, while everything based on organic chemistry was standardized and automated, much of what was based on microbiology remained artisanal.

A few decades later, just as microbiology was about to slow as a fount for new discoveries, recombinant DNA technology would suggest another wave of new knowledge, bringing new opportunities for companies that were willing to invest in them and exploit them. That's how the Swiss drug makers stayed ahead of other copycats. The pioneers didn't just master the old, but also forged ahead into the new. By leaping from one scientific discipline to another, they left latecomers scrambling to catch up.

Still, advances in science and technology always rely on old knowledge. The new discipline of microbiology did not negate the importance of traditional organic chemistry; new discoveries were attained because the scientists already possessed certain prior knowledge. Bacteriologists would not have uncovered antiseptics had there not been a wealth of chemical compounds to pour onto the different bacteria in experiments. The discovery of human chromosomes would not have been possible had there not been appropriate dyes to stain the cells' nuclei for improved visibility under a microscope. The new discipline of microbiology and the old one of organic chemistry informed each other in lockstep as progress was steadily made.

Market competition is therefore akin to mountaineering. Rival companies seek to reach the peak. In industries where the knowledge base changes slowly or not at all, the newcomers can eventually reach the same altitude as the incumbents. By contrast, in industries where the knowledge base evolves, new discoveries resemble constant mudslides. No one ever reaches the mountaintop; everyone is constantly being pushed downward. In such a race, experience and prior knowledge matter. Ambition is important, but fortune favors the prepared.

So, what if a company found itself in an industry in which breakthrough discovery was all but impossible? Would it be condemned to the brutal fate of the textile firms? Could a manufacturer of everyday, largely unchanged products, such as dish soap and laundry detergent, prosper over the centuries? As implausible as it might seem, Procter & Gamble has managed to do just that. Somehow, the firm has fended off compettitors for more than a century by making products seemingly commonplace and mundane. How did it do it?

A SMALL-TIME BUSINESS IN PORKOPOLIS

The year was 1857. At six in the evening, an exhausted James Gamble staggered into the back parlor of his company's office, located on the northeast corner of Sixth and Main Streets in downtown Cincinnati. There, he saw William Procter just finishing his bookkeeping, having recorded the daily expenditure and sales volume.

"Plenty of light from the fire, William," Gamble teased as he turned off the gaslight that his business partner Procter had recently, and reluctantly, installed.[56] Procter, a candle maker himself, had never been fond of the gas contraption. He complained that the "home improvement" had robbed him of a favorite evening pastime: reading to his family by the glow of a fine, fat candle.

William Procter and James Gamble were not just any business partners; they were brothers-in-law. For a long time, Procter & Gamble (P&G) did not bother to brand its soap and candles. There was no such need. Household items, from soap to garments to paint to perfume, were made and sold locally. For general stores and small shops, and even for itinerant peddlers, face-to-face selling was all that commerce required.[57] P&G gave its products simple, factual names: tallow candles, rosin and palm soap, pearl starch, or lard oil.[58]

To make soap, Mr. Gamble would arrive at the factory every day as early as 4:30 a.m. to light the kettle fires. He would send his employees to collect meat scraps, leftover fat, and wood ashes to produce lye— an intermediate step in soap making. Then, the boiling, creamy blend would be poured into wooden frames for another four to five days to harden.[59]

Everyone, including Gamble himself, had only a vague idea about the chemistry at work, and, quite frankly, understanding the science behind the product made no difference. All one needed was access to raw materials. Located conveniently in Cincinnati was the city's preeminent meatpacking industry, where more than 100,000 hogs, cattle, and sheep were driven into the local slaughterhouses daily. P&G thus got all the abundant and cheap animal fats at this "Porkopolis," "the Empire City of Pigs."[60] Instead of bothering themselves with the basic science of soap making, the two frugal founders poured their energy into developing labor-saving machinery to increase their factory's production volume.

To speed up the cutting of big blocks of soap for instance, Gamble installed a table on the packing line that came equipped with evenly spaced piano wires to divide the soap into long slabs in one pass. The slabs would then be turned at a right angle and separated into 1-pound bars on the second pass. The bars would then be sent to a foot press that stamped the company's logo onto them. Sixty bars at a time were boxed, wrapped, and shipped to the warehouse.

This pioneering approach to the industrial production of con-sumer goods was highly unusual. Both men had been trained as traditional artisans and had done most of their work by hand. Domi-nating the country's villages were job shops and little town mills that hummed with small-scale activities. Henry Ford's assembly line, or "progressive assembling," was still decades away.[61] So, it must have been the local meat-packers who inspired the two founders to auto-mate. In the absence of refrigeration, meat-packers had had to come up with a processing system efficient enough that the packaged meat wouldn't spoil before shipping. Pulleys and conveyor belts moved the meat around the factory, and workers stood at fixed stations to complete one specific task: removing carpal bones, separating con-nective tissues, or cleaning up waste.[62] The close-up observation of this "dis-assembly" line of hogs, located within the nexus of trade for tallow and lard, likely became the blueprint for P&G's ramping up of its production capacity.

By the 1870s, P&G had grown to sixteen production facilities, oc-cupying an area of about 67,000 square feet and employing more than three hundred men. More elaborate apparatus was installed. Seven kettles, each towering 10 feet high, were commissioned, and instead of manually scooping out the boiled liquid with a copper ladle, P&G designed a chain device that was suspended from the ceiling and con-trolled by a foot pedal. Automated vertical mixers, equipped with rotary blades, churned the boiling liquid, thoroughly creaming it to a smooth consistency. The cream was poured into an oblong wheel-mounted iron frame to congeal into soap. The resultant slabs were then subdivided by the steam-powered cutter that spat out individual bars that were exact in size and shape.[63]

Here is where the concept of the knowledge funnel comes in again in Figure 2.2. The expansive strategy to build ever-larger production facilities was a decisive move from "early craftsmanship to mass pro-duction and automation." Mechanical engineering reigned supreme. Hundreds of process engineers went up and down the facilities every day, inspecting the continuous flow of products. The most pressing concerns of the day were product quality and production capacity.

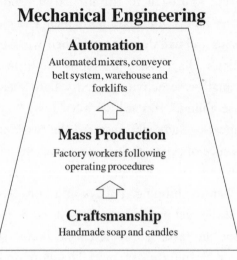

Figure 2.2 The knowledge funnel

SELLING A GOOD LIFE

When the second generation took over, headed by Harley Thomas Procter and James Norris Gamble, the company was struggling to ramp up to big-business proportions. P&G's famous Star Candle, having been dealt a severe blow from the gas lamp, was now mortally wounded by the advance of the incandescent electric lightbulb introduced by Thomas Edison. P&G needed to double down on soap making to make up for the inevitable loss of candle revenues. Harley Thomas had been trying to convince his relatives and elders for several years that good advertising was crucial for a turnaround. He was particularly infuriated at a company decision to call a superior white soap that James Gamble had reformulated, simply "the P&G white soap." "Scores of companies are marketing 'white soaps,'" he slammed. "Grocery stores are so full of them that neither merchants nor customers have any reason to care which they buy."[64] The restless Harley finally managed to convince the family in 1882 to allocate $11,000 (or $200,000 in contemporary terms) for his first advertising campaign.[65] He went to work immediately with an independent consultant in New York to clarify the scientific claims behind product purity.[66] There was, it turned out, no agreed definition of soap quality. The consultant had to check a textbook and

An original bar of Ivory soap and one in its original wrapper, right, sit on a shipping crate inside the Archives Center at the Procter & Gamble headquarters on Friday, June 18, 2004, in Cincinnati, next to a modern green package of an Ivory bar that also floats. *Source:* Associated Press.

suggested that soap should be all fatty acids and alkali. Anything else should count as "foreign and unnecessary substances."[67] The consultant also noted that the P&G white soap, when compared to three other leading brands,[68] had the least amount of impurities, with a mere trace of 0.56 percent: uncombined alkali (0.11%), carbonates (0.28%), and mineral matter (0.17%).[69] With the true flair of a marketing genius, Harley subtracted that residual amount from the overall content and came up with the headline "99 44/100% pure."[70] An ad pronounced on December 21, 1882, that "The IVORY is a Laundry Soap, with all the fine qualities of a choice Toilet Soap, and is 99 44/100% pure."[71] Appearing in the religious weekly the *Independent*,[72] the ad depicted a woman's delicate hands holding a stout string at the notch of a large bar, poised to effortlessly cut it into two cakes. The advertisement ended with the endearing catchphrase, "It floats!"

Harley's endeavor couldn't have had better timing. Throughout the 1840s and 1850s, chromolithography—a new printing method—had gained rapid popularity. Based on the principle that oil and water did not mix, chromolithography allows artists to draw their design directly on a limestone plate, using an oil-based medium, such as a wax crayon. This new printing technique eliminated the expensive and laborious engraving of wood and copper plates. The result was stunning, eye-catching graphics in bold tones at an affordable price.[73]

In a world without film, television, or radio, chromolithography quickly became associated with book illustration, advertising, and other commercial endeavors. The images charmed, captivated, and transfixed the nineteenth-century American public. Manufacturers generously supplied retailers with chromolithographed posters and trade cards along with other advertising materials, in the hope that shopkeepers would stockpile their merchandise.[74] Consumers, in turn, fervently collected them as souvenirs, making scrapbooks and albums. The printing press, which benefited the most, was propelled into a gigantic industry, from sixty companies in 1860 to seven hundred in 1890.[75] Referring to the United States as the "chromo-civilization," the New York Times observed in 1882 that "the rage for picturesque advertising which has marked the present popular renaissance in art has excited the keenest competitions in the production of beautiful designs and attractive novelties. The business in advertising cards has grown to enormous proportions, and the best talent in the country is employed in designing them. . . . The more beautiful and artistic a card or plaque is . . . the longer it will be kept in sight and talked about."[76]

Changing, too, was the business formula that newspapers employed. Instead of relying on readership revenue as they had previously, newspapers now tried to sell as cheaply as possible and make up the profits from advertisers who would pay more money for higher circulation. Under Harley's prodding, P&G tripled its advertising budget from $45,000 in 1884 to $146,000 in 1886,[77] turning it into one of the country's largest advertisers,[78] as colorful chromolithography made inroads into magazine advertising.[79] In one ad that ran in the Journal of the American Medical Association, P&G gave explicit advice to young mothers: "Much of the chafing of children under the joints where the skin lies in folds is due to the use of Soap containing too much alkali. In the Ivory Soap there is no excess of alkali, so it can be used in the nursery with the most satisfactory results."[80] And in October 1919, as millions of Americans pored over one of the most influential and widely read magazines of the time—the weekly *Saturday Evening Post*—they saw a full-page ad with color, depicting an elaborate upper-middle-class domestic scene with a maid cleaning objects round the house under the watchful eyes of the madam. Underneath the copy, it read, "Use IVORY Soap for renovating the prized possessions that a harsh soap would ruin. . . . IVORY has been cleaning such things as Oriental rugs, oil paintings, fine mahogany, enamel, gilded frames, statuary, silken hangings and valuable bric-a-brac."[81] P&G even resorted to running a contest for advertising ideas. At one point, Harley simply offered $1,000 for any "new, unusual, and improved method of using IVORY soap." So enthusiastic was the public's response that P&G compiled a compendium of the collected testimonies, ranging from soothing muscle aches to polishing jewelry.[82]

All these advertising efforts, to a modern observer, might sound unruly and chaotic, as they were aimed at a bewilderingly wide range of audiences, with inconsistent images and different messages going out each month.[83] But eventually, the disparate array of advertisements did settle for a single audience, namely, the white, predominantly Protestant, suburban population. This new advertising focus had much idealized Victorian America, embracing women, children, and babies in traditional family settings, emphasizing purity, femininity, and domesticity as core values, and projecting a sense of trust in an age of rapid industrialization. The message had created a loyal customer base upon which the company could solidly rely. The calculated move, however, was no longer Harley's personal directive, nor was it the result of the impulsive whim of a flamboyant executive. Instead, it was the fruition of countless refinements and painstaking calibrations by low-key, methodological analysts. It was an effort that codified flashes of ingenuity into something repeatable and dependable.

THE EARLIEST DATA WIZARDS

At the age of forty-five, Harley decided to retire and devote his time to enjoying life, traveling, and living in Paris, London, and Egypt.[84] In his place, Hastings L. French, an upright Cincinnati native,[85] stepped up and took over the entire sales organization. Together with Harry W. Brown,[86] the head of advertising, they pored over mountains of data in an effort to identify discernable patterns of marketing initiatives that would lead to positive results. In one instance, French and Brown sought to investigate an 1896 promotional event in Buffalo, where they had distributed samples. Despite its $3,700 budget, the event had failed to spur any observable demand.[87] Unlike John Wanamaker, the twentieth-century department store tycoon who famously quipped, "Half the money I spend on advertising is wasted; the trouble is I don't know which half,"[88] information at P&G with humdrum detail soon filled cabinet after cabinet of company notebooks. If marketing was to be transformed into a rigorous, reliable activity, then the effect of advertising, the two executives believed, would need to be measured in a reliable, replicable way. Personal insights must be extracted and formulated into repeatable procedures. Data collection, analysis, insights, and action—the four basic steps in data-driven decision making—became the corporate norms at P&G. And it was this scientific approach to advertising—generating and collecting data, searching for patterns, and looking for causes and effects—that enabled French and Brown to take advantage of the burgeoning new field of consumer psychology.

In the article "The Psychology of Advertising" in the January 1904 issue of the *Atlantic Monthly*, Walter D. Scott, the first prominent American applied psychologist, argued, "To advertise wisely the business man must understand the workings of the minds of his customers, and must know how to influence them effectively—he must know how to apply psychology to advertising."[89] *Fowlers Publicity Encyclopedia* recommended that managers designing a mail-order catalog "try its contents on a dozen or so of the common people, and see that they understand it"—arguably a primeval view of the modern market research methodology. All these were radical ideas, ideas that were ahead of their time. P&G, nevertheless, fervently adhered to them.

It's worth noting that P&G could have easily outsourced most of its marketing efforts to an independent agency if it had chosen to. Ad work usually involved multiple highly specialized illustrators—one to provide the technical drawing of the product with the highest fidelity possible and another responsible for creating an idealized or even romantic vision of the environment in which the product was used. The names of prominent illustrators often lent additional prestige to the product being advertised to the benefit of the paying client. But some of the earliest advertising agencies, including J. Walter Thompson and Lord & Thomas (which later became FCB) provided something beyond good drawing and harmonious coloring. They produced ad content, and they provided clients with creative expertise and media-buying insights.[90] Some operated research and information departments, others undertook sociodemographic market segmentation, and still others ran studio kitchens in New York and London, where housewives were observed as they tried out new products.[91] In fact, many legendary ads and slogans—Sunkist oranges, Sun-Maid raisins, Goodyear tires, Marlboro Man, Lucky Strike, Volkswagen's Beetle, "Nothing gets between me and my Calvins," "I'd walk a mile for a Camel," "Winston tastes good like a cigarette should," and "Fall into the Gap"—would not have existed without the help of the advertising creatives.[92]

Against this general trend was P&G's resolve to master consumer psychology in-house, rather than outsourcing the new knowledge discipline to others. It had been an internal survey that told P&G that American women doing household chores at home would appreciate radio entertainment. Out for something big, the company experimented with radio drama aired during the daytime, using the local Cincinnati clear-channel powerhouse in 1933, and launched the first domestic comedy in broadcasting history.[93] The results were immediate. Throughout the Great Depression of the 1930s, while competitors cut ad budgets, P&G increased its spending on radio. Not only did P&G stay well ahead of the other mass-produced soap makers, its earnings swelled from $2.5 million in 1933 to $4 million in 1934. As radio brought P&G's message into more homes than ever, managers mastered the new medium, and subsequently, created a whole new genre of radio entertainment: the soap opera.[94]

None of these would be possible unless the firm embraced consumer psychology as its second foundational discipline. This new emphasis, though gradual and subtle, was most evident in the CEO's expertise and background characteristics. "When P&G had to pick a new president, they went back to the place where they found the old one—the advertising department,"[95] reported *Advertising Age* in 1957. Not to factories, and not to sales. And it was the new knowledge rooted in consumer psychology that enabled P&G to innovate so differently from all other consumer package brands. It gainfully became the vanguard in advertisement using new media—from radio broadcasting to color television to social media marketing—for decades.

Meanwhile, manufacturing continued to forge ahead. When Ivorydale opened its doors in 1886 to replace the company's original production site, skeptics gawked at its extravagance. Designed by Chicago architect Solon Spencer Beman, Ivorydale comprised a cluster of twenty buildings on a 55-acre plot, 7 miles north of downtown Cincinnati.[96] To the people of Cincinnati, the factory was a sensation: A broad lawn separated it from the street, and trees were planted, flower beds set, and ponds and fountains filled. Limestone buildings with gables and red brick were all trimmed to a height of one story, except for the two-story buildings that housed the kettle boilers. Monster smokestacks rose above town, each towering more than 200 feet high, as they billowed exhaust into the sky.

Inside the factory, visitors marveled at the steam-powered conveyor belts that carried empty boxes and soap cakes to workers for wrapping. At the gate stood a bright red locomotive that P&G owned, its boiler front emblazoned with the Moon and Stars trademark. Soon after the first year of operation in 1886, Ivorydale helped make P&G a multimillion-dollar company.[97]

But large-scale manufacturing alone would never afford P&G the kind of protection it needed in the face of new competition. Recall how

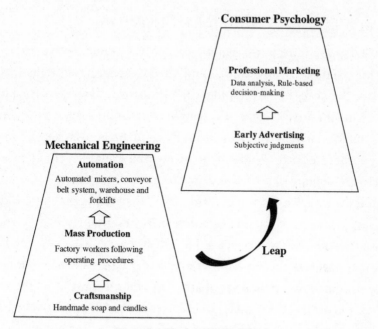

Figure 2.3 The knowledge funnel

new arrivals from Japan and then companies from other Far Eastern countries displaced the southern mills that had driven the northern mills in the United States out of business. Had P&G clung onto its initial knowledge discipline, namely mechanical engineering, no matter how much it expanded, the enterprise would not have lasted long. A single path of volume expansion would only have led to a ruinous state of price competition.

That is why, when Harley renamed P&G's white soap "Ivory," wrapped it in a black-and-white checkerboard-patterned covering, and declared, "It floats!" he effectively leaped onto the emerging field of consumer psychology. His early attempts, summarized in Figure 2.3, were inevitably sporadic, mostly based on guesswork and subjective judgment. But he was smart enough to later let professional managers take over and systematize his approach. Before the dawn of the twentieth century, P&G, the firm that had begun as a small-time artisanal enterprise, had leaped from mechanical engineering to consumer psychology.

"DUMPSTER-DIVING" WITH THE PHENOMENA

Thus far, we have seen two major leaps: P&G's—from mechanical engineering to consumer psychology, and the Basel pharmaceuticals'—from organic chemistry to microbiology. In business academics, a strong bias favors quantitative data sets: researchers assemble large sample sizes and employ "mean" analyses to understand ways of achieving high-level corporate performance. A quintessential example is Jim Collins's 2001 best seller, *Good to Great*. Starting with more than 1,400 companies, his research team identified eleven that went from a period of average performance to one of strong performance. He then found a matching set of companies in similar industries that had only managed to remain average the entire time. By comparing the mediocre and the great, Collins discovered a set of attributes that distinguished the winners. Chief among them was the character of the CEO: relatively humble leaders who generally shunned the limelight led the good-to-great companies, whereas more egocentric hired-in "superstar" executives tended to lead the mediocre companies.

Although intuitively appealing, many of those great companies have since fallen, struggled financially, or been forced to shut down. Among the eleven former stars were Circuit City, which filed bankruptcy in 2008; Fannie Mae, which the government bailed out; Wells Fargo, which got mired in banking scandals, and Kroger, a grocery chain, which is struggling in the face of e-commerce.

In the business world, managers face complex and dynamic environments. Things that worked a few years ago won't necessarily work forever. That is why overreliance on correlation as a research methodology can be misguided: correlations are often incomplete; there may also be factors that would be difficult to include in a quantitative sample; for instance, a specific decision that a CEO made together with the immediate reports. Conducting research from a distance without crawling into the firm could lead any scholar to draw erroneous conclusions. Does having a humble CEO lead to higher corporate performance or does a high-performing company with less financial pressure lead the CEO to act less aggressively? We simply don't know.

This is not to say that in-depth historical accounts are always superior. Rather, large-sample research often cannot tease out the underlying causality to show how and why certain managerial decisions can lead to different outcomes in different situations. When comparative case histories over long periods are done properly, researchers can confidently deduce unambiguous guidance about what actions will or will not lead to the desired results given the circumstances in which managers find themselves.

Before we look ahead, let's reflect on what we have learned so far from dumpster-diving into the histories of Novartis and P&G. Our observations have revealed that sustainable advantage is not much of a utopian position for a company to attain after all. Trade secrets or proprietary know-how eventually transfers to copycats. More evidence: the average time it takes for developing nations to catch up with developed countries in their use of standard technology has dropped from well over one hundred years (for the spindle, when it was first invented in 1779) to thirteen (for the cell phone).[98] Similarly, in 1922, the US tire industry comprised 274 firms, but by 1936, the number of companies was down by 80 percent to 49.[99] Today, only two US-owned tire companies remain, competing in the global market.

Only when the pioneers kept pace with the knowledge base as it shifted from one discipline to another, as was done in the pharmaceutical industry, could they exploit the opportunity to realize their first-mover advantage. Maintaining this perspective, let's ask the following questions: Has your company leaped from one knowledge discipline to another in the past? If so, what was the consequence? If not, what were the barriers? More generally speaking, if leaping toward a new knowledge discipline is so important to the long-term prosperity of a firm, why don't we see it more often?[100]

To answer that last question, we have to explore the process by which resources are allocated within a large complex organization. The next chapter explores the final leaps of the Swiss pharmaceuticals and P&G that brought them well into the twenty-first century. These final episodes among the century-old firms serve two purposes. First, the more modern history provides us with an inside perspective on how tumultuous changes and difficult trade-offs were actually made. Second, by amassing more data points over the long histories of these firms, we can be more confident that our conclusions have not been inadvertently cherry-picked.

Strategy, of course, is never about achieving perfection: it's about shortening one's odds, at best. Here we're about to see how the senior leaders of large established organizations maximized their chances to prosper.

3

THE SECOND ADVANTAGE OF A PIONEER: HOW KNOWLEDGE IS HARNESSED

It's not hard to make decisions when you know what your values are.

— Roy E. Disney, former senior executive
of the Walt Disney Company (1930–2009)

It's kind of fun to do the impossible.

— Walt Disney, American entrepreneur (1901–1966)

THE NEW SKILLS

UP UNTIL THE 1980S, PHARMACEUTICAL COMPANIES OFTEN HAD to rely on naturally occurring microorganisms to produce different drugs—penicillin by penicillium, ergotamine by the ergot fungus. That's why we saw Pfizer and Sandoz going to great lengths to set up soil-screening programs around the world. For insulin or other growth hormones, extraction from animal parts or even dead human bodies was sometimes the only option. As the twentieth century wore on, pharmaceutical research was also fast becoming the priciest science. If there is one word to summarize the whole process of drug discovery, it is *attrition*. Biomedical research has been fraught with exciting studies in animals that cannot be replicated in humans.[1] Roughly 95 percent of potential medications, or candidates, fail when they enter clinical trials because they are not potent enough or cause too many side effects.[2] These unfavorable statistics have dramatically increased the financial costs involved. For the Basel-based pharmaceutical companies, pooling and sharing resources was the only way to keep pace with the latest developments.

On March 7, 1996, CIBA-Geigy and Sandoz announced what was then the largest merger in the history of modern corporations. After decades of acquisitions and alliances among them, CIBA, Geigy, and Sandoz were about to amalgamate into a single entity. The resultant conglomerate was named Novartis, from the Latin term *novae artes*, which means "new arts" or "new skills."[3] The new skill that Novartis sought was none other than the recombinant DNA technology, a medicinal manipulation that helped to usher in the biotech revolution two decades before.

In 1973, two California researchers, Stanley Cohen and Herbert Boyer, demonstrated the possibility of bypassing natural evolution to directly insert selective genetic variations into a simple bacterium commonly found in the human intestine, *E. coli*. Before they met, Cohen of Stanford University had been studying bacterial resistance to antibiotics, while Boyer at the University of California, San Francisco (UCSF), had been studying the restriction enzyme, a molecular tool that could be used to slice and dice DNA at specific points. In a joint experiment, Cohen and Boyer produced a bacterium that simultaneously possessed resistance genes against two antibiotics, not through the evolutionary process of natural selection, but by recombinant DNA, proving DNA could be artificially recombined—the golden key to modern biotechnology. Using recombinant DNA, scientists could "order" bacterial cells to grow and mass-produce complex protein-based molecules even if they don't exist in nature, so as to create important medicine for humans. The bacterial biomolecular machinery can thus be harnessed to make pharmaceutical drugs that would otherwise be too expensive or complicated to be synthesized in the traditional chemical processes. Boyer went on to found the world's first biotechnology company—Genentech, short for Genetic Engineering Technology. The age of biotechnology had arrived.

When Novartis was formed in 1996, it was not only the second-largest corporation in Europe but also the second-largest pharmaceutical company in the world, with 360 affiliates in more than 140 countries.[4] Daniel Vasella, the former CEO of Sandoz, was appointed to head the new enterprise. His top priority was reviewing the research pipeline from both CIBA-Geigy and Sandoz in search of the next blockbuster.

A physician by training, Dr. Vasella was born in Fribourg, a city that straddles the border between the German-speaking and French-speaking regions of Switzerland. The son of a history professor, Vasella knew no one who practiced medicine in his childhood.[5] But the medical problems that plagued his early years stoked his lifelong passion for medicine. At eight years old, Vasella suffered attacks of tuberculosis and meningitis. He was forced to spend a year in an isolated sanatorium, far away from his family.[6] His parents, reportedly, didn't visit him during that year. His two sisters came only once. Lonely and homesick, Vasella remembered the horror of a spinal tap, a procedure to extract fluid surrounding the spinal cord. Nurses had to hold him down "like an animal" so that he couldn't move.[7]

One day, a new physician arrived and took the time to explain each step of the procedure, and Vasella was allowed to hold a nurse's hand, rather than being held down. "The amazing thing is that this time the procedure didn't hurt," he recalled. "Afterward, the doctor asked me, 'How was that?' I reached up and gave him a big hug. These human gestures . . . made a deep impression on the kind of person I wanted to become."[8]

Two years later, Vasella experienced yet another tragedy at the age of ten years. His sister, Ursula, was diagnosed with lymphatic cancer, or Hodgkin's disease.[9] He remembered seeing the burn marks all over his sister's body from the aggressive radiation treatment. And when her cancer spread to the liver, Ursula became too weak to even sit up in bed. Still, Ursula refused to give up high school and graduated before the final summer as her life was slipping away. In her last words that would forever be etched in the young man's mind, Ursula pleaded, "Daniel, do well in school."

In life, a thin line separates destiny from coincidence, or more poignantly, misfortune. Vasella didn't understand the disease that had taken his sister away. He only truly came to understand cancer later in his years at the medical school of the University of Bern, in Switzerland. After four years serving as the chief resident in internal medicine at the University Hospital, he joined the Sandoz pharmaceutical business and then worked in the United States for three years, including a three-month stint at Harvard Business School.[10]

While reviewing the research pipeline of Novartis after becoming its CEO, Vasella met Alex Matter, to whom he would later refer to as "a real intellectual bulldozer."[11] Tall, reserved, and acerbic, Matter spent more than a decade at CIBA-Geigy building up its cancer research, an area that had been regarded as a "backwater of medical science."[12]

For most doctors, the standard way to combat cancer was to surgically remove the tumor, then to employ chemotherapy and radiation—essentially injecting toxic substances or radioactivity into the body. If the doctor managed to kill off the cancerous cells faster than the healthy ones, the patient might just survive. Although cancer drugs could be effective at forestalling the growth of malignant cells, they did so indiscriminately, destroying normal cells and making patients overwhelmingly weak. Anyone who has had to soldier through the punishing regimen can attest that the whole process, from tumor removal to chemotherapy, is almost like having a limb cut off to avoid the spread of an early infection before antibiotics had been invented.[13]

To Alex Matter, the brutish bodily assault on cancer patients was outrageous. He saw the drug discovery was no more than "shooting compounds into mice and hoping for the best—maybe the lump would decrease in size. That was about it."[14] Cancer biology was so poorly understood that the only way to test one's hunches was to put them into practice and see what happened.

IN SEARCH OF THE MAGIC BULLET

In every company, there are two competing approaches through which corporate strategy can be realized. One is deliberate; the other, emergent. Deliberate strategy tends to be highly methodical and analytical. Senior executives set out to rigorously analyze everything they can and ferret out answers related to their business: data on market growth, segment sizes, customer needs, competitors' strengths and weaknesses, and technology trajectories. Deliberate strategy making usually ends with a rigorous assessment of the financial plausibility. A high net present value or internal rate of return helps to generate confidence that the strategy chosen is indeed worth implementing.

But not all opportunities can be adequately captured by this top-down approach. Former Intel chairman Andy Grove observed, "In my experience, [top-down strategic plans] always turn into sterile statements, rarely gaining traction in the real work of the corporation. Strategic actions, on the other hand, always have real impact."[15] What Grove referred to as "strategic actions," is in fact the emergent strategy. That is, the cumulative effect of day-to-day periodization and investment decisions that middle managers, engineers, salespeople, and financial staff make, and they can have a disproportionate impact on the long-term trajectory of corporate development. Although these decisions tend to be tactical, and they often fall outside the purview of official corporate scrutiny, they collectively represent the initial seeding of the next big thing. At Intel, the key historic decision to abandon memory chips and to concentrate on microprocessors was the result of a host of decentralized decisions taken at divisional and plant level that were subsequently acknowledged by top management and promulgated as strategy. Intel allocated a key resource, wafer fabrication capacity, according to the gross margin per wafer that was earned in each of its product lines. Once each month, Intel's production schedulers at the factory would meet to allocate the available production capacity across their products, which ranged from memory chips to microprocessors. When Japanese manufacturers intensified their attack on the US market in the early 1980s, the pricing of memory chips dropped precipitously. It was the resource allocation process at Intel that shifted the company from a memory chip company into a microprocessor company. That strategic shift, however, emerged only through the daily decisions made by middle managers as they allocated resources, not the result of an intended strategy articulated up front by the executive ranks. And once this new business opportunity had become clear, Intel's management then committed to a new, deliberate strategy with full force.[16]

This was strategy making at its best, where the intended corporate strategy actually succeeded the emergent strategy, which, if stifled by corporate rigidity, would have spelled disaster for the company. Organizations that inhabit relatively stable environments can plan their strategies in some detail. Organizations whose environments cannot be forecasted can only articulate a few strategic principles and guidelines; the rest must emerge as circumstances unfold. In other words, the role of emergent strategy relative to deliberate grows in its importance as the business environment becomes increasingly unpredictable. Borel's early experimentation on immunosuppression, driven largely by his own passion, was exactly the sort of emergent strategy that pushed Sandoz toward a new trajectory. Decades later, Alex Matter followed exactly the same footsteps as Borel, by pursuing an autonomous initiative that would eventually lead to a major corporate renewal at Novartis.

❖ ❖ ❖

In the 1960s, the genetic cause of chronic myeloid leukemia (CML) gradually began to come to light. CML is a rare form of leukemia that affects the blood-forming cells of the bone marrow. Pinpointing the genetic cause of CML was a major breakthrough from a research perspective. For the first time, scientists had identified exactly how a set of displaced DNAs inside the chromosomes of a cell nucleus triggered the production of an unusual enzyme called Bcr-Abl tyrosine-kinase.[17] Kinases are enzymes that regulate much activity within cells. And it was this wrong Bcr-Abl that caused the myeloid cells—the cells that make red blood cells and white blood cells—to multiply uncontrollably, leading to an unstoppable increase in their number, as if the immune system's production switch was stuck at full on. In fact, uncontrollable cell growth was the root of all cancers. In the case of CML, as leukemia grows, the patient would experience fatigue, fever, chills, occasional bleeding, bone pain, and, finally, death.[18]

With the fundamental biology of CML pried open, it became feasible, at least in theory, to engineer an attack on a specific molecule inside the cancer cell. Alex Matter saw within the cell an infinite universe that comprised molecules that selected partners like intricate locks, designed only to fit a specific key. He had in mind designing a compound that would inhibit the Bcr-Abl protein by chemically binding to it, thereby breaking the chain of unbridled cell proliferation. The mix-and-match characteristics of molecules should therefore allow a clever engineering of a compound to stop a specific chemical chain reaction without disturbing others, like using a false key to jam a lock. "Based on this concept," Matter recalled, "I put together a small team of people to see if we could design such a molecule."[19]

To many contemporaries of Alex Matter, developing a compound that would cross a cell membrane and reach its nucleus, where the Bcr-Abl protein was located, sounded as untenable as a scientific fantasy. At that time, chemical complexity at the molecular level remained obscurely overwhelming. Matter, however, possessed a rare kind of fixated resolve, to the point of galvanizing others to undertake the impossible along with him.

Jürg Zimmermann, then an ambitious thirty-two-year-old chemist, described their undertaking as almost "archaic" and "a little embarrassing" when the project was first under way. "We didn't actually know the structure of an enzyme, so when I drew them [on papers], I'd create an image of what I thought it should look like. Then I'd draw it again, trying to envision on paper what it might be shaped like."[20] Like a locksmith trying to forge the right key, Zimmermann created thousands of compounds and handed them over to Elisabeth Buchdunger, a cell biologist on the team, to verify the results. Little by little, Zimmermann learned about how the nuanced alteration in the molecule's structure might affect its chemical properties, and hence, the effectiveness, toxicity, and solubility of the compound. "Throughout this period, the scientific journals were saying that it will never be possible to engineer a selective compound [that binds only Bcr-Abl]. . . . Perhaps the best thing we had going for us was that all of us believed we would eventually succeed, and we refused to give up."[21] And every day, Zimmermann and the team was getting closer to solving the chemical riddle.

Some nine years later, in February 1994, the team confirmed that it had synthesized a compound that could inhibit 90 percent of leukemia cells in vitro—in a test tube experiment. The compound was shown to be effective at warding off cancer cells by binding to the Bcr-Abl protein without harming the normal cells. It would be the first cancer drug developed based on the precise understanding of the underlying biological pathway—dramatic news, not only because of the invention itself but also because of how it was invented. The targeted compound, labeled STI571, had achieved new drug candidate status pending animal studies and human patient trials.[22]

In medicine, when scientists manage to unlock a box, they often find another locked box inside it. To exploit a discovery in biology, one needs to be good at organic chemistry. To take advantage of the emerging understanding of human genetics that underpin the molecular pathway of a cancer, one needs to first master microbiology and so on. The ability to make these fundamental shifts in knowledge over time is the ultimate reason that the Swiss pharmaceutical companies have been able to ward off new competition. Figure 3.1 summarizes the multiple leaps the Basel drug maker has made.

These transitions, however, are fraught with challenges, even when one is armed with rich knowledge. No company can get it right every time. Those who have made it have done so with persistence, audacity, foresight, and sometimes luck. But, precisely because the transition is so difficult, the most experienced companies stand a better chance of remaining at the top. Inventions and discoveries stand on the shoulders of their predecessors; hard-won progress is usually built on experience and prior knowledge.

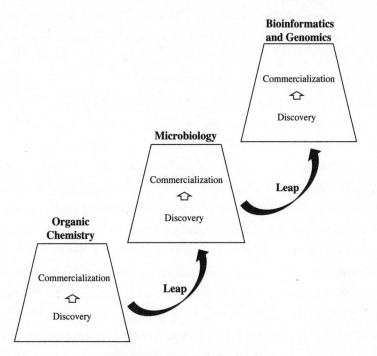

Figure 3.1 The knowledge funnel

As noted earlier, however, only very few compounds can successfully move beyond the initial candidate status. Most drug candidates don't succeed during clinical trials. The same applies to STI571, the new compound engineered by Matter's team. But beyond the clinical uncertainties, the market size for treating CML also looked severely limited. As a rare form of cancer, CML affects about 8,200 American adults each year, compared to the estimated 165,000 cases of prostate cancer and 250,000 cases of breast cancer in the United States. And in events similar to those that Borel had experienced at Sandoz three decades earlier, managers at Novartis were concerned that STI571 would offer little financial return. The animal studies and clinical trials alone would cost between $100 million and $200 million.[23] "The pharmaceutical team and I had some agonizing decisions to ponder," Vasella wrote.[24]

Still, when he saw the favorable results of the initial trial on STI571, the CEO decided to move ahead with development. "Ultimately, we are a business, and business decisions are often based on some form of statistical analysis and the chance to make a profit," he admitted. "But, as a management team, when there is a fair chance that a product on the market will change the practice of medicine, we have a duty to put that product out there. . . . I told our head of global technical operation, 'Money doesn't matter. Let's just do it.'"

Money, of course, matters a great deal in the pharmaceutical business. Novartis ended up running the biggest clinical trial in history, in large part because CML sufferers represented a small, closely knit patient community. They were vocal about expanding the trial as quickly as possible to include late-stage sufferers for whom STI571 was the only real hope. This targeted molecule, unlike conventional chemotherapy, attacks only cancer cells without disturbing the healthy ones, and thus bypassing many side effects: no more hair loss, no more sloughing of skin and gut lining, no more clogged veins, and no more nausea and vomiting. So negligible were the drug's side effects that many patients thought they had been given a placebo, except that they were also experiencing the real medical benefit and lives were prolonged far beyond the initial prognosis. Facing public pressure, the US Food and Drug Administration (FDA) completed the process of approving the new drug—Gleevec—in record time, after only two and a half months of review. In a news conference on May 10, 2001, the secretary of Health and Human Services, Tommy Thompson, emphasized, "We believe such targeting is the wave of the future."[25] In 2009, three creators of Gleevec won the Lasker Award, one of medicine's highest honors.[26]

THE EPIC QUEST FOR NEW KNOWLEDGE DISCIPLINES

The Gleevec approach, by chemically binding the Bcr-Abl protein because of a specific set of displaced DNAs, turned what had once been an acute cancer—CML—with a median survival time of three to six years into a chronic condition. As long as patients took the oral medication every day, many of them could expect to live, on average, for thirty years after the first diagnosis.[27] This improved life span of individuals meant that, ironically, the overall sales volume of Gleevec took off, even as CML remained a rare disease. It was estimated that, by 2030, there would be 250,000 living CML patients in the United

States who would require the daily medication.[28] By 2012, CML treatment had already grown into a $4.7 billion business, making Gleevec Novartis's best seller.[29]

The most profound impact, however, was the reshaping of the industry's research focus. There are more than one hundred types of cancer, each with distinctive genetic and molecular underpinnings, exhibiting different trajectories and personalities and, thus, demanding very different treatments. Unlike bacterial infections, cancer has no single pathological cause and no single mechanism, so is it impossible to create a uniform response to it. Shortly after the launch of Gleevec, the Novartis Institute for BioMedical Research (NIBR) was established with a focus on chemical biology and computational methods that aimed to inform drug discovery. Anxious not to be outdone, Novartis's Swiss archrival, Roche Holding, acquired Genentech—the first biotech superstar we saw earlier[30]—for $46.8 billion in 2009, instantly turning Roche into the world's largest biotech company.[31]

If leaping toward a new knowledge discipline is so important to the long-term prosperity of a firm, why is it so rare? The main reason, I've come to believe, is the complex process by which corporate resources are allocated within a large organization. In circumstances where the future is hard to read and it isn't clear what the right strategy is, an emergent process should dominate. That's exactly why when Alex Matter took on the task of establishing Novartis's cancer research, he had to be accommodated with a high degree of freedom and unhampered by bureaucracy. With full authority over the work of his staff members and the budget, Matter could approximate an entrepreneurial enterprise—a quasi-independent business for a temporary period.

And yet market leadership can't be achieved through an undirected process of boundless experimentation. Nor can it result purely from the efforts of skunkworks, or corporate ventures directly imported from Silicon Valley. Behind any unfocused effort lies a bleak prognosis: the established organization has become so dogmatic and unchangeable—insidious at its worst—that the only way to innovate is to put a few bright people in a dark room, pour in some money, and hope that something wonderful will happen.[32] That freewheeling approach may work well for venture capitalists because they invest to exit, either through initial public offerings (IPOs) or by selling startups to large firms. But an established organization should invest and innovate to rejuvenate its ongoing business ahead of competition. Integration between the old and the new becomes unavoidable. For this reason, sooner or later, the senior executives of an operating company have to call the shots and turn the emergent exploration into a deliberate execution. Once the winning strategy becomes clear, a firm must pursue it aggressively. Not doing so is tantamount to failed leadership.

Indeed, besides what Novartis has demonstrated, the more recent history of P&G reveals that top executives can and should personally intervene and commit their organizations to leaping toward new knowledge disciplines. Without their direct commitment, all activities by the rank and file, however innovative they may be, will fail. But the reason why so few companies have managed to leap is easy to understand: executives are often asked to trade secured, near-term profits for uncertain, long-term prosperity. No one can tell for sure whether a seemingly audacious move is a well-thought-out determination or a foolhardy idea. Most challenging of all is the impossibility of rendering investment decisions into positive financial forecasts when a company needs to leap. Only someone at the very top of a company can legitimately say, "Money doesn't matter. Let's just do it."

Today, it takes extravagantly equipped laboratories, huge budgets, and large teams of investigators to stay at the forefront of the industry. Novartis alone spent a staggering $10 billion on research and development in 2013. But capital expenditure itself is never enough to stave off newcomers' efforts to overtake pioneering incumbents. Remember that money was hardly an issue when the southern mills overtook Great Britain as the leading textile exporter. When the underlying knowledge discipline remains unchanged, newcomers possess the advantage of leapfrogging, thereby developing more advanced manufacturing capacities. Chapters 1 and 2 are littered with the disastrous outcomes of this situation, and it affects all sectors, including those devoted to the manufacture of personal computers, mobile phones, automobiles, solar panels, and, of course, textiles. That was how Yamaha outcompeted

Steinway in piano making, first through low wages, and then through automation. Among these "mature industries," the underlying knowledge discipline, even when improved incrementally, never quite leaped into an entirely different field.

❖ ❖ ❖

Despite the transformative effect of Gleevec, some 20 to 30 percent of CML patients do not respond to the drug,[33] signaling that the hideously ingenious malignancy can become resistant to sophisticated interventions.[34] "The fight against cancer continues. . . . Each time we come up with a new, effective drug, it's a small victory in a much larger, ongoing war," Vasella noted. "The more we know about the body, the more we realize how little we know." It should therefore be little surprise that leading pharmaceutical companies have continued to snap up biotechnology companies in their race for gene therapies, leapfrogging one another toward the latest frontier. An independent biotech upstart might possess a few interesting drug candidates. But, without the backing of an experienced pharmaceutical firm that can expertly navigate regulations and clinical trials, the path to commercialization remains all too perilous. In this environment, it would be nearly impossible for a newcomer from China, for example, to suddenly outrun an experienced pioneer in Switzerland.

All in all, the biotechnology revolution of the late 1970s that ushered in the new age of bioinformatics and genomics that is evident today has fundamentally changed scientists' approach to tackling disease. This, in turn, has opened up new possibilities for chemical intervention at the molecular level. From targeted cancer drugs to HIV treatment, transformative therapies unimaginable a decade ago have reduced abhorrent illnesses into manageable conditions. Astute readers may now ask, where else could P&G leap after consumer psychology with products so mundane and low-tech?

By 2012, only seventy-one companies that had appeared on the original Fortune 500 list in 1955 were still on it.[35] The life span of a Fortune 500 company is about thirty years. And yet, P&G still occupied the top shelf at number 34 out of 500 in 2016, commanding more than $200 billion in market capitalization.[36] What's so special about the way the Cincinnati centenarian is managed?

STIRRING THE NEXT WAVE

By the 1930s, P&G had perfected just the kind of manufacturing process that was expected of an industry heavyweight. With high-speed churning, whipping, and freezing, soaps were produced in a matter of hours rather than days.[37] P&G, however, remained a traditional soap producer, employing the same old ingredients and methods it knew since the 1800s: animal or vegetable fats combined with water and an alkali base at a high temperature. Such "natural" soap comprised long chains of fatty acids. But one common problem was its inability to clean when mixed with hard water, which was high in mineral content such as calcium or magnesium. The soap left a residue that looked like scum or curds. It was a nuisance to consumers and a problem that deeply troubled the company's engineers.

In April 1931, Robert A. Duncan, a P&G process engineer, was touring Europe on a scouting expedition "to learn anything concerning processes or products of interest."[38] In Germany, he learned about a laboratory-grown synthetic soap called Igepon,[39] which was described as "a good wetting agent, a fair detergent, not affected by hard water, and resistant to acid."

Chemically speaking, a wetting agent or a surfactant is an effective detergent. But since it isn't derived from natural fats, it doesn't contain the long chains of fatty acids that bind with hard water. During the same trip, Duncan located yet another company, Deutsche Hydrierwerke, which was about to launch a competing product, exclusively marketed to textile manufacturers. He ordered one hundred samples on the spot and shipped them express to Cincinnati for analysis, noting that the Germans "had no notion as to what value, if any, it had as detergent for home use."[40] With the Igepon sample in hand, P&G engineers discovered a way to synthesize a similar stringlike molecule, one end of which would bond with oil and the other end of which would bond with water. It was, thus, capable of breaking up grease that water could then wash away. Absent the fatty acid chains, no scum would form in hard water.

In 1933, P&G launched an alkyl sulfate–based synthetic detergent called Dreft. A year later, Drene, the first synthetic-based shampoo, was also launched. Inside P&G, however, a convulsive worry was immediate. Managers feared that the new products might cannibalize their much-cherished Ivory soap. But chairman William Cooper Procter, the last family manager of P&G, became a staunch supporter of the work on synthetic detergents. In a memorable remark to his staff, he said, "This [synthetic detergent] may ruin the soap business. But if anybody is going to ruin the soap business it had better be Procter & Gamble."[41] Management doubled down on the investment, and the technical center at Ivorydale effectively became one of the first analytical labs in the field of consumer goods.[42]

To an outside observer, one salient form of managerial behavior ran through the long history of P&G: the willingness to embrace self-cannibalization. Resistance to this counterintuitive strategy is natural. Managers often fear that a company's new products and services with lower profit margins may cut directly into the sales of existing products. Money should be invested in areas that are demonstrably most profitable without lowering overall profitability. But to cite a Steve Jobs almost-cliché, "If you don't cannibalize yourself, someone else will."

It turned out that Dreft and Drene were too mild to ruin any soap business. P&G scientists had yet to find a way to tweak the formulae so that they would be strong enough to remove heavier dirt. Hampered by the chemical limitation, Dreft was confined to being a light-duty product for delicate fabrics and baby clothes. It was popular in the area stretching from the Midwest to the Rocky Mountains, where hard water caused constant problems in washing.[43] Dreft was nevertheless a mere niche product. Another decade would pass before an important breakthrough occurred.

P&G researcher David Byerly, who led the development of synthetic detergents, including Tide. *Source:* Procter & Gamble

THE UNSTOPPABLE TIDE

During the intervening years, the Ivorydale technical center sought to create a "builder," a chemical compound that would emulsify oil and grease into tiny droplets[44] and boost the performance of the basic detergent when used in tandem with it. Sodium phosphates had been hailed as that complementary compound. But this builder suffered an unfortunate attribute: it stubbornly deposited particles that left clothes like sandpaper, stiff and rough.

After holding out for ten years, and spending more than 200,000 hours on mind-numbing tests to get the formula right,[45] the research team was all but quietly disbanded with key personnel reassigned elsewhere. Managers shunned their association with the failing venture. But there was one single-minded scientist, a maverick who refused to give up on what would later be known as Project X.

David "Dick" Byerly, who eventually filed the key patent for Tide, continued with his line of research at a time when the management had explicitly ordered a phase-out. His supervisor, Thomas Halberstadt, took notice of the young man's tenacity. "I was very fond of Dick but you've got to understand the man to understand what he did. . . . Dick was an obstinate cuss in some ways. Tenacious as all get out,"[46] he later recalled.

Understandably, Byerly approached Halberstadt with great suspicion when they first met in 1939. One day, Byerly showed up at his boss's office and revealed his big secret: "Now that you're here, I want to know, am I going to be allowed to work on what I think I should be working on?"[47] Byerly ushered his confused supervisor into the laboratory and spent the next two days going through his work records from the past five years. Dumbfounded, Halberstadt went up to ask Herb Coith, the associate director of the Chemical Division, for a green light. In a characteristically P&G fashion, Byerly was allowed to continue but was warned to keep Project X under tight wraps and never "make a big deal about it." Byerly was expressly forbidden to ask process development for "samples made in their pilot plant,"[48] so as to avoid drawing any unwanted corporate attention.

The outbreak of the Second World War brought on a severe shortage of many supplies and input materials. When a senior executive got wind of Project X, he lambasted, "How you fellows can fiddle around with a product that P&G [has] no intention of making when we've got more unanswered problems out here in the factories." All P&G facilities were forced to retool during wartime so as to continue with production using more rationed formulas. Engineers and scientists were firefighting every day. Coith demanded that Halberstadt shut down Project X immediately. But when Byerly sank into depression and threatened to resign, Halberstadt relented: "There was a great deal of work done that was never reported. We knew we couldn't [report]. That was that."[49]

The gamble paid off. In 1945, Byerly identified sodium tripolyphosphate (STPP) as the ideal builder when an important discovery came to light. To yield the best washing results, conventional wisdom had always suggested keeping the ratio of detergent higher and using only a modest dose of builder. But Byerly overturned this orthodoxy, using one part of detergent (the alkyl sulfate) to three parts of builder (the sodium tripolyphosphate).[50] The formula worked and delivered beautiful results.[51]

By now, even Coith could not suppress the whispers and was asked to present the findings to top executives. Without knowing it, P&G was about to leap to its third knowledge discipline: from manufacturing enhanced by mechanical engineering to advertising informed by consumer psychology to research and development rooted in organic chemistry.

A product demonstration was staged. Among the attendees were Richard Deupree, the company's president; Ralph Rogan, VP of advertising; and R. K. Brodie, VP of manufacturing and technical research.[52] The three had no doubts about the market potential of Project X. The only question was the timetable for the commercial launch. Although what follows is a reconstruction, every quoted word is verbatim and is in the historical record of multiple sources, thus presenting a rare opportunity to be a fly on the wall of this particular meeting.

To Rogan, a marketing expert, a typical launch should take at least two years: several months to prepare product samples, another six months to run blind tests in selected cities, and then additional time to tweak the formula based on the new findings. Still more time would be needed to develop an advertising strategy, poll consumers, prepare for a national launch.[53] President Deupree thought of Rogan's assessment and turned to Brodie. "Kirk, do you fit into that schedule?" "We could," Brodie demurred, "but Lever and Colgate will get samples of our product shortly after we start blind testing. Then they will put together some kind of product. . . . Surely their product will not be as good as ours, but they will crowd the market with similar advertising. . . . We will not be alone." Brodie counterargued that, if P&G were to bypass both the usual blind tests and the shipping and advertising tests, "this would give us a two-year start over Lever and Colgate."

At that point, Rogan promptly rejected the idea: "Kirk, you know we've never done that!" He reminded his colleagues that moving in that direction would commit P&G to $15 million to $25 million dollars' worth of investment with no proof that it would work—a significant amount in 1945, when the company's sales were less than $500 million a year. Brodie was unmoved: "But this product has so many advantages," he said. "It is in a different class from any other new product we have ever introduced. Certainly, there are risks, but the potential is so great, I think we should take those risks."

President Deupree looked at Brodie then to Rogan and then turned to Neil McElroy, a young advertising manager who would eventually succeed him as president, "Mac, what do you think?" "It sure is a tough one," McElroy said, "but from what I have seen and heard today, I think it's the best prospect I have ever seen in P&G. For my money, I would take the chance and blast ahead as Mr. Brodie suggests. If the product turns out to be a winner as it appears to be, a two-year lead would be like a license to steal."

Deupree nodded. "Okay, Kirk," the president declared, "crank her up. Full speed ahead!"[54]

So, when the first boxes of Tide went on sale in 1946, it was the first synthetic detergent that could deep-clean clothing—removing mud, grass, and mustard stains "without making colors dull or dingy."[55] The benefits of "making white clothes look whiter" were so apparent that Tide outstripped all brands in the market and became the number one detergent in 1949. P&G's own Oxydol, Duz, and Dreft were all pushed aside.

When confronted with the plummeting sales of other P&G products, McElroy, now president of the company, simply acknowledged that "If we don't [use this technology], someone else will."[56] The marketing team was tasked with trumpeting the "Modern Washday Miracle," promoting Tide as a product that eased the "burden of washday drudgery" for millions of American households. The initial demand swelled, limited only by internal production capacity. By 1955, the United States was consuming 2.5 billion pounds of synthetic detergents a year. Eight out of every ten packages of washing products were synthetic.[57] The floating Ivory was swept away in the rising tide.[58]

THE P&G PARADOX

Novartis and P&G could not be more different. Novartis spends fearsome amounts of money designing and testing drugs for therapeutic treatment, jumping over the highest regulatory hurdles. P&G creates common household goods that clean. One saves lives; the other helps people look nice. Both companies, however, have thrived for more than a century; both have rewritten the rules in their respective sectors and transformed themselves, not just once but again and again. Most important, in both cases, is the fact that when new knowledge was ushered in, the existing knowledge became not redundant but critically complementary.

In the case of Novartis, external trends drove the shifts in scientific discipline. And these trends were reflected in the changing research focuses and discoveries by major universities and scientific communities. By contrast, P&G raced ahead by taking advantage of what emerged from other settings, dutifully assimilating this knowledge. The directional shift, in other words, was largely determined and driven from within. As we have already seen, being a first mover rarely confers any substantial advantage that promises ultimate success. Had P&G relied solely on a single discipline (say, mechanical engineering) and stuck to its original Ivory soap, it would have become, at best, a low-cost supplier of a commoditized product, desperately fending off other newcomers by competing on price—not the global leader that we recognize today.

Assessing the impact of Tide, Halberstadt pointed out that P&G would "no longer be a soap company" but "would become an industrial corporation with its future based on technology."[59] At that point, P&G was employing more than 1,500 graduates from technical colleges, with the number of technical staff tripling that of the pre-Tide year of 1945.[60] A family firm whose founders stirred cauldrons by hand had now become an enterprise built on three knowledge foundations: mechanical engineering, consumer psychology, and organic chemistry. And it was that combination—the totality of three knowledge disciplines—that had created the unstoppable Tide.

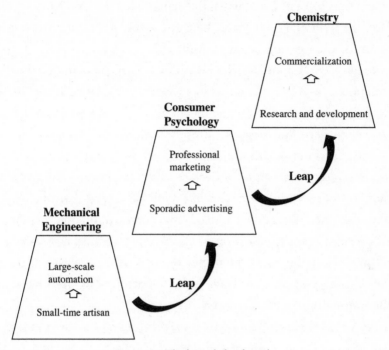

Figure 3.2 The knowledge funnel

Of course, our world has changed dramatically since Tide's early days. Even for P&G to prosper for another decade, waves of new knowledge are necessary. But the history of P&G, as well as that of Novartis, reminds us of the importance of embracing self-cannibalization. Self-cannibalization occurs when a company chooses to proactively replace one product or process with another that is potentially worth less. This is especially important, given any structural advantages a pioneer possesses—manufacturing scale, brand recognition, or trade secrets—are transient at best. To leap into a new knowledge discipline is to de-emphasize the old, and quite often, the new product or services launched will exert substitutional pressure on the old ones. That's why it's difficult for an established company to leap forward. And yet, as William Procter argued, "This [synthetic detergent] may ruin the soap business. But if anybody is going to ruin the soap business it had better be Procter & Gamble." This willingness to cannibalize a company's existing business before its decline was, in fact, eerily similar to Apple's under Steve Jobs. In 2005, when the demand for the iPod Mini was still huge, the iPod Nano was launched, effectively destroying the revenue stream of the existing product. And while iPod sales were still going through the roof, Jobs launched the iPhone, which combined the iPod, a cell phone, and Internet access in a single device. Three years after the iPhone's launch, the iPad made its debut despite the risk that it might one day cut into Mac desktop computer sales.[61]

The goal is not to encourage reckless behavior. But if the CEO's sole role in strategy making is to declare a new corporate direction only when entrepreneurial successes have fully emerged from below, the value that the CEO adds is indeed low. Forward-looking incumbents must recognize the need to continually branch out into new categories and must have the discipline to put the new venture ahead of the existing business—instead of leaving the opportunity to latecomers who will eventually become disruptive.

Now that we understand why it's critical for companies to leap and how some of the most successful ones did, the next three chapters will examine the direction in which one should leap in the future. What are some of the emerging trends or new knowledge disciplines that are critical for future companies' survival? Where are the next frontiers? In this world of heightened interconnection, where talent, knowledge, and capital move incessantly across national borders, the future always seems to arrive quicker than we expect. And precisely because the speed of development seems to have quickened, we need to identify the underlying drivers. Where exactly are the most powerful leverage points? Where should we leap?

REFLECTION ON PART 1

B EFORE WE MOVE ON TO PART 2, LET'S TAKE A MOMENT TO reflect on what we've learned.

Competitive Advantages Are Transient

When industry knowledge matures, copycats will catch up. Because latecomers often inherit a lower cost structure without the legacy assets, they exert competitive pressures on industry pioneers. That's why Steinway can't compete against Yamaha even though it has always made the finest pianos in the world.[62]

It Is Possible to Maintain Your Competitive Advantage

To avert this trajectory requires executives to reassess a firm's foundational or core knowledge and its maturity. Circumventing the seemingly inevitable begins by acknowledging where we are. Managers must therefore ask themselves what knowledge discipline is the most fundamental to their company. What is the core knowledge of your business? And how mature or widely available is it?

You can see this at work among business schools, including IMD. It used to be the ability to deliver a compelling classroom experience that attracted the corporate clients who would then send promising managers for executive training programs. That know-how in classroom delivery existed in the minds of professors. And yet, the sort of craftsmanship possessed by rock-star faculty is quickly being replaced by online learning, which automates the classroom experience to deliver content at almost zero cost over the Internet. That is why online learning is giving academics a strong sense of foreboding: it devalues the competency of a professor. How likely will the core competencies of your business be devalued, and how soon?

If Leaping Is So Important, When Is the Best Time to Leap?

A performance crisis, whether perceived or real, legitimizes top leaders' push for an abrupt reorientation. In breaking the grip of the existing organization, top management may simultaneously announce a new strategy and centralize resource allocation to make major investments in new areas or to force divestiture of unpromising projects. But such an abrupt change with such a wide scope also incurs huge risks because it leaves no margin for errors. It is therefore better to experiment, making small bets, while time is still on our side. In fact, one doesn't need to be a super-forecaster to know where to leap next. The inevitable is often quite apparent. Companies just need to leap while time is still on their side.[63]

Steve Jobs knew this. He said, "Things happen fairly slowly, you know. They do. These waves of technology, you can see them way before they happen, and you just have to choose wisely which ones you're going to surf. If you choose unwisely, then you can waste a lot of energy, but if you choose wisely, *it actually unfolds fairly slowly*. It takes years."[64] Jobs was referring to when he waited for two years for broadband, and then when it finally arrived, he jumped into the window of opportunity with the iPod. Countless others went earlier than Apple with their own MP3 players, but failed miserably. Before the 2000s, music sharing was mostly an illegal affair—on Napster—and it would take hours to download an album. With connectivity that poor, even the best-designed hardware made for hopelessly sluggish downloading. Jobs was waiting for the inevitable improvement of broadband to materialize.

This is an important lesson. Successful executives often exhibit a bias for action. But it's even more important to separate the noise from the signal that actually pinpoints the glacial movement around us. Listening carefully to the right signals requires patience and discipline. Seizing a window of opportunity, which means not necessarily being the first mover but the first to get it right, takes courage and determination. To leap successfully is to master these two seemingly contradictory abilities. The discipline to wait and the determination to drive, in balanced combination, often pay off handsomely. Cultivating this paradoxical ability at the individual and organizational levels is a major theme of the rest of the book. Now, let's turn to the next chapter and spot the inevitable.

PART II

WHAT WILL HAPPEN

4

LEVERAGING UBIQUITOUS CONNECTIVITY: FROM LONE GENIUS TO THE WISDOM OF THE CROWD

Western civilization, ever since the invention of the steam engine, has proceeded on the assumption that society must adjust to new technologies. This is a central meaning of what we refer to when we speak about an industrial revolution; we think about a society being transformed, and not just a new technology being introduced.

—AMITAI ETZIONI AND RICHARD REMP, *TECHNOLOGICAL SHORTCUTS TO SOCIAL CHANGE*, 1973

A BOOK BY HUNDREDS OF AUTHORS

FROM GALILEO GALILEI TO ALBERT EINSTEIN, FROM ISAAC Newton to Stephen Hawking, from Alex Matter of Novartis to David Byerly of Procter & Gamble, we tend to believe that human ingenuity resides in the minds of a few individuals. They are the prime movers who shape the world as we know it. Friedrich Nietzsche would say, "One giant calls to another across the desert intervals of time and, undisturbed by the chattering dwarfs who creep about beneath them."

But with our world becoming ever more connected, that may no longer be true. In fact, the chatters among the dwarfs can outsmart an intellectual giant.

Alexander Osterwalder was hooked. Having founded a startup and worked in nonprofits, he was consumed by a simple question: How can entrepreneurs change the way existing services and products are delivered? He had become so preoccupied with the question that he decided to enroll in a PhD program at the Faculty of Business and Economics (HEC) in Lausanne, Switzerland, to find out. He finished with a dissertation obscurely titled "The Business Model Ontology: A Proposition in a Design Science Approach."[1] In the ensuing years, Alex maintained a personal blog, interacted with a small group of business managers, and shared his interest with scholars and academics. He posted his original dissertation online for like-minded people to download. He posted YouTube videos of his talks. He gave free lectures to any companies that cared to listen. His followers steadily grew in number.

A few years later, Alex met his former dissertation adviser, Yves Pigneur, to discuss publishing his original dissertation, updated with new examples and additional insights. He wanted to publish the book and he wanted it so badly that he forgot just how slim the chance was of becoming a successful author. "There are one million books published in English every year; eleven thousand are business books, on top of two hundred and fifty thousand existing ones," Alex recalled. "It's very hard to stand out in such an ocean. . . . Nobody is waiting for another book; nobody is waiting for our book. But at that time, I just went ahead with my ignorant determination."[2] All Alex knew was that he needed to market his book as a field guide with animated visual graphics and complementary online content, all packaged in an unconventional manner to set it apart from the competition. The problem was that he lacked funding, and no major publisher would bet on him being a first-time author. He approached my school—IMD— and spoke with a colleague of mine, who couldn't help but burst out, "Don't waste your time on it!"

Fortunately, that sage advice went unheeded. The unfazed Alex went on to ask his online community to contribute. Or, more precisely, he invited them to pay to become coauthors of what he described as "an international bestseller 'yet to be written.'" For a $25 subscription, followers could receive draft sections of the book, on which they would then provide feedback.

As it turned out, many were eager to pay and to pay way more than $25. Every two weeks, Alex jacked up the price by 50 percent. By the time he was done finalizing the book, he had pooled 470 coauthors from some forty-five countries and raised $250,000 including presales. He used these funds to pay for a graphic designer, an editor, and a printer. And here's the surprise: everything happened in 2008. "It was a Kickstarter project, before Kickstarter," Alex mused.

The book's popularity grew with each coauthor scrutinizing and commenting on the content.[3] By the time the *Business Model Generation* was self-published, *Fast Company* magazine named it the best book for business owners in 2010, describing it as "by far the most innovative book on how to think about putting together a business." Success then fed on success. In short order, Wiley, a medium-size publisher that specialized in academic writing, acquired the global distribution rights and marketed Alex's book through major book retailers, including Barnes & Noble and Amazon. The 470 coauthors then undertook the most concerted and longest-lasting book promotion the industry had ever seen. They relentlessly trumpeted the final product through their personal networks on Facebook, LinkedIn, and Twitter.

Sales eventually topped one million copies and the book was translated into more than forty languages.[4] This was far in excess of the average twenty thousand copies that major publishers typically sold on any business topics. Ninety-two percent of all books sell no more than 70 copies, according to the Independent Book Publishers Association. In 2015, *Thinkers 50*, an annual ranking that the *Financial Times* deemed the "Oscars of Management Thinking," ranked Alex and Yves fifteenth.[5]

Today, Alex regularly lectures at Stanford and University of California, Berkeley, and delivers keynote speeches at major companies around the world. Because of the wisdom of the crowd, an obscure first-time author was catapulted into international stardom. Or, as

Tom Kelley, partner at the design firm IDEO and a professor at Stanford University, would say, "Enlightened trial and error succeeds over the planning of a lone genius." Ironically, when Alex went back to Wiley and asked whether they would have allowed him to do what had been done from day one, the publisher was adamant about its implausibility. "'No chance: you have practically broken every rule in book publishing possible.' Though we didn't know then, that was actually the only way to create the kind of book that we wanted to do," recalled the now celebrated author.[6]

THE RULE THAT REALLY MATTERS

While the viability of crowdsourcing has been demonstrated since the early days of Wikipedia, the heightened degree of today's connectivity was barely imaginable a decade ago. The accelerated improvement in how people are connected has profoundly changed how smart creatives can collaborate on ever-more-sophisticated projects, which in turn influences nearly every business prospect. What was once the personal foray of a single mind can be transmitted and distributed widely, allowing a whole community to participate. And this inexorable progression was underpinned by a convergence, first observed by one company.

In 1965, Intel cofounder Gordon Moore made a bold prediction about the exponential growth of computing power.[7] From vacuum tube to discrete transistor to integrated circuit, miniaturization of computer hardware had progressed rapidly. Extrapolating the trend, Moore asserted that the number of microchip transistors etched into a fixed area of a computer microprocessor would double every two years. And since transistor density correlated with computing power, the latter would double every two years. Intel has since delivered on that promise and immortalized it as "Moore's law."

So, whereas the IBM 650—the world's first mass-produced computer—could process less information than a single bacterium could, the computing power of the latest Intel Core i7, by the same analogy, would be close to that of a lab mouse.[8] Exponential growth also explains how a single iPhone today can summon more computing power than that of the entire spacecraft for the Apollo moon mission back in 1969.[9] And if Moore's law were applied to the auto industry, cars would by now get half a million miles per gallon, go 300,000 mph, and be so cheap that a driver would simply dump a Rolls-Royce rather than park it.[10]

Still, were it only computing power that rose exponentially, the extent of connectivity we enjoy today wouldn't exist. Network speed is also critical. Laying down fiber cables and setting up radio towers are easy. The difficult part involves negotiating who owns "rights of way" with the local government before broadband infrastructure can be placed above or below public and private property.[11] In other words, the speeds of communication networks—such as those involved in cellular telephony, Wi-Fi, or Ethernet—depend as much on technology as on government regulations.

Remarkably, despite market uncertainties beyond the technologist's control, network speed has risen just as quickly as computing power.[12] Fifteen years ago, wireless ran at about 5 to 10 kilobits per second (kbit/s). By the mid-2000s, wireless technology routinely delivered 100 kbit/s through cellular networks, and today, wireless can achieve speeds of 5 to 10 megabits per second (Mbit/s).

This exponential growth in connectivity, which industry experts refer to as "Edholm's law of bandwidth," has shifted the way we consume content and how information is transmitted. Take real-time movie streaming, which wasn't practical on a home desktop in the early 2000s. Most people would download an entire movie file overnight because the Internet bandwidth was not good enough to watch it in real time. By the late 2000s, many could stream movies with standard resolution on a laptop in a coffee shop. Today, we watch high-definition videos during our hour-long commutes on our smartphones, using 4G.

The new behaviors surrounding Internet usage are thus driven by connectivity that has become ubiquitous, voluminous, and smart; these behaviors, in turn, have spurred other component technologies, including GPS, gyroscopes, and accelerometers, found in every wearable and smartphone in our hands. A gyro sensor that measured angular velocity in the 1990s was a metal cylinder about 1 inch in diameter and 3 inches long, costing about $10,000, and it monitored only one axis of movement. These sensors are now reduced to tiny chips that cost an average of three dollars each. An autonomous drone typically comes equipped with two dozen of these sensors.[13] Such technological convergence is what enables self-driving cars and collaborative robots.

On the human side, the convergence has changed the way we work. Individuals and organizations can innovate very differently. Like Alex, companies no longer need to invent everything by themselves. When properly connected, an outside novice can be just as competent as, if not wiser than, internal experts. A company could therefore leverage external knowledge, previously diffusely distributed outside, to help it market and even design a product. And this leverage point is most relentlessly exploited by an Internet firm, hailing not from Silicon Valley, but from across the Pacific Ocean.

WE TWEET, WE GOOGLE, WECHAT

In Guangzhou, in southern China, the Canton Tower stands across the Pearl River from the city's main business district. Built in 2005, the skyscraper consists of two elliptical shapes twisting around each other at 45-degree angles, like a DNA double helix. The iconic structure that punctuates the city's skyline was China's tallest building for a brief period until a new construction went up in Shanghai in 2013.

In the shadow of the Canton Tower lies the TIT Creative Industry Zone, a neighborhood dotted with a dozen newly refurbished former industrial buildings. A plaque hanging on the red brick wall outside building #84 explains that it used to be a textile factory in the 1950s, then a military building in the 1960s and 1970s, and was repurposed back for civilian use in the mid-1970s. Its penultimate tenant was a metalworking shop that supplied the local auto industry.

Inside, there is nothing to suggest that the place was once a poorly lit shop floor with exposed lightbulbs and deafening noise. There are no machines that could churn out metal widgets. The original multistory structure has been stripped bare. What exists instead is a modern office with an open layout and white furniture. An atrium floods the interior with natural sunlight. Potted plants, toys, stuffed animals, and beanbags are scattered throughout the lounge areas. Young men and women wearing hoodies, designer sneakers, and angular spectacles wheel across the floor on ergonomic desk chairs like those made famous by Herman Miller, except that these are, of course, copies made in China. At the company's café and restaurant, people pay by tapping on their mobile phone. Credit cards and cash have all but receded into a bygone era. The cashless, cardless transactions are the direct result of WeChat's foray into electronic commerce. Building #84 and three neighboring buildings make up the headquarters of WeChat—China's largest messaging app.

When Facebook bought WhatsApp for $19 billion in 2014, Credit Lyonnais Securities Asia (CLSA) wrote, "If WhatsApp is worth $19B, then WeChat's worth at least $60B."[14] Because WeChat is privately held, any estimation of its true value would be, by definition, purely speculative. But it doesn't hurt that its parent company, Tencent, surpassed Alibaba in 2017 to become China's, as well as Asia's, most valuable company. Valued at more than $300 billion,[15] Tencent is ranked alongside the best of corporate America, including General Electric ($260 billion), IBM ($165 billion), and Intel ($170 billion). An early investor in Snapchat, Tencent also bought a 5 percent stake in Silicon Valley electric-vehicle maker Tesla in April 2017.[16]

As with all things China, the most astounding aspect of WeChat lies in its rapid ascent. Skeptics dismiss WeChat as merely a Chinese WhatsApp or iMessage. Many outside the country may not have even heard of the service. Still, there are 938 million monthly active WeChat users, a number larger than the entire population of Europe, let alone that of the United States.[17] So, it came as an additional surprise when Juliet Zhu, head of marketing at WeChat, reminded me that the size of the user base "doesn't tell the whole story. You need to count engagement." WhatsApp, for instance, has more than 1.2 billion users worldwide.[18] Facebook—WhatsApp's parent company since 2014—has over 2 billion users.[19] But to Juliet, WeChat has proven itself to be more enticing, for more than one third of its users spend four hours or more per day on WeChat.[20] By contrast, users average thirty-five minutes on Facebook, twenty-five minutes on Snapchat, fifteen minutes on Instagram, and one minute on Twitter.[21]

How does WeChat capture so many eyeballs and such long stares? Like Alex, WeChat did it by enabling end-users to be creative; but unlike Alex, it did it in a uniquely Chinese way, with engineers focusing as much on user experience as developing new tools for third parties to invent new features on their own.

IF CHARLES DARWIN WERE TO SURVEY THE INTERNET

In *The World Is Flat*, published in 2007, Thomas Friedman describes how the Internet transcends national boundaries and narrow ideologies by bringing billions of people online. In reality, the Internet has made the world anything but flat. The online world is still a rugged landscape with cloistered communities and echo chambers. The Beijing government, for example, has long warded off foreign websites it deems suspicious. Because of widespread Internet policing and mysterious censorship practices—collectively known as the Great Firewall—you won't spot Google, Twitter, YouTube, or Facebook in the Middle Kingdom.[22]

In their place, a slew of apps that initially bore some resemblance to their Western counterparts have evolved into entirely different species. Western companies have long been accustomed to mobile advertising. Facebook, Google, Twitter, and Snapchat have amassed copious user data to fine-tune ever more powerful algorithms and to help advertisers better target end-consumers. But in China, storing user data could pose a political risk so high that local firms have chosen to find other ways to get consumers to pay, either by charging transaction fees or through in-app purchases—why mine data when customers would pay directly for services? Because consumers across the world have vastly different habits even when using similar technologies, tech giants also resemble a collection of zoological species with functional features highly adapted to their local environments. Companies must specialize as they fight over and protect their market shares.

Take mobile payment as an example. In 2013, WeChat debuted its first payment system—WeChat Pay. One hugely popular feature is the "red envelope," which lets consumers send virtual packets stuffed with digital cash to families and friends during the Lunar New Year, using their mobile phones. To add a twist to the festive tradition, anyone can preset a fixed amount and distribute it at random to a selected number of recipients. Say you send three thousand yuan to thirty friends; some get bigger hauls than others, leading to grins and cringes all around. It's part social networking, part gaming, and part casual gambling. Between February 7 and 12, 2016, some 32 billion red envelopes changed hands, up from 3.2 billion during the same period in the previous year.[23]

Besides sending each other money, WeChat users can also pay utility bills and invest in wealth funds. WeChat's parent company, Tencent, had invested billions of dollars in Didi Chuxing (China's Uber) and Meituan-Dianping (China's Groupon) so that people could order rides or shop for group deals without ever leaving the app.[24] In recent years, WeChat has expanded further, including an impressive list of traditional retailers—McDonald's, KFC, 7-Eleven, Starbucks, Uniqlo, and many other well-established names, well beyond the countless mom-and-pop stores that have long embraced WeChat Pay. In describing this social and economic phenomenon in China, the *New York Times* wrote, "cash is rapidly becoming obsolete."[25]

Today, shaking one's phone via WeChat is a popular way to find new friends who are also users. Waving it in front of a television allows it to recognize the current program and gives viewers the opportunity to interact. WeChat has effectively rolled Facebook, Instagram, Twitter, WhatsApp, and Zynga all into one. Rather than being a stand-alone messaging app, WeChat is an indispensable mobile tool for booking doctors' appointments, settling hospital bills, filing police reports, reserving restaurant tables, accessing banking services, holding video conferences, playing games, and much more. To fuel the growth of this monster app, self-reliance would never be enough. WeChat needs to enable users to be creative, far more aggressively than Google and Facebook, to develop new services that run on top of its social media platform.

MASS-PRODUCING DECISIONS

In late 2012, seventeen people inside WeChat experimented with a new idea on the concept of "official accounts," with the goal of targeting companies and corporations. At that point, WeChat already had a solid following among end-consumers, but the team envisioned using open application programming interfaces (APIs), to turn WeChat into a communication pipeline for third-party products and services.

In the simplest terms, an API is an official set of rules and guidelines that facilitates information exchange between two pieces of software. The software routines, protocols, and tools can allow third parties to tap into WeChat's massive user base. Lake Zeng, vice general manager of WeChat's open platforms division, explained to me, "In the past, WeChat had successfully connected people, but we were not clear how companies could also leverage WeChat to connect and communicate with their own customers. We needed a vehicle to achieve this goal, and we thought 'official accounts' could be that very means."

Understandably, none of the team members was sure about what services to include in the beginning. As engineers fanned out to look for promising ideas, China Merchants Bank (CMB) came knocking on the door. To Lake Zeng, the project goal with CMB was simple—go wherever the customer wanted:

At the time, our idea about official accounts was very rudimentary. We only had a few demos. We thought that traditional companies might send messages or coupons to customers and promote sales. All our initial ideas had revolved around "broadcasting" functions. But the discussion with CMB changed the way we think.

Banks have high data security standards, and they have to keep these data on their own servers. If we wanted to make it work, we had to provide [an] open connection. From then on, we've pivoted

WeChat toward the role of a "connector" or "pipe." We let companies pump information from their servers to end-users on WeChat.

That openness proved crucial in attracting other adopters. Before long, China Southern Airlines, the country's largest airline by fleet size, launched its WeChat official account. When a user says, "Beijing to Shanghai, tomorrow," WeChat displays all flight information that fits those criteria. Clicking on a flight takes the user to a server that China Southern Airlines hosts where one can book and pay for the flight. Although all the data transactions happen on the airline's server, users get the impression that they are operating entirely through WeChat. This drastically simplifies the mobile user's experience. A user no longer has to download a new app or toggle across multiple windows on a tiny screen. A new proposition thus emerged: companies can create an unlimited number of new functions on their own and keep all the data if they want, with a user interface that is already familiar to hundreds of millions of Chinese.

When I was first told by an employee that WeChat only stored, on average, five days of user data, I was skeptical that any company would choose to erase its customer information. So was my research collaborator, who proceeded to ask about the size of the firm's computer server room. The limited physical footage, however, was consistent with the earlier assertion that beyond real-time monitoring and feature usage analysis, traditional data mining was all but impossible because of the relatively paltry storage. But WeChat's inability to store customer data is precisely its attraction for Western brands that might otherwise shun any tighter integration with a tech giant. Big brands don't like to surrender information control.

WeChat's major breakthrough, therefore, is the realization that a product's best feature will never be invented in-house. Killer apps must be invented by users instead. But that should not come as a surprise. As perceptive as Steve Jobs was, he couldn't have predicted that some of the most prominent functions of his iPhone would be hailing a cab (Uber) and taking automatically erased pictures (Snapchat). No single company could have come up with both of these

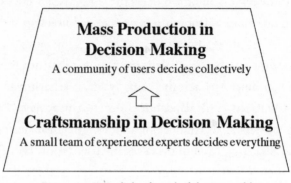

Figure 4.1 Knowledge funnel of the intangible

killer apps. Under most conditions, decision quality is enhanced when there are varied, independent inputs.[26] And if we draw upon the concept of a knowledge funnel from Part 1 of the book, we can see that both Alex and WeChat have decentralized decision making. They have effectively "mass-produced" decisions as outputs, just as Yamaha mass-produced pianos when competing against Steinway & Sons in the manufacturing world.

Yet herein lies a challenge: the level of technical sophistication involved in book writing and mobile app development doesn't seem all that demanding when compared to the engineering feats associated with building rockets or jet engines. Can critical decisions really be mass-produced when the goal is to develop something technologically complex and organizationally specific? Can we mass-produce decisions of all kinds?

This was the challenge faced by DARPA.

WHEN ENGINEERING BECOMES REALLY COMPLICATED

The Defense Advanced Research Projects Agency (DARPA)—the Pentagon's brain, as some would say—is the research division of the Department of Defense. President Eisenhower established the agency in 1958 to undertake high-risk research in an attempt to find solutions to real problems. Some forty years ago, DARPA went on to invent the Arpanet, the origin of today's Internet. And in 2012, it decided to crowdsource the next generation of fighting vehicles: a tank that could swim ashore carrying marines and move inland directly.

The concept of an amphibious infantry fighting vehicle—a fancier name for a swimming tank—is not new. In military warfare that requires beach landing, operations have historically been conducted using ships' boats to deliver troops to shore. To protect the soldiers, naval ships would protect the ground and air, aiming at hostile targets. But the risk involved in an exposed beachhead operation is so great that the marines have not stormed a hostile beach since the Korean War.[27]

The development of an amphibious fighting vehicle—a roaming tank that can also swim, capable of bringing foot soldiers ashore without the need for unloading and disembarking—has been the dream among military experts since its conception in the 1980s.[28] As is the case in the automotive industry, military vehicles are the product of development by teams organized around components and subsystems. Such division of labor is considered to be natural and even beneficial given the intricacies of modern vehicles. At Toyota, for instance, parts often have been designed as modular components called black boxes that are then assembled into a final product. The principle of modularity facilitates faster and more accurate troubleshooting. The well-known image of a GI in World War II trying to fix a jeep by taking everything apart in a remote jungle is a vivid reminder of the problems of nonmodular design. In the battlefield, when time is limited and mistakes are unaffordable, a more effective design should allow users to discard a defective component entirely and replace it with a black-box module.[29]

Of modern-day manufacturing, the personal computer is possibly the most modular system ever designed. Data passing through a hard drive to a microprocessor (CPU) conform exactly to industrywide protocols. Uniform design rules apply to the LCD screen, memory storage, and other peripherals such as keyboards, mice, and Bluetooth speakers. Thanks to modularity, it doesn't matter whether Seagate or Toshiba makes a hard disk; either way, it works just fine with an Intel CPU.

When an interface is standardized across components, these components become interchangeable. As long as the interface remains unchanged, component designers can be creative within their own black boxes. And when innovation occurs across all components simultaneously, the overall performance rises dramatically.

But modularity comes with limitations. Due to compliance to a standard interface, serious problems can emerge when radical innovation is required, and in the case of DARPA, trying to make a land-roaming tank swim. The new performance outcome requires new components be added, existing interfaces redrawn, and system architecture redefined. But because everything interacts with and depends on everything else, small problems can quickly compound and become intractable.

This intractability lies at the heart of the challenge that DARPA faced. Although modularity has facilitated an in-depth understanding in a few focused areas, it has prevented the interaction of components and subsystems beyond existing paradigms. Most damningly, experts have long been separated to precisely mirror a system's specialized modules.[30] As the performance for each component has continued to rise, the related uncertainty has increased, and even the best engineers have become overwhelmed by the overall complexity. "The propulsion people work on the propulsion system, the data people work on data management, and so forth,"[31] Nathan Wiedenman, an army lieutenant colonel, DARPA program manager, and armor officer, observed in Wired. "Nothing is just a data-management system or a power or thermal system. All the components of a complex system like this have mechanical, power, data, thermal, and electromagnetic behaviors that affect other sub-components around them." When a new system needs to be designed, built, and tested, and redesigned, rebuilt, and retested again and again, the development table grows longer, and costs go higher.[32]

At the height of the debt-ceiling crisis in 2011, under congressional pressure, former defense secretary Robert Gates promised to rein in the budget by saving $100 billion over the next five years. In the process, he was forced to shut down the amphibious vehicle project, which had already cost some $13 billion after running for over twenty years.[33] "The only entities able to contribute to the design of these important systems are corporations with the [resources] to build multimillion-dollar prototypes. That limits us to a handful of companies and maybe a few hundred brains," Wiedenman said. In fact, throughout DARPA's history, innovation had been concentrated among defense contractors, such as Lockheed Martin and Boeing. "In a nation of 300 million people, we can do better."[34]

IN COMES CROWDSOURCING

In October 2012, DARPA swung its doors open to innovators of all stripes to design a new amphibious infantry fighting vehicle—the Fast, Adaptable, Next-Generation Ground Vehicle (FANG). There would be three competitions: The first would focus on the design of the vehicle's drivetrain, the second on its hull, and the third on the complete mobility system. Stages one and two would come with $1 million cash prizes; the final round would double the amount.[35]

With help from Vanderbilt University, DARPA set up an online portal that served as a collaborative work system—a free-for-all candy store for techies—containing every engineering tool imaginable: qualitative reasoning, static constraint analysis, computational fluid dynamics, manufacturability analysis, and much else.[36] Even Lockheed Martin was impressed by what DARPA had built. "It's not about connecting just the people," observed Mark Gersh, a program manager at Lockheed Martin Advanced Technology Center in Palo Alto, California. "It's also about integrating the analysis capabilities with the tools, models, and simulations that integrated project teams use."[37] Users could download the tools and explore the component model libraries to start putting their designs together, simulating the overall performance of thousands of potential mobility and drivetrain subsystems.[38] The goal was to design a vehicle capable of self-deploying from a home ship and delivering seventeen marines from at least 12 miles from shore.[39] Four decades after inventing the Internet, DARPA had found new ways to leverage its invention.

The three-person team who took that prize in April 2013 were dispersed across Ohio, Texas, and California.[40] Team Ground Systems, as it was called, comprised Eric Nees; his father, James Nees; and their longtime friend Brian Eckerly. All three had engineering backgrounds: Eric worked for a military contractor in California, having done projects on conventional ground vehicles. His father, James, had spent more than two decades in the air force as a research engineer and later worked as a project manager at the Air Force Research Laboratory in Ohio. And Brian, who lived in Texas, went to high school with Eric and graduated from Ohio State University with a bachelor's degree in electrical and computer engineering.

"We did select a lot of components from the repository, but so many times we had to go research individual components on the DARPA site to make sure that they were at least close to being compatible," James recalled. While Team Ground Systems' design relied almost entirely on existing components in the library, they still found significant work was involved in finding the right ones. "It's nice to say you can just take all the LEGO blocks and stitch them together, but some components, though they look similar, are different. They just don't work with the rest of the system."[41] Team leader Eric emphasized that his background in automotive systems had been essential. "There's jargon that wasn't necessarily accessible to people not familiar with automotive systems in this project."[42] For Brian, who had worked for two big banks, contributing by crunching numbers came naturally. He described the banking industry as "mostly data analysis": "I was good at trying a lot of different combinations, collecting the data, and then providing the results back to my teammates on what was working well and what wasn't."[43]

That combined expertise was exactly what DARPA was looking for. While Lockheed Martin might have the best engineers, its inputs and existing process are primarily limited to internal experts already familiar to the field. Individual judgment that reflects the narrow insights and skills of a single organization will always pale in comparison to the collective wisdom of multiple parties. That's why in 2009 the National Aeronautics and Space Administration (NASA) had also crowdsourced when developing a new prediction algorithm for solar flares. NASA's previous model could achieve no more than 55 percent prediction accuracy and NASA needed improved prediction to better protect astronauts and equipment floating in space. After posting the challenge and receiving hundreds of submissions, NASA got an answer within three months from a retired wireless communications engineer living in New Hampshire. The man's algorithm reached 85 percent accuracy, using only ground-based equipment instead of the orbiting spacecraft NASA had traditionally used.[44] It was his unconventional thinking and new perspective that surpassed all the experience of world-class astrophysicists that NASA could claim.

Toward the end of the FANG challenge, DARPA had similarly attracted more than one thousand participants in two hundred teams. The fifteen finalist teams averaged about 1,200 hours on the project. Assuming a hypothetical hourly rate of $200, which would include administrative overhead, the collective design efforts would have cost about $3.6 million, making the $1 million pretax payout a great bargain.[45] "We really want to open the aperture to non-traditional design entities; folks who have the skills, but don't traditionally have a mechanism by which they can participate in the development of military vehicles," said Wiedenman. "I can be a transmission engineer for a civilian firm who really knows my stuff, [and] I can log on, join and participate in a meaningful way."[46]

Ultimately, Team Ground Systems settled on a design that traded automotive performance for manufacturing lead time, since the overall goal was to significantly speed up the design and manufacturing practice. Team Ground Systems was rewarded for quickening manufacturing by a factor of two compared to the runner-up, by selecting components, including the main engine, that were more quickly obtainable from the supply chain.[47] When asked how the prize money was divided, Eric laughed and said that there was only one fair way: a simple three-way split.

SOLVING THE RIGHT PROBLEM

To effectively harness the wisdom of the crowd, it is often insufficient to just describe the technical problem and then send people off to work. The famed Gates Foundation, for instance, has made repeated attempts to advance health science by running "Grand Challenges." These well-intentioned efforts are aimed at previously intractable problems—such as malaria prevention in rural villages—and encourage scientists to collaborate in a single place where "half-baked" solutions and partial advances are made accessible to the entire scientific community.[48]

Ten years on, few payoffs were seen. None of the funded projects has made many inroads, as reported by the *Seattle Times*. Bill Gates himself admitted having underestimated what it would take to implement new technologies in countries where millions of people still lack access to basic necessities such as clean water and medical care. In other words, it wasn't that the solution itself wasn't clever enough, but that the context of the problem hobbled its implementation. "I was pretty naïve about how long that process would take," Gates said.[49] External parties, after all, don't have the insider's perspective.

It's therefore not enough for companies to ask employees or customers to generate ideas without creating mechanisms to do something with them, or to push for answers without defining a problem worth solving. One can't demand disruptive ideas without ring-fencing resources, and DARPA has shown us how much more is needed.

Critical to DARPA's crowdsourcing effort was the online platform that spanned the entire design process. Contestants had full access to the entire component library and online tools to virtually simulate and validate their specific designs.[50] Through the system, competing teams received real-time feedback, incorporating it before resubmitting their designs.[51] DARPA's online platform, conceptually, had *decontextualized* a military-related question, turning it into a generic engineering problem.[52] One needn't know everything about military deployment—whether a tank is used for scouting, facing infantry and light armored vehicles, or assaulting bunkers and fortification. The requirements of these operations were embedded in the online simulation, built into the system as objective criteria, including stresses, strains, temperature, accelerating, and braking. What all the contestants focused on was making component trade-offs, attaining previously un-

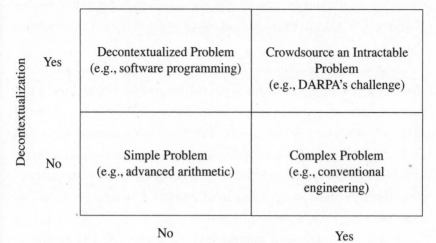

Figure 4.2 Problems of different names

thought-of, combinatorial kinds of optimization. The winner was then chosen based on a final score against system performance and ease of manufacture.

❖ ❖ ❖

Imagine a two-by-two matrix, as shown in Figure 4.2, in which the X-axis depicts how much a problem has been broken down and the Y-axis depicts how much it has been decontextualized. Assuming the matrix represents all solvable problems in the world, the bottom left corner would contain simple problems, problems whose solutions required neither division into smaller chunks nor a new perspective. An example would be a straightforward arithmetic question. Simple problems don't have to be easy to answer. They could be difficult, but don't require insights from a multidisciplinary perspective.

Engineering problems that demand a division of expertise usually fall into the bottom right corner. Building a car, putting up a skyscraper, and developing a new drug are complex tasks, and these tasks must be broken into subtasks, or modules, that call on different domains of knowledge. Employees across different disciplines must keep well informed about organizational context and industry know-how. Without this collective understanding, everything would descend into chaos.[53]

More interesting is the top left corner, which describes decontextualized problems. A decontextualized problem, even when extremely difficult, requires no organizational understanding. As long you are good at what you do, say, writing a piece of software code, you can solve that problem. By definition, such problems are mostly general and abstract in nature. And because everyone can participate, a decontextualized problem is the most suitable target for an open tournament—it's a call to let the smartest and the brightest win.

Google Code Jam—an international programming competition—consists of a set of algorithmic problems that must be solved in a fixed amount of time. The competition began in 2003 as a means for Google to identify top engineering talent whom the traditional recruitment channel would easily have missed. The winner in 2014, for instance, was an eighteen-year-old from Belarus, who beat twenty-six other coders from around the world in his first attempt at the annual competition, and who went on to win the competition four years in a row.[54] Such open tournaments, by design, enlarge the circle of problem solvers to the maximum. No one is required to understand the context of an industry or a company. Raw intellectual horsepower reigns supreme.

But for organizations that seek to tap into this external expertise, the biggest challenge lies exactly in translating an organizational, domain-specific problem into something sufficiently general for the large pool of external talent to contribute to. Charles Kettering, the famed inventor and head of research at General Motors, once said, "A problem well stated is a problem half-solved." The importance of stating a problem in a way that rids itself of organizational context is even truer when a company attempts to crowdsource. Syngenta, a global Swiss agribusiness that produces agrochemicals and seeds, understood this well. As noted in Part 1, research in drug making has leaped from the traditional domains of microbiology and chemistry to those of recombinant DNA and computational biology. Agribusiness is no different. It was the genetic manipulation pioneered by biotechnology seed companies that resulted in various herbicide- and insect-resistant crops. Syngenta, a $13-billion-a-year company, also a spin-off from Novartis since 2000, fully recognizes the primacy of data analytics in improving seed breeding and plant yield. But the firm lacks one critical resource. "We have a great many biologists and chemists who can do traditional bench work in our labs, but data scientists and software programmers are scarce resources globally," one manager told me. "We can never compete against Google or Facebook when recruiting certain talents." And so, Syngenta experimented with a crowdsourcing project.

Joseph Byrum, senior research and development (R&D) and strategic marketing executive at Syngenta, wrote, "We wanted to replace that instinct [of trial and error in a lab] with hard data and statistics, but doing so required delving deep into mathematical questions that had never before been raised in agriculture."[55] Like DARPA, Byrum realized that leveraging the wisdom of the crowd required more than just an online campaign: "A manager who posts an online challenge, walks away, and expects the solution to be waiting in the email inbox a few days or weeks later is going to be disenchanted."[56] This is because software programmers lack familiarity with plant biology and agriculture. Things that look familiar to an agronomist are foreign to a statistician. Lost in translation, lost in the crowd. "It took numerous one-on-one discussions to carefully walk each participant back onto the same page, but this time was well spent."

In 2014, Syngenta ran an online tournament, inviting computer scientists to devise machine algorithms for automating assay analysis, a labor-intensive process that biochemists traditionally carried out to measure the presence, amount, or functional activity of a target molecule. Beating more than 154 contestants and five hundred submissions, the winning algorithm demonstrated a 98 percent screening accuracy, resulting in annual labor savings of at least six bench workers. Still, Syngenta was most surprised by the variance in submission quality.[57]

Great programmers are rare. The received wisdom in the tech world asserts that the productivity of a great developer is at least three times that of an average developer and ten times that of a bad one.[58] Whether or not this is empirically true, Syngenta observed a similarly wide variation in the performance accuracy of submitted algorithms. When the results were lined up in descending order, the performance curve resembled a steep cliff, with the best submissions concentrated among a handful of programmers.

Some of these top coders turned out to be previous winners of Google's Code Jam tournament who had adamantly refused to join the Internet giant, preferring a freelance lifestyle instead. And that suited Syngenta just fine. The company ended up paying the cash prize to only the top three contestants but gained access to the greatest minds that even Google couldn't employ.

Viewed through the two-by-two matrix in Figure 4.2, the FANG challenge became especially interesting. Historically, DARPA had decomposed the task of tank-building into component modules with standard interfaces. But the online simulation had further decontextualized the design challenge. System constraints well understood by internal engineers were now codified into the online tool set. Consequently, outsiders could focus on solving an abstract optimization problem. Had DARPA not modularized and decontextualized the engineering problem, it would have been forever mired in its own intractable complexity. "[Just like] all multidisciplinary design spaces, this was an awesome experience and has my team reconsidering our *tool sets* for our day jobs," commented one contestant as he contemplated emulating DARPA's approach in his own business. "I think it was a great experience."

With the help of the online collaboration tool, a nonmilitary engineer like Eric can now rival a system expert at Lockheed Martin.

DOING GREAT THINGS WITHOUT GETTING PAID?

At some level, we all know that salary alone will not sufficiently motivate people. Most of the contestants at DARPA and Syngenta knew their chance of winning was slim. Many of Alex's coauthors would never have thought their self-publication would one day become an international best seller. Police officers, firefighters, and soldiers do not risk their life for a weekly paycheck. And yet they all pushed on.[59]

In a fascinating study, Mark Muraven—at the time, a psychology graduate student at Case Western—designed an experiment to understand how willpower operates, which was later entertainingly capitulated by the author, Charles Duhigg: Why do some people exhibit stamina when facing a tedious assignment and persist, while others quickly become distracted and give up? Is "grit" an inner capacity or something strongly influenced by the environment?

Muraven and his coauthors recruited seventy-seven undergraduates to a laboratory and tempted them with cookies (cookies and undergraduates remain the constant staple of psychology experiments). They were asked to skip lunch. As the students arrived with an empty stomach at the laboratory, they were shown two bowls of food. One was filled with warm, freshly baked cookies, soft to touch and sweet to smell. The other was heaped with cold, stale radishes in a pile. Without stating the true intention of the experiment, a white coat–wearing researcher stepped in and told half of the participants to eat the cookies and ignore the radishes. For these cookie eaters, concentrating on the cookies did not feel like a task at all. They savored every moment of it. Then, the second group was told to ignore the cookies and concentrate on eating the radishes.

After five minutes, the researcher returned and asked the two groups of participants to solve a puzzle that appeared easy but was actually impossible to solve. It involved tracing a geometric pattern in one go without lifting the pen off the page or repeating a line twice. Muraven wanted to find out whether willpower resembles personal character or behaves like a reservoir of resource, and to what extent willpower can be influenced. Would the radish munchers, who had used a lot of willpower to resist the temptation of the sweet cookies, be so depleted of their willpower that they would no longer have the stamina to stay focused on solving the impossible puzzle?

The cookie eaters, with their faces relaxed, some humming songs, attempted the puzzle repeatedly. They spent on average nineteen minutes before giving up. The radish eaters, however, looked agitated, showed palpable frustration, shifted restlessly in their seats, and complained about the setup of the experiment. They quit after just eight minutes,

60 percent less time than the cookie eaters spent. One hurled insults at the researcher. Turns out willpower can be depleted like any other resource. Once it is exhausted, we can no longer focus on difficult tasks. We lose our patience and succumb to all kinds of temptation. After a long day at work closing the accounting books and filing endless complicated expense reports, most of us end up slouching in front of the TV, eating a tub of ice cream. Going to the gym is for tomorrow; let's relax tonight.[60]

When Muraven became a professor at the State University of New York at Albany, he ran the same experiment with a new twist. After a new group of unsuspecting undergraduates was asked to skip lunch, Muraven assigned the cold, stale radishes to the first group and asked them to ignore the warm, sweet cookies. This time, however, a kind-looking researcher came in to discuss the purpose of the experiment and described how the research team was trying to understand the human ability to resist temptation. She asked the students nicely, and she expressed gratitude to them for their time and effort in advancing the knowledge of modern psychology. She also told them that they would have an opportunity to provide feedback on the experimental setup to the research team.

After much radish munching by participants, the researcher came back and had the students sit in front of a computer screen. Random numbers were flashed for five hundred milliseconds each. Every time a four followed a six, participants were instructed to hit the spacebar on the keyboard. It was a classic mundane task designed to measure people's ability to stay focused. The computer program lasted for twelve minutes.

To everyone's surprise, this group of students was able to concentrate the entire time, despite their supposedly depleted reservoir of willpower.

The second group of students was subject to the same treatment but with one exception: this group was not told about the purpose of the experiment. The researcher looked rushed and unconcerned, flipped through papers, and instructed them in a commanding tone with a stern face: "You must not touch the cookies." When the students were seated in front of the computer screen, they performed terribly during the test. They missed hitting the spacebar, despite explicit instructions;

they complained that they felt tired and that the numbers were flashing too quickly. They were exhausted.

As Muraven later explained, "If people feel like it's a choice or something they enjoy because it helps someone else—it's much less taxing. If they feel like they have no autonomy, if they're just following orders, their willpower muscle gets tired much faster."[61]

Choice and enjoyment also explain the Wikipedia phenomenon. Computer scientist Martin Wattenberg estimated in 2008 that 100 million hours were spent on the project by people around the world. At the time of writing this, some thirty-one thousand "Wikipedians" were identified as active editors, spending on average one hour per day editing, seven days a week. The top 20 percent were spending more than three hours per day in addition to whatever they might do as a day job.

The world's number one Wikipedian was until recently a resident of Indiana named Justin Knapp, who holds a degree in philosophy and political science. After editing anonymously for months, Knapp finally joined Wikipedia in 2005 and went on to become the first person to have a million edits. Today, he has accumulated a staggering record of more than 1.3 million entries. Although Knapp is obviously an outlier, his motivation and that of many other avid Wikipedians are not that alien to us. It's easy to see the purpose of Wikipedia, of "bringing free educational content to the world," as valuable.

To be sure, not everyone can be sufficiently motivated by a sense of purpose alone. For some people, the act of altruism and the sense that they are contributing to and cataloging the growing body of human knowledge is enough to propel them into slaving for countless hours on Wikipedia. For others, it is because Wikipedia has given contributors social bragging rights about what they have written online. We all want to look good in front of others and feel good about ourselves. There is nothing more powerful than disclosing a piece of interesting information unknown to others. That's why people exchange secrets and spread rumors around the water cooler. Somehow, we are hardwired to dispense insider information in exchange for no more than a vague sense of admiration from our peers. We do it to gain social recognition and status.

The genius of Wikipedia is to transform the mundane tasks of writing and editing factual articles into a golden opportunity for anyone to tell anything to the entire world. Top contributors are recognized for their sheer effort. They see how many times their articles are viewed and their relative position in terms of the number of entries that they make, all published in a league table for public examination. For hardcore Wikipedians, that is a big deal.[62]

That's why before pushing problems out to a vast group of people, I've often found asking the following three questions can be enormously helpful:

Why is the problem important?

The crowd needs to understand why it should take notice and get involved. Wikipedia beat Encyclopaedia Britannica not because of better compensation to its writers and editors—it pays nothing. Instead, Wikipedia promises its contributors a purpose that is boldly displayed on its website: *bringing free educational content to the world.* Similarly, for most DARPA contestants, the sense of nation-building, valiantly ensconced in heroism, looms large. People need to be moved to take action.

What does a good idea look like?

Define up front the objective criteria, such as implementation time or feasibility. This helps the crowd submit and identify ideas that are truly actionable. Illustrate the types of solutions that you are seeking and the success metrics you'll use. Frame the challenge in a quantifiable way. DARPA, NASA, and Syngenta succeeded in large part because of the way they articulated their problem statements—what they are and aren't.

Does the problem need to be broken down?

If the problem is significant, it helps to break it down into smaller segments. Make sure that the crowd is aware of any constraints, or better still, embed those constraints in the collaboration tool. All these help lower the barrier to entry. As an organizer, you don't have to spend time re-creating the wheel. Often you can use one of the existing platforms (e.g., Spigit or InnoCentive, among many others) or borrow materials from those willing to share.

HOW WECHAT IS CHANGING EVERYTHING
WE KNOW ABOUT THE INTERNET

In January 2017, WeChat created yet another stir by rolling out WeChat "Mini Program," which allows users to experience many mobile apps without having to download or install anything. In less than twenty-four hours, such headlines as "Super App WeChat Plans to Lock Out Foreign App Stores," "WeChat Beats Google to the Punch," and "Tencent Takes On the App Store" began to circulate on the web.[63]

As any smartphone user can attest, most of us use only a handful of apps every day, though we often have dozens of them stored on our devices. Localytics found that, typically, one in four people abandoned a new app after just one session.[64] The big idea of WeChat was to lessen the burden consumers experienced when downloading an app and to reduce maintenance costs for app developers. Juliet Zhu, head of marketing at WeChat, explained, "If you build an app from ground up, you might be spending 70 percent or more of your effort sorting out the backend programming, [an] operation that end-users don't see or even notice. We think developers should dedicate the majority of their efforts [to] thinking about content and services they are trying to provide to customers. Right now, it can cost an app developer up to a hundred thousand dollars to build a generic iOS or Android app prototype. There must be a better way."

Market feedback also drove the development of mini-programs, as it did for many other inventions. Among WeChat's business users, the most popular usage remained the subscription accounts, through which business owners could send media content, including promotional offerings and discount vouchers, to end-consumers. Service accounts, which allowed consumers to transact directly, languished. Chale Chen, product manager on the Mini Program Team Open Platform, explained to me, "In our previous official account setting, we built the system around conventional HTML5. Essentially, our direct API pump[ed] data in and out. In China, however, connectivity can be unsteady. Delays and wait times are common. Online transaction[s] at times may get lost because of timeout[s]. This represents a challenge [to the] user experience."

A team of a dozen programmers thus began to rethink how they could re-architect the official account. Soon enough, the concept of a mini-program emerged. Using a proprietary language, similar to the approach of Apple's iOS ecosystem,[65] Mini Program packages common user-interface components into standard modules—swiping, jumping to next, dropdown menus. The modular setup dramatically lessens data usage and makes programming far easier than that under the iOS or Android systems. In short, developers can focus on building content.

To be sure, some advanced developers scoff at the resultant limitations. They lamented that the simple-to-use standard restricted their creativity, bemoaning that the new mobile apps had all but fallen into a vanilla format. But that's exactly the point: to lower the bar for small businesses to jumpstart their digitization strategy. Chale recalled, "We had one engineer from an FM radio broadcaster who decided to try to build out a mini-program. He basically spent one weekend learning how to code and launched the new application the following Monday. That's what we try to achieve. We want to tear down any obstacles that bar entrepreneurs [from] launch[ing] their own apps."

Not all mini-programs receive approval. WeChat still vets the work developers submit. Tellingly, WeChat's criteria appear to be even more stringent than the gold standard that Apple set forth. Games and advertising are all but forbidden. Although developers can provide services, such as booking a hotel, and then charge customers for them, they are not allowed to sell virtual goods, such as screen savers, emojis, or games. And all mini-programs have to be free. As Juliet described it,

> Mini Program is not designed to monetize. The idea is to help service providers to become more effective in serving their own customers by making their services more accessible whenever the purchasing occasions arise.
>
> That's also why the function of a mini-program doesn't appear on one's WeChat interface until it is used the first time. Either it can be

discovered socially through friends or in the real world by scanning QR codes. If Mini Program is not something consumers use anyway, the button has no place to show up. User interface should always be kept clean. We don't want to confuse our users with the new rollout.

Despite the strict limits, on the eve of the launch of Mini Program, WeChat had already gathered one thousand apps, a number that has continued to grow. Arguably, WeChat's greatest achievement lies in its ability to increasingly open its business model to outsiders. Where DARPA and Syngenta tapped into the wisdom of the crowd to help solve complicated technical issues that were defined up front, WeChat empowered its business users to invent new functionalities that have not been foreseen.

By May 2017, more than 200,000 third-party developers were working tirelessly for the WeChat platform.[66] Ubiquitous connectivity turns out to be a major leverage point for its business growth. What began as a scrappy ICQ copycat has evolved into a social media platform that is democratizing e-commerce for third parties, and in so doing, turning itself into the biggest superapp in the world.

But if crowdsourcing is a means to mass-produce solutions and solve complex problems, the next leverage point must be to automate the process by which these solutions are generated. How companies can not only crowdsource important decisions but also automate those decisions will be the subject of the next chapter.

5

LEVERAGING MACHINE INTELLIGENCE: FROM INTUITION TO ALGORITHM

> Count what is countable, measure what is measurable, and what is not measurable, make measurable.
>
> — GALILEO GALILEI, ASTRONOMER (1564–1642)

> Not everything that can be counted counts, and not everything that counts can be counted.
>
> — WILLIAM BRUCE CAMERON, *INFORMAL SOCIOLOGY*, 1963

THE COMING OF THE COMPUTER OVERLOADS

FOR DATA SCIENTISTS AND MACHINE-LEARNING EXPERTS, MARCH 2016 was a momentous month. AlphaGo, a computer program that Google developed, beat world champion Lee Sedol 4 to 1 in a series of games of the ancient Chinese board game of Go.[1] In Western chess, players make about forty moves on a sixty-four-square chessboard. In 1997, IBM's Deep Blue trumped chess grandmaster Garry Kasparov by deploying a brute force approach, by calculating all of the possible endgames, rifling through millions of scenarios per second, and then determining the winning move.

That brute force method won't work for Go. On the nineteen-by-nineteen grid, Go players proceed to play up to two hundred moves.[2] The permutation of outcomes quickly compounds to a bewildering range—10^{761} to be exact—more than the total number of atoms in the entire observable universe.[3] It had been thought that it would take at least another ten years before a machine could beat a human at Go. And yet, Google has managed to create just the kind of machine algorithm that approximates humanlike qualities, or to play the game by intuition. Not only is it possible to technologically replicate the intuition of a human expert, but also to surpass it. Most remarkable is that AlphaGo has become a machine that could improve its performance every day, on its own, without the direct supervision of a human programmer. And this inevitable rise of intelligent machines is already affecting nearly every company in some way. How did we get here?

Until very recently, computers required programmers to write instructions. Computers generally don't learn autonomously; they follow rules. The earliest iterations of so-called machine learning required heavy support and constant monitoring by computer scientists or statisticians. Humans had to label data and explicitly set end goals. Under the umbrella of this early form of machine learning came the statistical mining of big data, which helped uncover previously unknown patterns and recommended remedial actions. This approach of data analytics, though labor intensive, has proved incredibly powerful in predicting consumer behaviors: how we click, buy, or lie. Machines have improved the way companies e-mail, call, offer a discount, recommend a product, show an ad, inspect flaws, and approve loans. Credit card companies can detect, in real time, which transactions are likely to be fraudulent, and insurers can identify which customers are likely to file a claim or who is likely to die. The downside is that these algorithms are context dependent. They are machines built for a single purpose. Deep Blue, which played chess well, wasn't very useful for anything else.

During the earliest days of Amazon.com, an editorial group composed of real writers hand-sold products with witty taglines and decided what to promote. Over the years, a competing group used a machine algorithm called Amabot to generate recommendations based on customers' web searches and previous purchases. Characteristically Amazon, CEO Jeff Bezos let the two groups fight on, pitting personable, handcrafted messages against standard, automatic recommendations. Before long, the commercial results showed that humans couldn't compete in driving sales. Amabot handily won a series of tests and demonstrated it could sell as many products as the human editors, with the ability to scale up transaction volume without incurring additional cost. The human team, of course, would need to hire and train new employees if it were to meet increasing demand.[4] In 2002, one employee placed an anonymous three-line ad in the Valentine's Day edition of a local Seattle paper, the *Stranger*, addressed to the algorithm:[5]

DEAREST AMABOT: If you only had a heart to absorb our hatred. . . . Thanks for nothing, you jury-rigged rust bucket. The gorgeous messiness of flesh and blood will prevail![6]

The editorial group was soon dismantled.[7]

Still, as powerful as Amabot was, it couldn't be used for other situations. Nor could the algorithm be applied to unstructured data expressed in natural human language. Before being spoon-fed into a machine, data need to be neatly formatted in a relational database— orderly rows of numbers and words—like an Excel spreadsheet. It would take another decade before the limitation in data format was resolved.

MORE THAN A SOUPED-UP SEARCH ENGINE

In February 2011, IBM made a deep impression on the American public when its supercomputer Watson beat human contestants in the popular game show *Jeopardy!* About 15 million viewers watched live as Watson triumphed over former champions Ken Jennings and Brad Rutter. It was also an episode that made clear in the public mind that machine learning could go beyond the single-minded focus of number crunching. *Jeopardy!*—like most TV programs of its genre—features trivia on a wide variety of topics. The game has a unique answer-and-question format: the clues are presented in the form of answers, and the contestants have to phrase their responses in the form of questions. On the topic of classical music, for instance, a clue might be "Mozart's last and perhaps most powerful symphony shares its name with this planet." The correct answer would be, "What is Jupiter?"[8] Playing *Jeopardy!* is akin to scouring a dictionary for a word and then looking for a crossword puzzle in which that word might fit.

Visible through a horizontal window, behind the contestant podiums, was a room where Watson's computers churned, with mountains of microprocessors calculating zeros and ones, and roaring fans cooling them.[9] Watson was rummaging through 65 million pages of text per second during the competition.[10] The meaning in these texts, as expressed in the natural language, often depends on what has been said before, the topic itself, and how it is being discussed. The exact meaning in everyday English is never completely or precisely stated. To properly read a news article, one must distinguish between "parking in driveways" and "driving on parkways" or understand the fact that "noses run" and "feet smell." Competing on *Jeopardy!* thus requires the ability to understand subtle meaning, irony, riddles, slang, metaphors, jokes, and puns. And for Watson to become more than a souped-up search engine, the IBM engineering team had infused it with three capabilities so it could produce the right answers in split seconds: (1) natural language processing, (2) hypothesis generation, and (3) evidence-based learning.[11] "In *Jeopardy!*, built into the game is this notion of confidence that it is not worth answering unless you are sure. And in the real world, there are lots of problems like that," said Dr. Katharine Frase, vice president of Industry Solutions and Emerging Business at IBM Research. "You don't want your doctor to guess, you want them to have confidence in their answers before giving you a treatment."[12]

At the end of the two-day *Jeopardy!* tournament, Watson had amassed $77,147 in prize money, more than three times the amount its human opponents had accumulated. Ken Jennings, who had won more than fifty straight matches previously, came in second, just ahead of Brad Rutter. "Just as factory jobs were eliminated in the twentieth century by new assembly-line robots, Brad and I were the first knowledge-industry workers put out of work by the new generation of 'thinking' machines."[13]

To see why the human sense of self is so wrapped up in the history of computers, it's useful to note that computers used to be human. Before computers became the digital processing devices that dominate our twenty-first-century lives, the word referred to something else: a job description. From the mid-eighteenth century onward, computers, many of them women, were on the payrolls of corporations, engineering firms, and universities, performing calculations and numerical analysis.[14] The Harvard Observatory alone was one of the biggest computer recruiters at the time. Director Edward C. Pickering had long struggled to catalogue his astronomy data and finally decided to replace one of his male assistants with Williamina Fleming—a great early astronomer. Ms. Fleming proved to be so adept at computing and cataloguing that the entire observatory was soon staffed with female scientists, earning the place a less than noble name—Pickering's Harem.[15]

That was a far cry from gender equality. Computer, as a job description, was a simple euphemism for a performer of mental drudgery. The quest to create a thinking machine didn't really begin until the dawn of modern computing, around the 1940s. Pioneers Alan Turing and John von Neumann anticipated a time when mechanical computers could mimic human intelligence. If a machine could finally become indistinguishable from a human during text-based conversations, then it could be said to be "thinking."[16]

"If you actually watch that *Jeopardy!* episode, at the bottom of the screen, it provided the different answers that Watson came up with," observed Dr. Omar Latif, vice president of the health insurance company WellPoint. "Watson didn't just come up with one answer. Watson came up with multiple answers and each answer has a certain confidence level and I realized that this is exactly how physicians think! When I see a patient, there is usually not just one answer. There are probably four or five answers. But I tell the patient the answer that I think has the highest confidence."[17] The choirboy face and awkward grin of Ken Jennings also add a particular poignancy to the human defeat, especially since he had worked as a software programmer himself.[18] "I, for one, welcome our new computer overloads," Jennings later wrote. Unlike Amabot a decade earlier, Watson represented a machine that no longer blindly followed instructions. The machine could digest unstructured data in the form of human language and then make judgments on its own, which in turn has profoundly changed the way businesses value managerial expertise. One financial service executive put it most succinctly: "Consider a human who can read essentially an unlimited number of [financial] documents and understand those documents and completely retain all the information in those documents. Now imagine you can ask that person a question: 'Which company is most likely to get acquired in the next three months?' That's essentially what [Watson] gives you."[19]

THE (IN)FALLIBLE HUMAN

We live in a world with a knowledge economy that reveres subject experts. Central to modern health care, for example, is the total reliance on physicians to make decisions based on lifetime experiences. A key responsibility of a doctor is to diagnose patients when they present with symptoms. Despite uncertainties and incomplete information, doctors are expected to identify a patient's disease, usually on the spot, and to correctly prescribe the corresponding treatment.

And for many doctors, diagnosing a patient is an art that demands unending training. In a fascinating account in the book *Brotherhood*, by Drs. Deepak and Sanjiv Chopra, Sanjiv recalled his personal encounter with legendary clinician Dr. Elihu Schimmel, head of the gastroenterology division at the Boston VA Hospital:

> I flicked on the X-ray view-box light and . . . literally in seconds, Dr. Schimmel said, "Stop." I stopped. He stared at the X-ray for about thirty seconds.
>
> "Sanjiv, this patient is a chronic smoker and an alcoholic. He has diabetes. He also had polio as a child. He needs to have his gallbladder removed." I was stunned.

"Eli," I began," . . . how can you fathom all that from one X-ray?" He explained: "His diaphragm's flattened and his lungs are hyper inflated. That's a sign of his being a smoker, emphysema of the lungs. I can see pancreatic calcification, so he's got chronic pancreatitis from alcohol. He has aseptic necrosis of the head of the femur and kyphoscoliosis, which can be a result of polio in childhood."

There were six of us in that room listening to him, enthralled and mesmerized. Nobody said a word and I'm sure we were all thinking the same thing: We are watching a virtuoso performance.[20]

This virtuoso performance is what distinguishes the novice from the experienced, whose quick decisions can be every bit as good as a decision made cautiously and deliberately.[21] Renowned clinicians take great pride in their ability to make difficult, sometimes obscure diagnoses in the blink of an eye. Nobel Laureate Daniel Kahneman similarly recounted in *Thinking, Fast and Slow* a close call by an experienced firefighter: The commander of a team entered a house whose kitchen was burning. He stood in the living room with his hose, blasting water onto the smoke and flames. But the fire kept roaring back. The commander suddenly heard himself shout, "Let's get out of here!" without realizing why. The moment his crew reached the street, the living room floor collapsed. The fire, it turned out, had started in the basement. Had the men stayed inside, they would have plunged into the blazing inferno.[22]

To Kahneman, that was the glorious display of human intuition. Hot fires are loud, but this one was eerily quiet; the floor was muffling the flames that were raging underneath. "Only after the fact did the commander realize that the fire had been unusually quiet and that his ears had been unusually hot. Together, these impressions prompted what he called a 'sixth sense of danger,'" wrote Kahneman. The beauty of it all was that the commander could size up the situation in seconds without even being fully aware. He couldn't describe exactly what went wrong except that he recalled being gripped by a primal feeling of unease. And yet, the safety of his team was completely dependent upon all that meticulous assessment calculated behind the locked door of his consciousness.

The problem of expert intuition, however, is that it's hard to replicate and expensive to acquire. In a business environment, this is often the ultimate limitation to growth.

Consider the business of building and running a shopping mall. Besides the choice of the construction location, the tenant mix is crucial. The more brands, the better. Instead of sitting idly and waiting for retailers to come, a mall owner must hunt for the ideal brands, setting aside enough time for potential tenants to plan, fund, and allocate resources in advance. When working with an architect, the mall owner needs to specify the theme, amenities, facilities, and features of the construction and comply with all the legal and safety requirements, all while sticking to a reasonable budget and a realistic timeline to make the project profitable. And because an iconic mall is often the pride of a small city, a less than fully functional, fully occupied mall is not what a township would like to greet on its inauguration day.

Given the intricacies of all the commercial and engineering activities, it is little wonder, then, that mall developers tend to be local players who specialize in familiar markets where they excel, in large part, because of their unique managerial expertise. It's not the sort of global industry—like those of home appliances or consumer electronics—where a uniform product standard can be imposed across continents. There are simply too many everyday decisions that need to be made based on past experience. For this reason, the size of a property developer can be surprisingly modest when compared to other industries. Simon Property Group, the largest US operator and developer of shopping malls, generated about $5.3 billion in revenue in 2015.[23] In 2016, the group opened three new centers—two outlets and one full-price retailer.[24] In contrast, Whirlpool, America's largest home appliance company, was making $20 billion in revenue the same year.

Still, halfway across the world, the breakneck urbanization in China has forced a property group to come up with a unique solution to overcome the same barrier that had tripped up all its US counterparts. Wanda Group, China's largest commercial property company, reportedly added twenty-six shopping malls in 2015,[25] with the goal of opening at least fifty malls each year starting in 2016.[26] That same year, revenue topped $28 billion.[27] CEO Wang Jianlin, one of China's wealthiest men, has amassed an estimated net worth close to $30 billion[28] (Donald Trump, the first billionaire president in US history, has about $3.5 billion).[29] With such a steep ramp up, Wanda can't rely solely on experienced staff. The company simply doesn't have time to cultivate enough competent project managers to fuel its growth.

When I last spoke with Liu Mingsheng, the general manager of the Corporate Culture Center, I was surprised how little he talked about Wanda's culture but instead elaborated expansively on the role of Wanda's information system:

> Almost ten years ago, the group [began] with office automation, with all property projects driven by an information approach. The typical development time of a shopping mall is around two years. Our information system divides the entire cycle from construction to opening into three hundred major milestones, with each milestone further broken into another hundred or so sub-tasks.
>
> A green light on the system means that a given plan is completed successfully, and a yellow light means that a given plan is not completed as scheduled. When a yellow light is on, the vice president in charge must come up with ideas to catch up on the delay[s]. If the yellow light is on for a whole week, it will turn into a red light, and the responsible person will be punished or replaced.
>
> Similarly, property management is coordinated through a centralized system that monitor[s] fire control, water heating, air conditioning, energy conservation, and safety information, all displayed on a single, ultra-large screen.

When I visited a Wanda shopping center in Beijing later that afternoon, the facility manager showed me how he could review every critical real-time statistic on his smartphone, including a heat map that visualized customer flow. "By triangulat[ing] sales volume with the inflow of shoppers, we can predict which tenant might run into financial trouble months in advance. This helps us collect receivables better," explained the manager. Back at the office, he was reviewing a number of maintenance requests online, with pictures or videos attached. All the information and the approval are routed automatically to the designated employees. Nothing was left to chance over e-mail or an Excel spreadsheet.

"In the past, we need[ed] lots of experts to make sure projects could be opened for business on time. But with the IT system, the replacement of any general manager can occur at any time. In fact, anyone can start building a shopping mall tomorrow," Liu asserted. "You don't need to be an expert on everything. All you need to do is to focus on the specific plans that you are responsible for. If you get stuck, look at your computer for help. This is how we scale."

What Wanda illustrates is the fundamental limit when a business relies on experienced staff. That human brain cannot be copied exactly; training takes time. A business that relies on expert judgment will be forever confined to small-scale operation. To scale a business in the knowledge economy would require automating the workflow and instinct of an experienced manager.

But there is an additional benefit when businesses rid themselves of sole dependency on human experts. When the opportunity to exercise judgment is rare and feedback is hard to come by, human intuition can often be downright misleading. In these situations, the acclaimed experts are no masters—they are merely clueless pundits.

In my executive programs, I often ask my participants a puzzle described by cognitive psychologist Daniel Levitin. Imagine, you go out to eat at a restaurant and wake up with your face turned blue. There are two food-poisoning diseases, one turns your face blue and one turns your face green. There is a pill that will cure you. It has no effect if you are healthy, but if you have one of these two diseases and you take the wrong pill, you die. The color your face turns is consistent with the disease 75 percent of the time. The green disease is five times more common than the blue disease. Which color pill do you take?[30] After ten minutes of discussion, most participants would choose the blue pill. "Why?" I ask. "The face is blue," they respond, and "the color the face turns is consistent with the disease most of the time."

		YOUR FACE		
		BLUE	*GREEN*	
DISEASE	*BLUE*	15	5	**20**
	GREEN	25	75	**100**
	TOTAL			**120**

Figure 5.1 Face puzzle

At this point, I would pull out a four-cell table like the one in Levitin's example. Don't get me wrong, I also made the same mistake the first time I read the puzzle. But if we assume a population of 120, we can populate the table with the following information, as shown in Figure 5.1.

Now look at the first column on the left. It shows that even if the patient's face turns blue, one is better off taking the green pill because there is a higher prevalence of the green disease in the general population. In other words, we have focused on the wrong information all along. We should look at the base rate of the disease, not the potency of the specific pill in treating the disease. Unlike firefighters, who experience extensive drills day in, day out, questions surrounding probabilities are seldom asked and the long-term data are hard to come by. In medicine, it often takes years, if not decades, to ascertain the efficacy of a medical treatment in combating a chronic condition. The feedback between a decision made today and the observable future result is so tenuous that it translates into little learning.[31]

The problem of focusing on the wrong information is commonplace, whether it is kitchen table rambling or job interviews or boardroom politics. At companies, discussion of a management team often degenerates to "highest-paid person's opinion," or HiPPO for short.[32] And if applying rudimentary statistics could be critical to medical decisions, imagine how a souped-up search engine like Watson can change all the industries in which expert opinions had once reigned supreme.

WISE COUNSEL IN THE MAKING

Every day, medical journals publish new treatments and discoveries. On average, the torrent of medical information doubles every five years. Given the work pressure in most hospitals, physicians rarely have enough time to read. It would take dozens of hours each week for a primary care doctor to read up on everything to stay informed.[33] Eighty-one percent reported that they could spend no more than five hours per month poring over journals.[34] Not surprisingly, only about 20 percent of the knowledge that clinicians use is evidence-based.[35] The sheer amount of new knowledge has overwhelmed the very limits of the human brain and, thus, rendered expert intuition—once powerful machinery—powerless.

David Kerr, director of corporate strategy at IBM, recalled just how Patricia Skarulis, the chief information officer at Memorial Sloan Kettering Cancer Center (MSK), decided to reach out. "Shortly after she watched the Watson computer defeat two past grand-champions on the *Jeopardy!* TV quiz show, she said MSK had collected more than a decade's worth of digitized information about cancer, including treatments and outcomes," Kerr said in an interview. "She thought Watson could help."[36]

Being the world's largest and oldest dedicated cancer hospital, MSK had maintained a proprietary database, which included 1.2 million inpatient and outpatient diagnoses and clinical treatment records from the previous twenty-plus years. The vast database also contained the full molecular and genomic analyses of all lung cancer patients.[37] But unlike a lab researcher, hospital doctors routinely make life-or-death decisions based on hunches. A doctor has no time to go home and think over the results from all the medical tests given to a patient. Treatment needs to be decided on the spot. Unless there's an intelligent system to mine for insights up front and then make them instantaneously available for doctors, the deluge of information won't improve doctors' ability to make the right call.

In March 2012, MSK and IBM Watson started working together with the intention of creating an application that would provide recommendations to oncologists who simply described a patient's symptoms in plainspoken English.[38] When an oncologist entered information, such as "my patient has blood in his phlegm," Watson would come back within half a minute with a drug regimen to suit that individual. "Watson is a tool that processes information, fills the gap of human thoughts. [It] doesn't make the decision for you, that is the realm of clinician, . . . but brings you the information that you would want anyway," said Dr. Martin Kohn, chief medical scientist at IBM Research.[39]

For Patricia at MSK, the real aim was to "build an intelligence engine to provide specific diagnostic test and treatment recommendations."[40] More than a search engine on steroids, it would transfer the wisdom of experienced doctors to those with less experience. A physician at a remote medical center in China or India, for instance, could have instant access to everything that the best cancer doctors had taught Watson.[41] And if MSK's ultimate mission as a nonprofit is to spread its influence to deliver cutting-edge health care around the world, an expert system like IBM Watson is the essential carrier.

In early 2017, a 327-bed hospital in Jupiter, Florida, signed up for Watson Health precisely with the intention of taking advantage of the supercomputer's ability to match cancer patients with the treatments most likely to help them.[42] Since a machine never gets tired of reading, understanding, and summarizing, doctors can take advantage of all the knowledge that's out there. WellPoint has claimed that, according to tests, Watson's successful diagnosis rate for lung cancer is 90 percent, compared to 50 percent for human doctors.[43]

Cycling back to our original knowledge funnel in Part 1, all these developments should not come as surprises. They are the natural consequence of our long march toward the ultimate automation (see Figure 5.2). Dumb machines helped Yamaha beat the brawn at Steinway & Sons; now, smart machines are displacing the intelligence at MSK. But for most executives, all these technologies still feel foreign. How can an existing business, especially one in a non-IT sector, begin to leverage the shift toward knowledge automation?

As improbable as it might seem, a role model can be found in a Japanese publisher. Starting out in the early 1960s, Recruit Holdings

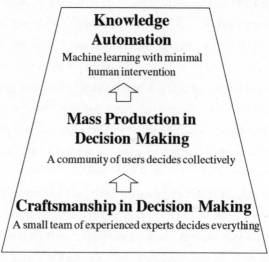

Figure 5.2 The ultimate automation

began as an advertising company publishing magazines for job seekers. Spurred by the internet revolution in the early 2000s, the company added business verticals, such as real estate, bridal, travel, beauty salons, and restaurants. By 2015, as Recruit's digital platforms were gaining popularity, the company noticed the enormous amounts of online data on types of transactions and end-user behaviors. By establishing an artificial intelligence (AI) research laboratory in Silicon Valley, the management aimed to apply the latest technologies in data analytics and machine learning. Still, the case history of the company is as much about AI as its determination to cannibalize its existing businesses through data-driven innovations to leapfrog into the future. What sets Recruit apart from its contemporaries lies in the process by which the strategy is managed. No one can leap overnight; it takes time. Recruit shows us how.

NOT YOUR GRANDPA'S CLASSIFIEDS

In 1962, Hiromasa Ezoe, a student at the University of Tokyo (Tōdai), launched a university newspaper with the idea of connecting job-seeking new graduates with prospective employers. The newspaper went viral and became Japan's first recruiting magazine. Ezoe named his company the Recruit Center.

Straight out of college, the ambitious entrepreneur would spend the rest of his career growing the tiny advertising sales agency into a sprawling conglomerate of twenty-seven subsidiaries with 6,200 employees. By 1986, Recruit was generating some $3 billion a year, owned office towers in the upscale Ginza shopping district, and engaged in businesses as diverse as human resources, real estate, telecommunications, restaurants, hotels, and information publishing.[44] For a long while, Ezoe followed a simple motto: In this world, money comes first.[45]

It was the era of Japan's economic miracle. Even so, not all of Recruit's businesses were equally successful. Recruit's strong suit remained classified ads, like those in the back of newspapers. For more than three decades, the company supplied job seekers with information by printing hard-copy magazines that comprised two publications: *Recruit Book*, an employment information magazine for college students, and *Recruit Shingaju Book*, which provided information on colleges and universities for high school students.[46]

In the mid-1990s, just as the Internet began to take off, Recruit started to deliver information over the web in a proactive effort to defend its leading market position. It launched *Recruit Navi*, an online job board for fresh graduates in 1996. As was the case for many book publishers and daily newspapers, migrating online proved nearly fatal. Discarding the traditional magazine meant that Recruit had to rely on online advertising revenue, which decimated corporate earnings.

"Before the transition, we had three formats existing in parallel—thick paper-based magazines (like telephone directories) that we sold through bookstores, a free paper magazine, and a web-based magazine," Takanori Makiguchi, an executive manager at Recruit, told me. "After the transition, we kept the free paper magazine and the online magazine, but we got rid of the books. Our sales dropped to one tenth. This was our very first experience in shifting from paper to online."

Fortunately for Recruit, Internet usage exploded at the dawn of the new millennium. The number of online users in Japan surged from 2 million in 1995 to an astonishing 69.4 million in 2002. The overall publishing market also completely shifted to favoring free online content. But it still took nearly four hair-raising years before the company could restore its overall revenue to its former level. That early experience, nevertheless, proved crucial. Recruit understood what it would take to succeed in the Internet economy, at a time when business consultants and many academics were still relatively clueless.

Among business school academics, the "network effect" is a common refrain that explains the rise of Uber, Airbnb, and Alibaba. In each of these cases, the company took on the role of a two-sided marketplace, facilitating selling on the supply side and buying on the demand side to enable the exchange of goods or services. The value of such a platform depends, in large part, on the number of users on either side of the exchange. That is, the more people that use the same platform, the more inherently attractive the platform would become—leading even more people to use it.

Consider for a moment any dating site or app (from OkCupid to Tinder to Match.com). Men are drawn toward them because they promise a huge supply of women and the high likelihood of a good match, and vice versa. Because of this network effect, users are willing to pay more for access to a bigger network, and so, a company's profits improve when its user base grows.[47] Scale begets scale. But beyond that, product differentiation remains elusive. Think Uber versus Lyft, or iMessage versus WhatsApp. Platforms often look alike, and competition is reduced to a game of "grow fast or die." This is why Facebook is obsessed with growth. This is also why, when Snapchat went public in March 2017, the number of daily active users became the single most important metric for potential investors.[48] The more people that hang out on Facebook or Snapchat—reading news and playing games—the more willing big brands, such as Coca-Cola, Procter & Gamble, and Nike, are to buy ads there. Only when a platform reaches a certain size, does its dominance then become hard to unseat.

Recruit followed the same logic. By being the first to convert to online, and being more aggressive than its competition in its pricing strategy, the company had cemented its leading online market share. It cast its lot with the first golden rule of all Internet businesses: with sufficient customer traffic, a firm can prosper despite lower gross margins than those associated with the traditional print form. That is, a high number of online transactions can eventually be converted into decent profits. In all subsequent migration projects, Recruit never lost money. Still, to secure victory in the long run, not only does size matter—quality does, too. And this would be the second rule that Recruit soon discovered.

BEYOND BECOMING BIG

Before Facebook, Myspace was the reigning king of social networks. Founded in 2003, Myspace commanded the allegiance of bands, photographers, and other creative people. As late as 2008, it was the top social network in the United States. News Corp's Rupert Murdoch purchased Myspace for $580 million[49] and thought the firm could be worth as much as $6 billion and anticipated as many as 200 million user profiles by mid-2007.

Myspace's fall from grace was striking. By April 2008, the site had lost some 40 million unique visitors per month. Some blame the website's anarchic design that resembled "a massive spaghetti-ball mess,"[50] others attribute the failure to the site's lack of technological innovation. But the core problem was its reputation. The network was filled with scantily clad would-be celebrities[51] flooding the site with scandalizing photos that led to the public perception of a tawdry digital basement.[52] Elite users were fleeing en masse to the next safe haven: "Facebook." Quality matters as much as size.

Recruit understood this well. Take its travel business, Jalan, as an example. It started off as an advertising catalog for hotels and hot springs. But when Jalan.net was launched as a booking website (think Kayak or TripAdvisor), it started to compete with other travel agencies. Now that the website was acting as an intermediary between resorts and travelers, Recruit could no longer highlight just the positive aspects of a resort, which it had done in the past with its magazines; the website also needed to display unflattering user reviews so as to position itself as a trustworthy adviser. In other words, what defines quality depends on the customer group. As products moved online, the value proposition shifted; the definition of quality evolved.

While reviewing the corporate development at Recruit, one gets the impression that the management team has resolved to disrupt itself ahead of competition. Its penchant for experimentation only grew in the coming decades. By 2015, Recruit employed more than one thousand software engineers who maintained two hundred websites and 350 mobile apps, serving restaurants, beauty salons, bridal and wedding venues, housing rental, and much more. And that was just within the company. Outside the four walls of its Tokyo headquarters was in fact the company's most important constituency—the millions of entrepreneurs out there who pushed Recruit to become one of Japan's foremost digital media companies. And here is the ultimate lesson: none of these changes look revolutionary overnight. They are incremental steps that edge the boundary of the firm gradually outward. But together, they have redefined the core mission of Recruit, altering the corporation's trajectory toward much better prospects.

FROM MAGAZINE PUBLISHER TO PLATFORM PROVIDER

Historically, proprietors who placed ads with Recruit were often small businesses. Although jealously independent, these entrepreneurs struggled with back-end administrative tasks, which they knew all too well. A beauty salon may benefit from voluminous reservations after signing up to an online booking system. But more often than not, a beautician ends up copying an online report by hand onto a paper scheduler to avoid double-booking by phone-in customers.

"If you're a hairdresser, you want to spend time with your customer cutting hair, styling hair. Or if you are a cafe owner, you want to spend your time serving that delicious cup of coffee," said an empathic Yoshihiro Kitamura, president of Recruit Technologies. "And yet, they have so many other tasks to manage that the time spent on the business is actually very limited. When you do the math and count off the hours that they spend on operational tasks, they have very little time for growing that business."

A veteran at Recruit, Mr. Kitamura has a fresh, boyish face. His thick, dark hair and lively brown eyes easily disguise his thrumming ambition. Under his lead in 2012, Recruit launched the Salon Board, a cloud-based reservation and customer management platform that enabled centralized management of both telephone and online bookings. The platform was an instant hit among beauty salons, with the killer feature being an automated reply function that eased administrative burdens.

A year later, Kitamura announced AirREGI, a smartphone and tablet-based point-of-sale cash register that was integrated with a similar cloud-based data management system (this time, aimed at restaurant owners). To spearhead deployment, Recruit tasked the thousand-strong sales staff to distribute forty thousand free tablets across Japan. The company then unveiled AirWAIT in 2014, an app that streamlined waiting by allowing customers to use their smartphones to queue virtually. And in 2015, AirPAYMENT went live, which took away the headache of payment processing and cash management that so commonly plagued small and medium-size enterprises.

Because of its budding operations across multiple platforms, Recruit was able to invest in capabilities that a stand-alone business couldn't justify. This, in turn, improved the overall customer experience and set the company further apart from the competition. "'Why us' is always the main question. Is there any quality that will give us the upper hand?" Ken Asano, a longtime colleague of Kitamura, said to me. "If it doesn't give us an upper hand, a Google App or Facebook Plugin is enough to kill us. So, when evaluating business opportunities, we must ask, 'Can we really do it better than everyone else?'"

That was why the company did not pursue all seemingly profitable services. "If the idea is for easy monetary gains, we have to reject it," Asano acknowledged with the fierce intensity of constant vigilance. "We need to know what will be the scale of the business in the future. It's not just short-term money, but the potential number of users across platforms."

This put tremendous pressure on the engineering team. Even the most introverted software programmers couldn't only do programming;

they had to visit customers, acquainting themselves with business realities. Programmers at Recruit routinely venture out with sales staff to observe a wide range of operations, from orthopedic clinics to gourmet restaurants, with the goal of extracting, for instance, a common denominator for a useful reservation process.

The other purpose of these visits is to rapidly prototype: putting something together quickly for testing. A prototype at Recruit typically meets 60 percent of the client's need. Only when the core offering gains traction would engineers look for other features to add. When AirREGI was designed, for example, many restaurants operated by former Recruit employees were selected as test sites. Much later came an auxiliary feature called AirRESERVE, which was a screen layout that mirrored the actual table settings at the restaurant. This customized representation helped restaurant hosts to speed up table allocation, especially during peak business hours. A small tweak, one might say, but that was exactly the sort of product feature that increased customer loyalty after the initial offering took off.

Amidst all the changes, one major shift at Recruit was the changing role of sales. In the past, customers placed ads to drive traffic to stores. Today, all of the digital platforms are new means to improve business efficiency. Sales personnel no longer mindlessly canvass towns, touting advertising space to proprietors. They instead collate customer insights and act as champions for technology requirements, effectively multitasking as general problem solvers.

BUILDING OR BUYING

Every time a company discovers the need to do something new, executives must decide to what extent the firm will outsource those activities. The rapid development we saw surrounding machine learning is no different: Should we build the capability in-house or outsource it to other technology creators? This is what General Electric's (GE) former CEO Jeffrey Immelt called the "make or buy" dilemma. "We as a company didn't go to bed one night and say, 'We can't be an industrial company anymore. We need to be more like Oracle. We need to be more like Microsoft.'" Immelt recalled when GE first began building a digital team in California. "It happened more on an evolutionary basis, really based on the industries we're in and the technology we serve. Do we want to partner, or do we want to do it ourselves? We have lots of good software partners, but, basically, we said, 'We need to do this ourselves. Let's err on the side of seeing if we could approach it in that way.'"[53] Although GE opted to build the software capability in-house, the boundary between the end of "make" and the beginning of "buy" can be less obvious in most cases. Even if a company decides to hire a few data scientists and step up its efforts in machine learning, this doesn't preclude the company from purchasing a third-party software. But there is certainly an advantage to cultivate the prerequisite knowledge base internally.

Consider the integrated circuits that revolutionized the touch and feel of many home appliances in the 1960s and 1970s. Led by Panasonic, Sony, Toshiba, and Hitachi, the Japanese manufacturers began to embed many electronic functions into home appliances that were historically based on mechanical and electrical engineering. Washing machines suddenly came with electronic displays, computerized switches, and synthetic sound alerts instead of mechanical dials and analog switches.

While many Japanese and, later, Korean manufacturers have developed their in-house capabilities in electronics, European and American manufacturers tend to "stick to their core," by outsourcing the design and manufacture of electronic circuitries to third parties. The result is that those with in-house capabilities can integrate products with new functionalities ahead of the competition, while others only follow existing market trends, incorporating features already commonly found in the marketplace. The choice that Kitamura and Asano would soon wrestle with is similar: To what extent should Recruit invest in machine learning as an in-house capability?

STEPPING OUT FROM THE SHADOW OF THE TECH GIANTS

To Kitamura at Recruit, the company was particularly well positioned at the intersection between offline and online activities. With the successive debuts of various digital platforms, the potential to glean insights from its valuable data became all the more apparent. "Say a customer is seated at a restaurant; such an offline action should trigger information online—[be it] pulling the customer profile to understand her food preference, or tallying up kitchen inventory for the waiter to make spontaneous menu recommendations," said Kitamura. To Asano, the future is to blend offline and online data to the point where the digital divide vanishes. "If we can grasp that moment of this second wave of digitalization, removing the final boundary between online and offline ahead of Google, Facebook, or even IBM, we can dominate the sphere across all SMEs [small and medium-size enterprises] in Japan, and that will be our winning card."

The lack of in-house data scientists, however, had hampered Recruit's progress. That's the same challenge that Syngenta faced, as we observed in the last chapter. And so, Recruit became the first Japanese company to collaborate with Kaggle—the world's largest community of about 300,000 data experts—to hold a two-and-a-half–month data prediction competition. In 2015, the company invested in DataRobot Inc., a provider of platforms for general machine learning. These platforms used massive parallel processing to train and analyze thousands of models in open-source languages, including Python, Spark, and H2O. The resolute commitment to data science eventually came in late November, when the board announced an artificial intelligence (AI) research laboratory in Silicon Valley, headed by Dr. Alon Halevy, a heavily cited AI researcher cherry-picked from Google. Like many of his contemporaries, Halevy espoused open software to expedite innovation. Under his watch, all AI development relied on open-source components. He also took a page from Recruit's existing playbook by co-locating his researchers with existing businesses. Data scientists wouldn't just write code, but embrace unplanned conversations with customers and sales—an approach that might look odd in Silicon Valley, but a long-established business norm at Japan's headquarters.

"We have a very interesting collection of datasets, but we don't have the appropriate tools. What you see at Recruit is that they are excellent at providing services, but they have not really focused on technology in a concentrated way," Halevy said to me. "It was and still is 'let us make the service better.' However, there is now this visceral sentiment that we have to leverage data to make a real difference." In that regard, Asano couldn't agree more: "We need Recruit to take high-quality data and turn it into value. We are unique in the sense that we can take a holistic view of our customers." Being thoroughly pedestrian and small business–oriented, the smiling Kitamura raised his voice in excitement, "We can now see exactly the kind of business opportunity for us to invent new services, in the very sector where we choose to compete."

THE SECOND MACHINE AGE

In my executive class, managers often express a grave concern about how fast artificial intelligence is unfolding—so fast that they become afraid of committing to a supplier, or any standard, since there might be a better solution tomorrow. But precisely because we are living in a world of accelerated change, as far as machine intelligence is concerned, one must stay in the know. That was the basic reason that Recruit decided to set up an AI lab in-house. Its scale can never rival that of Google, and, quite frankly, it doesn't need to. But management realizes Recruit must at least possess the ability to repackage new technologies that others might create.

One radical improvement in recent years is how machines learn. Back when Watson was trained to serve as a bionic oncologist, it was necessary to ingest some 600,000 pieces of medical evidence and 2 million pages of text from forty-two medical journals and clinical trials,[54] which included 25,000 test-case scenarios and 1,500 real-life cases,[55] so that Watson would know how to extract and interpret physicians' notes, lab results, and clinical research.[56] Conducting this case-based training for a brainy machine can be thoroughly exhausting and time-consuming. At MSK, a dedicated team spent more than a year developing training materials for Watson.[57] And a large part of this so-called training came down to the daily laborious grind: that is, data cleaning, program fine-tuning, and result validation—tasks that are sometimes excruciating, often boring, and altogether so mundane that they could hardly seem inspiring at all. "If you're teaching a self-driving car, anyone can label a tree or a sign so the system can learn to recognize it," explained Thomas Fuchs, a computational pathologist at MSK. "But in a specialized domain in medicine, you need experts trained for decades to properly label the information you feed to the computer."[58] Wouldn't it be nice if machines could teach themselves? Could machine learning become an unsupervised activity? Google's AlphaGo demonstrates how that unsupervised process is indeed possible.

Before AlphaGo played the board game Go against humans, Google researchers had been developing it to play video games—Space Invaders, Breakout, Pong, and others.[59] Without the need for any specific programming, the general-purpose algorithm was able to master each game by trial and error—pressing different buttons randomly at first and then adjusting to maximize rewards. Game after game, the software proved to be cunningly versatile in figuring out an appropriate strategy and then applying it without making any mistakes. AlphaGo thus represents not just a machine that can think—as Watson does—but also one that learns and strategizes, all without direct supervision from any human.

This general-purpose programming is made possible thanks to a deep neural network—a network of hardware and software that mimics the web of neurons in the human brain.[60] Reinforcement learning in humans occurs when positive feedback triggers the production of the neurotransmitter dopamine as a reward signal for the brain, resulting in feelings of gratification and pleasure. Computers can be programmed to work similarly. The positive rewards come in the form of scores when the algorithm achieves a desired outcome. Under this general framework, AlphaGo writes its own instructions randomly through many generations of trial and error, replacing lower-scoring strategies with higher-scoring ones. That's how an algorithm teaches itself to play anything, not just Go.

This conceptual design is not new; computer scientists have discussed reinforcement learning for more than twenty years. But only with rapid advancement and abundance in computing power could "deep learning" become practical.[61] By forgoing software coding with direct rules and commands, reinforcement learning has made autonomous machines a reality. Most remarkable about AlphaGo is that the algorithm continually improves its performance by playing millions of games against a tweaked version of itself.[62] A human creator is no longer needed nor able to tell how the algorithm chooses to achieve a stated goal: we can see the data go in and the actions come out, but we can't grasp what happens in between. Simply put, a human programmer can't explain a machine's behavior by reading the software code any more than a neuroscientist can explain your hot dog craving by staring at an MRI scan of your brain. What we have created is a black box, all-knowing but impenetrable.

In the second game of the match, at the right-hand side of the board, AlphaGo made a surprise move during the thirty-seventh turn that flummoxed even Lee Sedol. "I've never seen a human play this move," exclaimed Fan Hui, a three-time European Go champion, who was watching the game live. Repeatedly Fan uttered, "So beautiful."[63] One year after defeating Lee Sedol, AlphaGo went on to trounce Chinese Go grandmaster Ke Jie. "AlphaGo is improving too fast," Ke said in a news conference, commenting on his opponent's unique and sometimes transcendent style of play,[64] including, not infrequently, making reckless sacrifices that would ultimately prove part of a winning strategy.[65] "Last year, it was still quite humanlike when it played. This year, it became like a god of Go."[66]

No doubt, such breakneck advances in artificial intelligence irk many. Elon Musk, founder of Tesla, once posted a stirring comment, saying that AI could be "potentially more dangerous than nukes"[67] and likening it to "summoning the demon."[68] Musk's conviction has prompted him to donate millions to the ethics think tank OpenAI[69]— and he's urging other billionaire techies, including Facebook's Mark Zuckerberg and Google's Larry Page, to proceed with caution in their myriad machine-learning experiments. Apple cofounder Steve Wozniak has equally expressed grave concerns.[70] "The future is scary and very bad for people," he argued. "Will we be the gods? Will we be the family pets? Or will we be ants that get stepped on?" Perhaps the most ominous of all has come from none other than Stephen Hawking, the great theoretical physicist at Cambridge University. "The development of full artificial intelligence could spell the end of the human race," he told the BBC.[71]

While such disconsolate forecasts may be exaggerated, few can deny that, in our ceaseless march toward the age of machine automation, self-taught algorithms will play a far bigger role in organizing our economic activities. What will happen when the ubiquitous connectivity of sensors and mobile devices converges with such AI as AlphaGo or IBM Watson? Could a bevy of general-purpose, self-taught algorithms govern the world's economic transactions? "The thing that I believe is going to be really incredible that's going to happen next is the ability for artificial intelligence to write artificial intelligence by itself," said Jensen Huang, cofounder and CEO of Nvidia, whose graphic processing units (GPUs) crunch complex calculations necessary for deep learning. It has been the speedy number crunching that has enabled computers to see, hear, understand, and learn. "In the future, companies will have an AI that is watching every single transaction—every business process—that is happening, all day long," Huang asserted. "As a result of this observation, the artificial intelligence software writes an artificial intelligence software to automate that business process. Because we won't be able to do it. It's too complicated."[72]

That future isn't that much into the future. For years, GE has been working on analytics to improve the productivity of its jet engines, wind turbines, and locomotives, leveraging the continuous stream of data they collect in the field.[73] Cisco has set out the ambition of transferring data of all kinds into the cloud in what it calls the "Internet of Everything."[74] Tech giants, including Microsoft, Google, IBM, and Amazon, are making their internally developed machine-learning technologies freely available to client companies via application programming interfaces (APIs) which we discussed in Chapter 4. These machine intelligences, previously costing millions if not tens of millions to develop, essentially have now become reusable by third parties at negligible cost, which will only spur industry adoption at a wide scale. With unsupervised algorithms quietly performing the instantaneous adjustment, automatic optimization, and continuous improvement of ever more complex systems, transaction costs between organizations are poised to drop dramatically, if not disappear entirely. For this reason, redundancy in production facilities should be radically reduced and the enormous wastage that is so prevalent in the global supply chain today should vanish. Once the coordination of business transactions within and outside an organization speed up, from sales to engineering, from logistics to business operations, from finance to customer service, friction among companies will drop, and consequently, broader market collaboration can then be realized. In an economy where transaction cost approaches zero, traditional propositions such as "one-stop shop" or "supply chain optimization" will no longer be differentiating. These propositions will become commonplace, achievable by even the smallest players or new entrants in all industries.

This is akin to the cheap and powerful cloud computing upon which Netflix, Airbnb, and Yelp depend. Until very recently, any Internet businesses needed to own and build expensive servers and resource-intensive data centers. But with Amazon Web Services (AWS) or Microsoft Azure, a startup can store all of its online infrastructure in the cloud; it can also rent features and tools that are in the cloud, essentially outsourcing all of its computing chores to others. No need to forecast demand, or plan capacity—simply buy additional services as requirement goes up. The engineering team of a startup is therefore freed up to focus on solving problems unique to its core business.[75] Similarly, when fewer resources are required for organizational coordination, being big can only slow things down. No longer is it credible for big companies to claim conventional advantages by virtue of their being vertically integrated (an arrangement in which the companies own and control their supply chains). Instead, they are under tremendous pressure to match smaller players that are able to specialize in best-in-class services and deliver customized solutions in real time as orders are made. In other words, big companies need to act small in the second machine age, a topic we'll investigate deeper in Chapter 7.

WHAT ABOUT THE FLESH AND BLOOD?

Back in 2000, when Warren Buffett was asked why he couldn't find a way to make money on technology stocks, the Oracle of Omaha simply repeated his stock answer: "We will never buy anything we don't understand."[76] Fast-forward to the 2017 Berkshire Hathaway Annual Meeting. Buffett conceded that artificial intelligence could "result in significantly less employment in certain areas."[77] And that a jobless future will confront every manager in every industry.

Keeping in mind medieval monks, who had spent years hand-copying sacred texts, suddenly being confronted with the printing press, how will white-collar workers of the twenty-first century divvy up cognitive work, going forward? The traditional human advantage is eroding fast; humans who are currently relied upon for decisions—for instance, an art expert is needed to "sense" a forgery, and a medical specialist is required to offer a "clinical glance" for diagnosis—could become obsolete very quickly.

The story of Recruit has touched this very contentious area regarding the nature of managerial work. We have caught a glimpse of how salespeople at Recruit are becoming general problem solvers. The big question is this: In the age of bots and big data, are there functions of human expertise that can never be displaced? The next chapter will turn to this timely existential question.

6

LEVERAGING MANAGERIAL CREATIVITY: FROM BIG DATA TO HUMAN INTEREST

No great discovery was ever made without a bold guess.
— SIR ISAAC NEWTON, MATHEMATICIAN (1643–1727)

BETWEEN MYSTERIES AND PUZZLES

TWO TYPES OF QUESTIONS BOMBARD EXECUTIVES EVERY DAY. One is puzzles, and the other, mysteries. What your competitor is about to launch is a puzzle—a problem that can be solved only if you have the correct data. So is the question of whether Russia tried to influence the results of the 2016 election in Trump's favor. It's hard to know unless you have more information. The key to solving a puzzle is therefore better intelligence and sharper calculation. But when Albert Einstein said, "We can't solve problems by using the same kind of thinking we used when we created them," he wasn't complaining about the inability to look up a piece of critical information, which IBM Watson could perform miraculously. Rather, Einstein was referring to new types of problems that demanded a shift in thinking, a new way of seeing the world that was needed before one could imagine a potential solution. Einstein was referring to the second type of problem: a mystery.

Mysteries abound in the business world. The question of what your customers really need, for instance, is often a mystery. In most situations, corporate executives have an array of tools—from in-depth focus groups to large-sample surveys to big data from social media—to uncover the needs, wants, and aspirations of consumers. Challenges arise when consumers don't know what they want or cannot even articulate an approximate solution to address those unmet needs, or when the status quo of an industry has become so entrenched that it is impossible for anyone to envision an alternative. And so the old saying that railroad companies got into trouble because they let others—cars, trucks, airplanes, and even telephones—take customers away from them, assuming themselves "to be in the railroad business rather than in transportation."[1]

Unlike the solution to a puzzle, the answer to a mystery simply doesn't yet exist; it has to be invented. While computers excel in precision, rigor, and consistency, they are not designed to make sense, or integrate social interactions across domains, or traverse data online and offline, or come up with a working hypothesis that explains human behaviors and answers the question "Why?"

A young Steve Jobs in 1995 described just how Apple came to develop the Macintosh:[2] "The problem is that market research can tell you what your customers think of something you show them, or it can tell you what your customers want as an incremental improvement on what you have, but very rarely can your customers predict something that they don't even quite know they want yet. . . . So there are these sorts of non-incremental jumps that need to take place where it is very difficult for market research to really contribute much in the early phases of the thinking about, you know, what those should be." Two decades later, when an editor asked him how much market research had gone into the iPad, "None" was still Steve's reply.[3]

Of course, having someone like Steve Jobs would make life easier, as far as coming up with the next killer app was concerned. But for the rest of us mere mortals, when geniuses are few and far between, what kind of struggles must we endure before arriving at the "aha" moment? That struggle was what Rosanne Haggerty endured when she tried to pry open an intractable problem in New York City's Times Square: homelessness. And that endearing ability to persist in the struggle of sense-making about the human condition, paradoxically, is our biggest advantage in the age of smart machines.

THE GOTHAM UNDERCITY

An irony of New York City is the proximity between the haves and the have-nots. Times Square, an iconic tourist destination, historically had one of the highest densities of homeless individuals in the United States. During the late 1980s, the area was notorious for its peep shows and prostitutes. In the thick of it stood the massive, decrepit Times Square Hotel. The inside of the fifteen-story brown-brick building was littered with makeshift sleeping cubicles. These 4-by-6-foot rooms, each lit by a bare bulb, were just large enough for a narrow bed and a locker; with walls, long turned yellow from tobacco smoke, that rose to about 8 feet. Chicken wire made up the difference to the ceilings, which looked about to fall. Trash, mildew, and crack vials were everywhere.

The Times Square Hotel was in bankruptcy for years. A string of halfhearted administrators whom the court had appointed carelessly managed it. The building itself had been violating more than 1,700 building codes, and it was on the verge of being condemned and getting shut down. Living in the building were some two hundred single occupants, mostly elderly, some mentally ill, and others, Vietnam veterans. Shutting down the hotel, as ramshackle as it appeared ironically, would only cause an inevitable surge of homelessness in the neighborhood. "It was the largest single-room occupancy hotel in New York City," Rosanne recalled. "It was so big and so visible. My mind was drawn to what could be done with it."[4]

With sharp facial features and shoulder-length blond hair, Rosanne Haggerty speaks like a high-powered business executive—polite, measured but assertive, carefully choosing her words—not the gregarious social activist one would expect. She grew up outside Hartford, Connecticut. At seventeen, after her father passed away, she took care of her seven younger siblings, as recounted in a *WSJ Magazine* profile. She majored in American Studies at Amherst, and did her senior thesis on Thomas Merton, the Trappist monk and social critic. She volunteered after graduation at the charity for homeless teens, Covenant House, on Forty-Third Street in Times Square. She soon became involved with a group called Catholic Charities and learned how to apply the new Low Income Housing Tax Credit (LIHTC).

LIHTC, pronounced "lie-tech," was a dollar-for-dollar tax credit created under the Tax Reform Act of 1986 that gave incentives for the private sector to develop affordable housing for low-income Americans. "Part of it was timing," Rosanne said. "It was a relatively new program and not a lot of people knew how to use it."[5] She found herself courting major nonprofits and large corporations, touting the idea to redevelop the Times Square Hotel. Her enthusiasm warmed many, but none moved forward. So, she launched her own association— Common Ground, now known as Breaking Ground—in 1990, and used LIHTC as a funding source, to obtain subsidies from the federal, state, and city governments. She pulled together a gamut of daring investors, from JPMorgan to Ben & Jerry's, to acquire and renovate the Times Square Hotel.

By the time the building reopened in 1993, the 652 units had been turned into a state-of-the-art, supportive facility for low-income single adults. "The typical squalor of these [single-room occupancy hotels] was really a management problem,"[6] Rosanne insisted. The ingredients for a successful housing project, she believed, were "good design and committed management" that would connect residents to supportive services. In the case of the Times Square Hotel, it came equipped with a garden roof deck, a computer lab, a restored lobby area that matched the original chandeliers, a tight security system, medical facilities, a dining room, a library, and an art studio. Included on-site were counseling services for health care and job training by psychologists and therapists who helped residents to turn their lives around.[7] "For many years, the award-winning facility has become a showcase for doing things differently. We make it easy for people to succeed," Rosanne emphasized. On April 15, 1994, Ben Cohen and Jerry Greenfield, the two cofounders of Ben and Jerry's, opened an ice-cream shop on the ground floor and gave away some three thousand cones. The scoop shop was run by those who lived upstairs, and it would stay open for the next fifteen years. So successful had the operation become that the scoop shop extended into a satellite facility in Rockefeller Center.[8]

Still, for Rosanne Haggerty, homelessness in the Times Square neighborhood remained a mystery. Despite the widespread accolades and professional recognition that Common Ground received, and despite the innovative approach to developing the Times Square Hotel, she observed no significant drop in the number of people sleeping in front of her building. And on one morning in May 1998, she received a phone call from the emergency room of a local hospital. "Are you Ms. Haggerty, president of Common Ground? We have a patient who has identified you as the next of kin," said the social worker on the other line. "We think she's homeless, well, from Times Square anyway." "Ah." Without asking any more, Rosanne put on her work suit and left for the hospital.

"Here we have an extremely fragile old lady whom I saw pushing cardboards from Thirty-Fourth Street up to Times Square every day. We all recognized her for years, even though we never knew her name," recalled Rosanne. "From the hospital, we quickly brought her to our housing facility. When I inquired why she didn't apply for our service in the past, she smiled very sweetly but said, 'You guys never asked.'" Something had gone amiss. Rosanne's organization had not been able to help those she had wanted to help the most in the first place. Mysteriously, the system had failed to respond to those who needed help the most. And if having well-run, supportive housing did not translate into a real reduction of homelessness in the neighborhood, why bother?

COUNTING WHAT COUNTS

Most social workers believed in a conveyor belt model. According to the model, the homeless were to move sequentially from the streets to shelters and then to permanent housing: if one made a street person aware of the shelters, he or she should naturally gravitate toward them;

and those who lived in shelters were in turn inclined to move into permanent housing, as long as rules were made clear and options available. Few service providers ever questioned this basic assumption. And yet, any experienced social worker would concede a so-called service-resistant population—homeless individuals who refused shelters, and in New York City, even during the throes of a northeastern winter. In 2001, Common Ground experimented with an outreach program: a midnight winter count to assess firsthand the size of this very segment.

The identification of the service-resistant population seemed paradoxical. In the city, dozens of organizations had designed programs to help the homeless in various ways. Hospitals provided emergency room and detoxification services, a large soup kitchen was located just fifteen blocks away from Times Square, and faith-based organizations with well-intentioned volunteers routinely descended from the nearby suburbs to Manhattan to feed the hungry in the middle of the night. And yet, on that frigid January night, Rosanne's team identified well over four hundred individuals sleeping outdoors in Times Square.

Ending homelessness was important from both a humanitarian and a financial standpoint. Individuals who languished on the street often consumed enormous amounts of public resources. Murray Barr was a classic example. Practically a fixture on the streets of Reno, Murray cost Nevada's taxpayers a million dollars over ten years in substance abuse treatment, emergency room visits, and other services. But the state didn't spend nearly as much on housing. "It cost us one million dollars not to do something," observed Officer O'Bryan of the Reno Police Department.[9] Research out of San Francisco also indicated that providing stable housing to a homeless person could reduce emergency room visits by 56 percent. University of California researchers learned that fifteen homeless individuals could cost taxpayers over $1.5 million in hospital and law enforcement bills within eighteen months. Across the United States, nearly two thirds of high-cost Medicaid enrollees were homeless or unstably housed.

When Common Ground followed up the first midnight count with more in-depth interviews, the team was surprised to find out that many homeless people were in fact averse to shelters. They hated them. Featuring dank halls, the odor of urine, alcohol, drugs, and strangers in various states of coherence, shelters offered little respite from the dangers of the street. Whereas on the street, a community of street people know where to find food, where to get a weekly shower, and how to eke out a living. The street may present many problems, but homeless people equally valued their sense of freedom and jealously guarded their independence. They felt the rules that social service providers imposed were often arbitrary and downright disrespectful. Many felt trapped in the homeless state only because of existing bureaucracies. To be qualified for subsidized housing, for instance, one must produce copies of one's birth certificate, evidence of income, a credit standing document, or proof of sobriety for six months—a near-impossible feat for anyone who had been living on the streets for years. "Shelters were, in their minds, associated with broken promises and a number of barriers to housing, like admission criteria that appeared to screen out those most in need of services," said Rosanne.[10]

Common Ground thus took the next logical step with its findings. It put together a "Street-to-Home" initiative that targeted the service-resistant population. The goal was to identify these people and determine what it would take to get them into housing: "I reached outside the usual suspect[s] and hired someone different to figure this out."[11] That's when Rosanne hired Becky Kanis, a West Point graduate who had worked as a special operations commander, a military intelligence officer, with the army. "It occurred to me that we needed someone without pre-conceived ideas about the problem."[12] Rosanne tasked Becky with reducing street homelessness in Times Square by two thirds in three years.[13] Becky swiftly formed a formidable volunteer team together with other third-party outreach workers, and started by asking the homeless whether they needed food, medical assistance, financial support, a job, shelter, counseling, or housing. The team focused on finding new ways to work through the existing system, navigating everything inside the bureaucratic labyrinth: getting a medical screening, receiving a psychiatric evaluation, applying for welfare or disability benefits, and obtaining proof of a source of income. Becky's team streamlined the application process whenever possible, and they fought against many rules and regulations, which often discriminated against the very people they should have helped in the first place.

Meanwhile, Common Ground unveiled its third building, the newly renovated Andrews Hotel, which was once synonymous with the infamous Bowery in lower Manhattan. The Andrews Hotel was designed to offer only temporary, short-term housing, serving those who needed a "first step" off the street, unlike the Times Square facility that offered long-term leases. The Andrews Hotel was therefore able to adopt a much simpler intake procedure: no sobriety requirement, no curfews, no compulsion to enter rehabilitation or other support services. On-site services were available, but if residents did not want any, they did not have to accept them. All told, during its first year of Street-to-Home operation, Becky's team successfully housed forty-three homeless individuals who had previously refused shelters. It seemed that the initiative was finally working. But as Rosanne and Becky would soon discover, there was still much to learn. Driving down homelessness in a neighborhood was, in fact, devilishly hard.

ONE STEP FORWARD, TWO STEPS BACK

In contrast to the last chapter, in which we saw how AI automation was poised to replace even the mainstream professions—accounting, radiology, law, journalism, and stock trading—this chapter reveals areas that still call for judgment, creativity, and empathy, the sort of activities at which the human mind outshines computers. The jobs of recreational therapists, athletic trainers, and clergy have been shown to be relatively immune to automation, as highlighted in a study by Carl Benedikt Frey and Michael Osborne at the University of Oxford, precisely because these jobs require a lot of human interaction, and their nature tends to be relational.[14] But jobs that are transactional and routine—real estate agents, auditors, telemarketers—will be at high risk of being displaced by robots.[15] The impending setback that Rosanne was about to face also illustrates that there is always tricky stuff for which the human mind will continue to excel.

During the second midnight count in Times Square, one year after the launch of Street-to-Home, Common Ground discovered that street homelessness, instead of going down, had actually shot up by 17 percent. This dire statistic left Rosanne befuddled and brought the entire project to a halt: either the basic concept of Street-to-Home was flawed, or the implementation had been a fluke. On the hunch that the initiative still might have targeted the wrong audience, James McCloskey, director of Street-to-Home at the time, made a bold move. At five a.m. every day, for four consecutive weeks, he took his team members to canvass the streets and created a by-name roster with individual photos of all those who slept within the twenty blocks surrounding Times Square. Of the fifty-five individuals the team counted there that winter, McCloskey learned that only eighteen slept in Times Square regularly. The others were there only intermittently and were not consistently homeless. In other words, those eighteen were the only truly chronically homeless people in the neighborhood and the neediest, yet they were the ones who had somehow escaped even Street-to-Home so far.

It's hard to overstate the breakthrough of McCloskey's findings. The term *chronic homelessness* had not yet entered the public-work lexicon at the time. And most service providers were treating every homeless individual very much the same way. "It was like a doctor at [the] emergency room of a hospital saying 'everyone is equally sick,' which of course is not the case," Rosanne observed. It turned out to be this erroneous mixing of the transitionally and chronically homeless in the statistics that explained why the year-on-year figures had not decreased. What the team had finally brought to light was the fact that there existed a group of persistent members of the underclass whom everybody had ignored until then. Making housing easily available at Common Ground wasn't nearly enough. Absent targeted intervention, the chronically homeless would forever evade the existing system.

To concentrate its efforts on this group, Street-to-Home stopped accepting new referrals from third parties. These outreach organizations, which had previously been friendly and cooperative, turned hostile.

"All of these partners had been referring people to us. All of a sudden, we were saying that we would stop all collaboration and focus only on the most difficult cases. They were enraged. They protested. They complained how restrictive and uncaring we ha[d] become," Rosanne told me. "But we said, 'We could only handle the most difficult cases. The easy cases that you have been working on, you should work on [your] own.'" The Street-to-Home team then threw themselves into housing exclusively those eighteen homeless individuals. All of them had been living on the street for an astonishing fourteen years on average. They were known by practically every Times Square business operator, police officer, and service agency. They all had drug, alcohol, and medical problems, and had been contacted by at least one of the outreach teams previously. Yet no one wanted to handle, or had so far successfully handled, this most difficult cohort.

Rosanne speculated that housing these "iconic" homeless people could demonstrate that an intractable problem was, in fact, solvable, which would in turn create a ripple effect, spurring the transformation of the local neighborhood. "You can comfortably walk past a nameless guy in Harlem, but once you know that it's Ed, a Vietnam vet with cancer, you can't be comfortable anymore."[16] A year later, encouraging results began to emerge. As hypothesized, targeting the iconic homeless individuals and giving them exactly what they wanted—housing, not shelters—could persuade others who had been on the street for shorter periods to also seek help. This strategy of "housing first" paid off. In 2006, Street-to-Home saw a 75 percent reduction in homelessness in Times Square over a year, then another 50 percent the following year, resulting in a total sustained reduction in homelessness of 87 percent, as well as a 43 percent decline in homelessness in the twenty surrounding blocks. The result also led to an overhaul of all of New York City's outreach contracts, when then mayor Michael Bloomberg decided to adopt Common Ground's method in all five boroughs starting in 2007, ushering in an era in which the focus of service providers progressively shifted toward measurable outcomes rather than services delivered. Remarkably, Street-to-Home remained, up until this point, a small pilot, with eight employees and a budget of $350,000.

To be sure, homelessness has always been driven by multiple causes. Health and drug dependency and domestic violence can afflict the working poor, as can stagnant wages and soaring rents. The median New York City rent had increased by 19 percent between 2000 and 2014, while household income decreased by 6.3 percent.[17] During the same period, the city lost hundreds of thousands of affordable or rent-stabilized units.[18] These macro trends made the working poor ever more vulnerable. A job loss or a medical emergency could lead to eviction or home foreclosure. But the general trend doesn't mask a deeper, undeniable dynamic—that the chronically homeless were, in many ways, opinion leaders among the homeless. Rosanne proved the ripple effect she had theorized all along. To meaningfully reduce homelessness in a neighborhood, one must prioritize scarce resources to help those who were most entrenched in the most difficult situations, and stop avoiding them because they were difficult to deal with. That was, in many ways, the exact opposite of what other service providers had been doing.

What set Common Ground apart from other conventional approaches was its persistent inquiries into the life circumstances of a population who were once termed "service resistant." Without assuming what policy changes would help or armchair-theorizing what people might need, the Common Ground team went out to the field, and its members immersed themselves in the alien world of chronic homelessness. The team suspended judgment, postponed analysis, and drew conclusions only based on up-close observations and careful listening. Only then did Common Ground begin to arrive at an impactful solution. "The combination of stable housing and supportive services are the magic ingredients that make it possible for people who have frequently fallen through the cracks in the social safety net to regain stability in their lives and move forward," observed Steven Banks, the commissioner of New York City's Human Resources Administration/ Department of Social Services.[19]

UNDERSTANDING THE MYSTERY THROUGH EMPATHY

The late Bill Moggridge, director of the Cooper-Hewitt National Design Museum in New York City, once said, "Engineers start with technology and look for a use for it; business people start with a business proposition and then look for the technology and the people. Designers start with people, coming towards a solution from the point of view of people."[20] Tim Brown, the CEO of the world's largest design house, IDEO, went further. He referred to design thinking as "more than style," but "getting under the skin" of end-users, channeling innovation efforts through the empathic lens of a careful anthropologist. At Stanford's Hasso Plattner Institute of Design, or, as it's often known, "the d.school," two basic elements of design thinking are taught: empathy—understanding the human emotions, goals, and needs that a design must address—and rapid prototyping—developing quick and cheap solutions and updating them rapidly in response to users' actions and suggestions.

Although design thinking might have come naturally for Rosanne, the good news is, others can also learn it. And once you acquire it, the ability to decipher tiny cues of human behaviors can be as much a saving grace for Common Ground as for an industrial engineer when designing his medical device.

When Doug Dietz set out to visit a local hospital that had recently installed a new magnetic resonance imaging (MRI) machine, he had little idea of what life was like inside a children's ward.[21] A soft-spoken midwesterner with a wry, endearing smile, Doug is a twenty-four-year veteran of General Electric (GE). He works as an industrial designer at GE Healthcare, where he is responsible for the overall machine enclosures, controls, displays, and patient transfer units.

"I see this young family coming down the hallway, and I can tell as they get closer that the little girl is weeping. As they get even closer to me, I notice the father leans down and just goes, 'Remember we talked about this, you can be brave,'" Doug recalled.[22] As the MRI began to make a terrible noise, the little girl started to cry. Doug later learned that hospitals had routinely resorted to sedating young patients because they became too scared to lie still for long enough. As many as 80 percent of the patients had to undergo general anesthesia.[23]

After witnessing the anxiety and fear his life-saving machine had caused, Doug resolved to redesign the imaging experience. His boss at GE, who had visited Stanford's d.school while working at Procter & Gamble, suggested that Doug fly to California for a weeklong workshop. Doug knew he couldn't launch a big research and design (R&D) project to redesign an MRI machine from scratch. But at d.school, he learned a human-centered approach to redesigning the experience. Over the next five years, with a new team, Doug would elicit the views of staff from a local children's museum, hospital employees, parents, and kids and create many prototypes that would allow his ideas to be seen, touched, and experienced.[24] Testing and evaluation with young patients and interviews with their parents then revealed what worked and what didn't, helping Doug to generate even more ideas in a continuous cycle.

The result was the Adventure Series, through which young children were transported into an imaginary world where the scanning process was part of an adventure. Hospital wards included "Pirate Island," "Jungle Adventure," "Cozy Camp," and "Coral City."[25] In one of them, children would climb into the scanner's transfer unit, which had been painted like a canoe, and then lie down. The normally terrifying "BOOM-BOOM-BOOM" noise of the scanner became part of the adventure—it was the sound of an imaginary canoe taking off. "They tell children to hold still so that they don't rock the boat, and if you really do hold still, the fish will start jumping over the top of you," Dietz said.[26] Children loved the experience so much that they begged their parents to let them do it again. Sedation rates went down by 80 percent, while parent satisfaction rose by an astounding 90 percent.[27] A mother reported that her six-year-old daughter, who had just been scanned in the MRI "pirate ship," came over, tugged on her skirt, and whispered, "Mommy, can we come back tomorrow?"[28]

It was precisely this kind of small data,[29] the tiny cue of human behaviors observed in a single child, that led to the groundbreaking design. The human condition that Doug had come to grasp drove him to transform a harrowing ordeal into a fun event and, thus, boost the business performance of General Electric. When such circumspection is properly applied, as also in the case of Rosanne, it changes the way an industry views its customers, end-users, products, and services. But most important perhaps is the creative role of the human mind in both episodes. Millions of years in natural evolution have produced a human brain that is particularly adept in situations characterized by ambiguity and complexity, when the required understanding veers away from the material world and into the social realm. "In science, when human behavior enters the equation, things go nonlinear. That's why physics is easy and sociology is hard," astrophysicist Neil deGrasse Tyson has said.[30] And so with the rise of smart machines, managers must leverage the fundamental human advantage by staying creative. Established organizations must also find new ways to scale that human creativity so that a large part of the company can make the sort of creative leap exemplified by Doug. To stay competitive, it's no longer enough to rely on a handful of creative individuals—everyone needs to unleash his or her creativity. That's what P&G is determined to cultivate as we approach the second half of the twenty-first century: to unleash managerial creativity en masse.

SCALING UP CREATIVITY AT P&G

When Alan G. Lafley—or A. G.—was poised to replace the CEO, Durk I. Jager, in June 2000, Procter & Gamble (P&G) was practically in free fall.[31] After a botched attempt to merge with the New Jersey–based drug maker Warner-Lambert, investors whipped P&G by sending its share price into a 20 percent plunge.[32] The company issued a profit warning the following March, predicting a smaller-than-expected return for the year.[33] Later, in June, P&G missed its revised forecast earnings, falling behind its stated goal by another 15 percent.[34] Altogether, the company's share price had dropped by more than half in four months, wiping out $75 billion in market capitalization.[35] It had become too much for anyone to bear. CEO Jager, whose brief tenure was just shy of eighteen months, announced his immediate departure.

With the stock price in tatters and investor confidence destroyed, Lafley had no choice but to begin a brutal turnaround: laying off employees, slashing nonperforming brands, and culling new products. But as effective as those urgent actions might have been in the short term, they did not nearly address any of the fundamental issues. The multilayered approval process at P&G, so commonly seen in many conservative companies where "everything is tested to death,"[36] had resulted in a sluggish product pipeline, a declining product portfolio, and a lack of new customers. Even Pampers, Tide, and Crest—the gold-standard brands—had been languishing for years. More than simple wholesale downsizing, P&G needed a new knowledge base to yield relevant insights and regenerate new growth. Design thinking was just the helping hand that the "Proctoids" needed.

AN UNLIKELY CANDIDATE

Early in his career, Lafley spent years working in Japan, a country often described as having a very design-oriented culture. He came to believe in the power of up-close observation. He was never comfortable with "research-at-a-distance" methods such as focus groups convened inside corporate conference rooms or large-sample surveys sent to respondents. "When you [instead] ventured inside people's homes, you noticed funny little things that didn't show up in research surveys— like women having to resort to opening Tide packages with screwdrivers to avoid breaking fingernails," Lafley would say.[37] It was clear that P&G couldn't compete through technology and marketing alone; design would be the means to deliver superior experiences.[38]

In setting out "to build design into the DNA of the company," the CEO tapped Claudia Kotchka as the design chief in 2001. A twenty-two-year P&G veteran who punctuated her speech with a lot of "fantastics" and "awesomes," Claudia started as an accountant at the now-defunct Arthur Andersen.[39] Having gotten bored as a bean counter, she tried brand management, then marketing, and later headed P&G's package design department. Lafley chose her because she was someone who could speak the language of design as well as that of business.[40] To improve P&G's understanding of design, Claudia benchmarked the company against others that were far more design-sensitive. Mattel and Nike became the reference points. She then built a network of design experts, setting up a formal review board that included world-class designers, such as Tim Brown, the CEO of IDEO, and Ivy Ross, Gap's executive vice president of marketing. Claudia also sought help from a trio of deans: David Kelley of the d.school at Stanford, Patrick Whitney of the Institute of Design at the Illinois Institute of Technology, and Roger Martin of the Rotman School of Management in Toronto. "The external board works because members are not pursuing a personal agenda and have no legacy to protect,"[41] observed Claudia.

GENERATING GOODWILL

To circumvent resistance, design thinking was positioned as a proven method to save troubled businesses. No one could force design thinking on a business that did not want it. Which was why Claudia decided to start in areas where there was an existing interest, not necessarily the areas of the greatest need. Seeing and experiencing were also part of the process. In 2003, Lafley took his entire global leadership team of thirty-five to IDEO in San Francisco for a day and a half. "When [our] engineers were working on something," Lafley said, "they really didn't want anybody in the sandbox until they're ready to show it."[42] Claudia echoed, "Everything we've done has been about demonstrate, demonstrate, demonstrate."[43] One early effort involved tapping into consumers' frustrations with annoying cleaning chores. The team was instructed to focus on "extreme users," ranging from a professional house cleaner who scrubbed grout with his fingernail to four single guys whose idea of cleaning the bathroom was to push a filthy towel around the floor with a big stick. If P&G could make these people happy, it would achieve a home run. One idea soon gained traction—a cleaning tool on a removable stick that could reach shower walls and get into nooks and crannies.

Over the next eighteen months, the team made multiple iterations in record-breaking time and unveiled the Mr. Clean Magic Reach bathroom cleaner. Pointing at the blue lever that connected the pole to the cleaning head, Rich Harper, the design manager for household care, highlighted how the color blue, which was associated with cleanliness, was just the kind of subtle signal that helped consumers understand a product. Equally important was the audible *click* when the cleaning head snapped into place properly: "It's those little details that have really made a difference."[44] While pointing out the round holes on the blue foam head, Harper conceded that they had no real function, but they helped convince consumers that the head was squishy enough to fit behind the toilet. And the silver color of the pole? It signified that "touch of magic" associated with the Mr. Clean brand.

Consumers loved the prototype; some even refused to return it. One woman was overheard saying she had "lust in her heart" for it. Mr. Clean Magic Reach was launched in 2005. Although it did not become a blockbuster, it sold well enough to encourage managers to think about innovation differently, and it led them to try out product ideas beyond liquid detergent, which eventually led to the mega-hit Mr. Clean Magic Eraser.[45] Another example was Kandoo, a wet wipe with a kid-friendly button on the box. "Look at kids who are toilet training," Claudia observed. "Their line is 'I want to do it myself.' So, we said, 'OK, we know how to make a great wipe—what can we do to empower kids to use it themselves?' We made this clever pop-up box that lets a kid grab a wipe with one hand. And the kids went nuts for it."[46] Moms loved Kandoo, too, because kids would not waste an entire roll of toilet paper when they used it. It was a huge hit in Europe, and it subsequently became available in the United Sates. Soon after, the company launched a soap dispenser that kids could use with one hand. Kids pushed the top, and foam came out. Without wasting soap, the product helped teach children good habits.

Precisely because design thinking helped unleash creativity, Claudia simply tried to get as many people through the experience as possible. "I always say, 'Show, don't tell.'"[47]

CHANGING CONTEXT

Meanwhile, Lafley worked to change the organizational norms. He modeled design thinking in his own behavior and dedicated ever more time to in-depth in-home visits wherever he traveled. During one of his many trips to China, he insisted on chatting, through a translator, with rural Chinese women washing clothes in a river, just to learn how they used detergent. He also modified several key processes, including how business strategy was reviewed. "Ten, twenty, thirty years ago, you were greeted with a briefing book that [was] about two inches thick,"[48] he recalled. Presidents from each category were expected to demonstrate absolute conviction and to be prepared to answer every conceivable question that senior management hurled at them. Lafley mused, "I am not sure if that approach was all that different from what a lot of other industries and companies were doing."

The CEO saw the need to devise a new process to reflect the changing nature of the strategic conversation, a new kind of conversation that needed to be more exploratory and creative and less combative. Business leaders were now asked to submit their slides two weeks before any strategy review. Lafley would read the materials and issue a short list of questions that he wanted to discuss at the meeting, emphasizing that he wanted a discussion, not a presentation. Executives would then bring only three more pieces of paper—charts, graphs, notes—to the review. Lafley reasoned that forcing executives to toss around ideas with senior management would encourage them to become comfortable with the logical leaps needed to generate groundbreaking ideas. "What we try to achieve is a conversation, a discussion that focuses on the critical issues. . . . Do we have an idea? Do we have proprietary technology? Do we have a prototype? Do we have a few iterations with some consumers so that we know we've got something?" And if a project was already in the development phase, the conversation would take the following direction: "What are the critical milestones? What are the killer issues? What are the one, two, three most critical issues that, if we get them right, we have a success; if we don't get them right, we are going to shut down the project and move our resources on?"[49]

Between 2000 and 2008, P&G's revenue more than doubled from $40 billion to $83 billion, while earnings took a gigantic leap from $2.5 billion to more than $12 billion. This was the kind of growth expected from an IT company or a firm operating in an emerging market, not an almost two-hundred-year-old soap company based in Cincinnati, Ohio.[50] As for Claudia, she simply followed one overarching principle: "When big organizations scale well, they focus on moving a thousand people forward a foot at a time, rather than moving one person forward by a thousand feet."[51]

WHAT ARE PEOPLE FOR?

Very often, managers I come across hold the belief that machine automation—particularly that involving artificial intelligence, which we explored in the last chapter—would lead to mass unemployment or a "jobless future."[52] Yet such an apocalyptic outlook ignores an indispensable resource that continues to exist in the age of the algorithm: the creativity of the human mind. Rosanne at Common Ground relied on human intelligence to make sense of the chronically homeless and, in so doing, addressed one of our thorniest social problems. Doug at GE embraced deep, nuanced engagement with sick children at hospitals. And Claudia at P&G evangelized design thinking as a way of unpacking consumer behaviors at scale.

"Journalists and expert commentators overstate the extent of machine substitution for human labor and ignore the strong complementarities that increase productivity, raise earnings, and augment demand for skilled labor,"[53] wrote David Autor, an economist at MIT. "Tasks that cannot be substituted by computerization are generally complemented by it." The upshot is that artificial intelligence, machine learning, and cognitive computing can either exert a complementary effect or substitutional pressure. But that outcome is not predetermined. Atul Gawande—a celebrated surgeon, writer, and public health researcher—explained exactly why human interaction remains paramount in the age of AI. He painted a simple scenario of a local clinic. "I have pain," a patient complains. "Where?" the doctor asks. "Hmmm.

Well, it's sort of here." The patient points with a hand. "Well, do you mean there under your rib cage, or do you mean in your chest, or your stomach . . . ?" This intimate interaction, to Gawande, is as much about a patient telling her story as the doctor probing the patient. "It's more of a narrative than it is a straight set of data." A physician needs "not only to ask you to take off your clothes, but then to actually have permission to cut you open and do what [he] choose[s] to do inside you."[54] Trust, empathy, and dialogue are what make health care ever so human. Only we can fully grasp the meaning of compassion, pride, embarrassment, envy, justice, and solidarity.

As much as one might hope, expert systems are still built around major job functions and used only by specialists. IBM Watson has built its application for lung oncologists. Some other AI systems are built to help dermatologists detect melanoma, distinguishing cancer from such benign skin conditions as acne, a rash, or a mole. Still others interpret mammography for radiologists to screen breast cancers. Each of these specialized systems is tremendously powerful, but still needs someone to integrate the data and to choose which system to use. Meanwhile, patients carry with them four kinds of information: their DNA, their zip code (where we live tells a lot about our socioeconomic status), their individual behavior patterns, and other data that indicate what health-care options are available to them. Some of this information can be collected online, some can be captured via embedded sensors and mobile phones, and some will remain forever evasive as offline information. In fact, setting up a properly functioning system might sound easy in principle—just pour in the data and let the system make its association, as in the case of AlphaGo—but it's actually difficult and subtle work, vexing even to people with a strong background in computer science.[55]

For these reasons, AI, like so many other technologies that came before it, is in fact an augmentation technology. AI is the carrier of world-class knowledge and expert instinct. AI will augment professionals, offering them expertise and assistance. But that machine alone cannot resolve a mystery by itself. "When you use a phone, you amplify the power of human speech. You cannot shout from New York to California, and yet this rectangular device in your hand allows the human voice to be transmitted across three thousand miles. Did the phone replace the human voice? No, the phone is an augmentation device," explained computer scientist and self-driving-car pioneer Sebastian Thrun.[56]

Through this lens, the nature of artificial intelligence is much demystified. Earlier examples of a similar nature in fact abound in the business world. There existed a time when credit officers at retail banks evaluated personal loan applications based on their experience, sometimes in conjunction with corporate guidelines and policies. In 1956, Fair, Isaac and Company—a Minneapolis firm founded by Bill Fair and Earl Isaac—developed a formulaic method of determining creditworthiness and began calculating FICO scores that replaced the subjective judgments of a bank loan officer. The FICO scores were deployed for Sears's in-store credit cards, then for Visa and Master-Card, then for autos and mortgages, and are now used for evaluating small-business loans.[57] Today, virtually no human eyeball is needed to process any credit request below $50,000.[58] This is how an industry took off by ridding its dependence on a small group of human experts.

The recent advances in artificial intelligence undoubtedly have made expert systems far more powerful in accelerating knowledge transfer. These advances are enabling computers to "reason," and to manipulate data that are ill-structured, involving assumptions, approximations, and other heuristics. Still, a human is required to decide where and how AI is deployed; a human still needs to decide which key decisions be turned over to AI or to keep a human in the loop; a human still needs to imagine what new products or services could be created by combining the emerging capabilities of machines with a human touch. These are the sort of questions only we can answer. Although automation has made the process of turning data into useful information faster than ever, it hasn't done away with the human task of sense-making, to endow information with meanings, and to act upon them creatively. Former chairman Norman Augustine of Lockheed Martin, the world's largest defense contractor, wrote in the *Wall Street Journal*, "An education in *history* can create critical thinkers who can digest, analyze, and synthesize information and articulate their findings. These are skills needed across a broad range of subjects and disciplines."[59] To stay competitive, therefore, corporate leaders must proactively codify that which it is possible to routinize and, at the same time, engage managers to embark on creative work, leveraging their freed-up human capacity.

KNOWLEDGE REENGINEERING

When it comes to knowledge automation, Common Ground has achieved it even before the dawn of smart machines. Rosanne and her team had figured out a way to disseminate expert judgement across the wider community by codifying expert knowledge into an easy-to-follow playbook. By doing so, Common Ground managed to spread its influence beyond New York City to the rest of the nation.

After two years of working as the first director of Street-to-Home, Becky Kanis took on a new position at Common Ground as the director of innovation. She grew increasingly restless, having seen that the critical barrier to ending homelessness was often not the lack of resources per se but the fragmentation of knowledge, expertise, and the power to act. "We as a society ha[ve] set it up . . . with all the money that [is] taxed and the federal government gets it, they give little buckets to little groups of people," Becky observed. "The housing authority gets this. The mental health people get that. But it's so distributed, and so diffused, that no one actor in any community has sufficient resources or authority to [be] truly responsible to reduce homelessness."

After seeing the benefits of identifying the chronically homeless by their names and faces, Becky decided to expand the Street-to-Home concept to incorporate information on medical conditions. She reached out to Jim O'Connell, the founding physician of the Boston Health Care for the Homeless Program. "I still ride the van every Monday and Wednesday night from nine at night to five in the morning. It's unbelievably fun and important," said Dr. O'Connell, who has been providing medical care two nights a week out of a van since 1986. The experience of being a street physician has taught him the common causes of early death among the homeless. "I can actually see what's going on [on] the streets and where people are coming from." Together, Kanis and O'Connell adopted the eight distinct markers that identify those at extreme risk of dying on the street. They called the instrument a vulnerability index:

1. More than three hospitalizations or emergency room visits in a year
2. More than three emergency room visits in the previous three months
3. Aged sixty or older
4. Cirrhosis of the liver
5. End-stage renal disease
6. History of frostbite, trench foot, or hypothermia
7. HIV/AIDS
8. Trimorbidity: co-occurring psychiatric condition, substance abuse, and chronic medical condition

All of a sudden, the vulnerability index turned the conventional first-come, first-served, queue-waiting approach to helping the homeless on its head. Now included in the existing by-name roster were eight important markers signaling medical need. The vulnerability index was therefore a person-by-person record, creating a sort of health registry for any given community. It's the FICO scores equivalent for homelessness.

In a sense, the experience and knowledge that Becky accumulated through numerous midnight counts were now codified and translated into a simple survey instrument. It used to take a well-seasoned social worker with the tenacity of an army commander to identify the chronically homeless who needed help the most. This is no longer the case. The simplicity of the vulnerability index could mobilize communities to act. With the help of Common Ground, Los Angeles County and City launched Project 50; Washington, DC, adopted its own program; and Phoenix implemented Project H3. Collectively, these newly mobilized communities showed that individuals could be moved from the streets into housing in an average of ten days, demonstrating that what had started in crowded New York City was transferable elsewhere, even to less dense neighborhoods. The vulnerability index spurred cities and housing bureaus to act quickly for the most vulnerable first.

Meanwhile, Becky and Rosanne got wind of a wildly successful program called the 100,000 Lives Campaign. In just eighteen months, the campaign had successfully prevented 100,000 accidental deaths due to medical injuries and snowballed into a nationwide movement. At the heart of the movement were six simple interventions that hospitals had to prioritize, including paying attention to the first sign of patient decline, timely usage of antibiotics, and prevention of pneumonia. These procedures, though seemingly innocuous, often required cross-departmental collaboration between nurses, doctors, and surgeons. Without proper prioritization, these crucial steps could easily be forgotten amid a hectic schedule.

"The two of us exchanged a nod from across the room as if to say, 'We could do this with homelessness too,'" Becky recalled from that fateful meeting with Rosanne. "We asked IHI [Institute for Healthcare Improvement] to coach us on large-scale change and adapt the strategies and techniques." In 2010, Common Ground launched its own 100,000 Homes Campaign. It aimed to house the nation's 100,000 most vulnerable people by July 2014. The campaign focused on aligning resources across multiple sectors, including housing authorities, faith-based groups, public hospitals, local businesses, nonprofits, landlords, property developers, philanthropists, and concerned citizens. Newly enrolled communities, which were virtually all outside New York State, participated in a four-part online seminar followed by a three-day intensive training session on using the vulnerability index survey. These communities then independently conducted a "registry week" to identify individuals on the streets and solicit the information necessary to link them to stable housing.

In her characteristically determined style, Rosanne launched Community Solutions in 2011 as a spin-off. Community Solutions was to focus on disseminating know-how beyond New York. "I concluded, to my horror, that we had developed a way of attacking the problem that was inherently limited," said Rosanne when reviewing how

Common Ground had been operating some three thousand housing units since 1990 to serve the homeless population.[60] "It was good, it made a real contribution, but each of our initiatives took four or five years and could cost $40 million. That's what we were known for, that's what was unique. But the model couldn't scale." But through Community Solutions, 173 communities had enrolled in the 100,000 Homes Campaign by November 2012. These communities had administered over 35,000 surveys while helping over 22,000 individuals move into stable housing. That figure rose to 70,000 people a year later, with an estimated 88 percent of tenants maintaining their housing for a year or longer. By June 11, 2014, the campaign had housed 101,628 individuals, beating both their target and their deadline.

That same year, the Building and Social Housing Foundation, in conjunction with the United Nations, nominated Community Solutions for the World Habitat Award. It was the second time that Rosanne had received the honor, the first was during her time at Common Ground some fifteen years previously. "By diffusing a proven approach and partnering with local stakeholders across the country, we have ended up with a unique view on homelessness in the US," explained Rosanne. "If you want to understand certain patterns of homelessness around this country, we probably would have the answer."

MAKING A CREATIVE LEAP

Isaac Newton said, "No great discovery was ever made without a bold guess." Typically, innovators push forward, risking failure and harm to their own security and reputations. They have a dream that does not fit the norm. They accept long hours, personal expense, nagging uncertainty, and rejection. And when they succeed, their idiosyncratic views become the new normal. Their individual stories are then rightfully seen as epics. They become part of history. But there's more than this rhetoric. The spread of a new practice also requires a concerted effort to codify expert understanding into explicit knowledge, easy-to-follow instructions that others can adopt. What was once proprietary know-how is translated into widespread knowledge. The story of Common

Ground is as much about solving a mystery as it is about knowledge automation. What started as a midnight count in Times Square has turned into a national movement that has transformed the lives of 100,000 people. The real key has been the vulnerability index, which embodies expert knowledge and empowers the less experienced across the nation. And the vulnerability index brought us back full circle to our starting point of this chapter—that any trailblazing effort is, by definition, a uniquely human endeavor.

Machine learning and big data concern themselves with correlation, not causation. They do not have an embedded model of the world that can reliably distinguish between the truth and lies. Under the hood of IBM Watson, for instance, the algorithm establishes manifold statistically significant relationships, but never quite explains why they are so. What constitutes observable truth in law or philosophy may not in psychology. To achieve any groundbreaking insights regarding marketing, consumer desire, popular art, or even the user interface of a mobile app, it still takes an innovator to synthesize human experience, newspaper articles, and stories about how people have reacted, conversed, and complained. Extracting the hidden and ambiguous meaning in the social realm requires not just big data, which are often broad and shallow and devoid of emotional meanings, but small data—the thick and deep information about individuals, for example, about how a sickly child at the hospital is nervously waiting for an MRI scan.[61]

The way we assess the performance of computer systems can also be misleading. The notion of machine intelligence, strangely enough, remains ill-defined. Scientists tend to evaluate a computer on tasks that are difficult for humans, such as playing chess, Go, or *Jeopardy!* These tasks are unnatural and difficult for humans because they require deliberation and planning, the type of cognitive work that our evolutionary history has endowed us with only most recently. These are not the sort of tasks that human intelligence has evolved for—making very quick decisions using limited sensory data with limited calculation power. Consequently, a computer can play chess far better than it can recognize the face of its opponent. That's also why *captchas* are still used for secured online transactions: our ability to transcribe wavy, distorted letters is better than computers. Captchas require us to prove that we're human, not bots, in a kind of reverse Turing test.[62] Precisely because people are more agile and dexterous than the most advanced robots in identifying objects and understanding nuance, the results are always better when computers and humans work together, rather than either one working alone, whether it is playing chess, or solving other real-world problems.[63] You can try pushing a machine toward the bleeding edge, but it still won't beat an average machine that works alongside a human. The future is merging machine capability and human consciousness.

I am therefore not advocating a nostalgic return to human judgment. As we saw earlier, once Rosanne arrived at her groundbreaking insight to target the chronically homeless, she and Becky then launched the vulnerability index to capture the essence of that newfound wisdom. The codification of tacit knowledge helped to spur further innovation along the new trajectory, allowing other communities to emulate Common Ground's approach and culminating in the 100,000 Homes Campaign. And one doesn't need IBM Watson or AlphaGo to codify learning. Through the vulnerability index, Community Solutions diffused a new practice in its own way, transforming a profession once ruled by hunches, habits, and outdated practices into an applied science that relies on objective measurements. In fact, Community Solutions later partnered with Palantir Technologies, a computer software and services company in Silicon Valley, to develop an online platform that automatically matched the results from the vulnerability index to the available housing in the area. It not only identified the most vulnerable but also automated the once time-consuming housing-matching process. Supply automatically met demand. The *Economist* labeled Community Solutions "Just like Airbnb."[64] As for Rosanne, she decided to move on to investigate even thornier issues in Brownsville, Brooklyn, New York. Despite having one of the largest concentrations of public housing in the country, Brownsville also had a high rate of family homelessness historically. Community Solutions created the Brownsville Partnership to help vulnerable people remain stably housed as family units and to improve their lives in the places where they lived. The project sought to prevent homelessness at the family level before it occurred.

All these suggest that, against the tyranny of big data and machine learning, when automation inevitably displaces narrowly defined expertise, more general-purpose jobs will spring forth. In the early twentieth century, hundreds of thousands of workers who manually operated switchboards staffed the telephone systems at AT&T. When those systems got automated, the telephone operator job ceased to exist. In its place, the office receptionist, who answered general inquiries and relayed telephone messages, came into the mainstream in corporate America.[65] Similarly, when ATMs automated the routine tasks of a bank teller, it became cheaper to operate bank branches. Banks opened more offices, and consequently, the total number of tellers actually grew.[66] When tractors replaced manual plows, we were able to produce much more food. When weaving and spinning were mechanized, human labor in textile manufacturing was made redundant, but workers have gone on to build cars, airplanes, trains, and skyscrapers. New inventions have always been replacing human labor for centuries, but our standard of living rose when technology increased our productivity. Higher productivity has led to growth in employment in the long

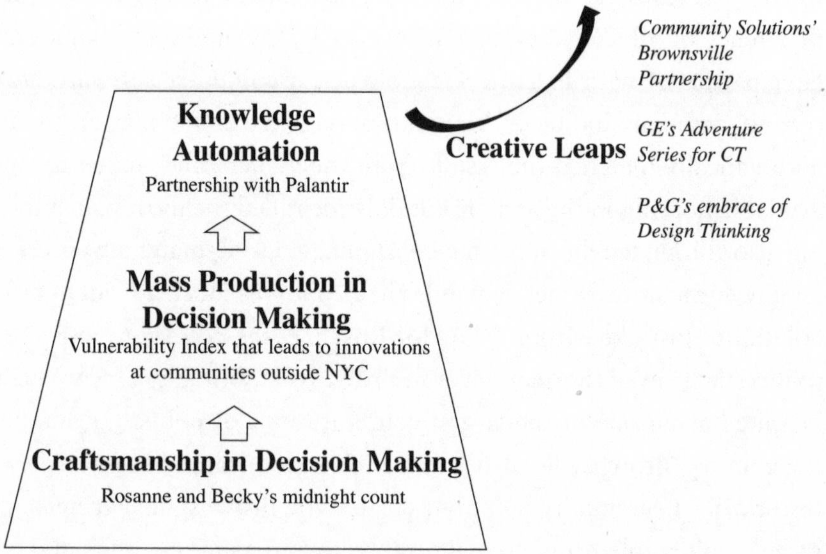

Figure 6.1 The creative leap after automation

run, not a decline. How we facilitate the transition is a societal issue that goes beyond the scope of this book. But as a society, we have every reason to be hopeful.

One last piece of supportive evidence. An investigation by Boston University economist James Bessen found that jobs and automation often grow hand in hand, that automation creates more jobs than it destroys.[67] Such findings have been corroborated by other more recent research. Many companies building AI systems have found that humans must play an active role in both building and running them.[68] And that's exactly the point: whether machine automation will complement or substitute human labor comes down to a choice. The imperative for companies is clear. Executives must infuse knowledge work with creativity while automating everything that is routine. Doug at GE showed us the importance of this. Rosanne at Common Ground demonstrated its possibilities. And Claudia at P&G proved that it could be done at scale (see Figure 6.1).

A. G. Lafley, when giving advice on how students could succeed in a fast-changing world, advocated a multidisciplinary approach that combined "art, science, the humanities, social science, and language." Writing in the *Huffington Post*, the former CEO argued, "The mind develops the mental dexterity that opens a person to new ideas, which is the currency for success in a constantly changing environment. . . . Completing a broad liberal arts curriculum should enable a student to develop the conceptual, creative, and critical thinking skills that are the essential elements of a well-exercised mind."[69]

So, what must executives do in the age of smart machines? The key is to automate as many routine cognitive tasks as possible. Free your people up from white-collar drudgery so as to leverage their fundamental human advantage, to solve problems of the next frontier creatively.

REFLECTION ON PART 2

Three Leverage Points Are Rewriting the Rules of Competition

To derive an integrated strategy, every effective leader must begin with the big questions: What world am I living in? What are the biggest trends in this world? How do I align my company's activities so my organization gets the most out of these trends and cushions the worst? Part 1 shows us the power of history, which acts as a prism to help us understand the past so we may leap into new knowledge disciplines. Part 2 takes to the future to pinpoint the two intertwining trends that are propelling all companies into the twenty-first century: the inexorable rise of intelligent machines and the emergence of ubiquitous connectivity. As new technologies are introduced, society is being transformed, and with it, the way we will work in the future. We saw that connectivity favors a decentralized mode of innovation; smart machines automate expert knowledge, and consequently, managerial activities that will still be ensconced in the human realm demand a heightened level of creativity, social understanding, and empathy.

Machine Intelligence Is Evolving

The current development of AI is akin to the early years of electricity as it replaced steam power in manufacturing. At the turn of the twentieth century, most textile factories were still powered by flowing water and waterwheels. Factories that installed steam engines had to accommodate pulleys, belts, rotating shafts, and a host of complex gear systems. Factories were built largely around a rigidly imposed steam engine, impairing all possible workflow efficiency. Interestingly, when manufacturers began to adopt electricity, engineers couldn't imagine an alternative layout like the modern-day assembly line. Rather, they grouped electric motors in a big cluster, forgoing the benefit of a decentralization of power in optimizing workflow. It took almost another two decades for manufacturers to unleash the full benefits of electricity.

Today, big organizations still tend to frame AI as a cost-cutting measure that substitutes human labor in paper processing. Although this can be all-important, the biggest potential is likely to be far more profound: self-taught algorithms will play a much bigger role in coordinating economic transactions, including energy management, health care, finance, legal, transport, and pretty much everything in our lives.

Companies Will Have to Make Big Bets

A bold decision always looks good—until it is wrong. To facilitate evidence-based decision making, managers must carry out frequent experimentation to diminish the dark space of ignorance and to arrive at conclusions with the required level of familiarity. Critical assumptions must first be identified and then proved right through rigorous experiments. Companies like WeChat, Common Ground, and Recruit Holdings took an evolutionary approach, ran numerous experiments, before hitting a pivotal moment. This is how the strategy process under uncertainty should be managed: create enough opportunities so that relevant evidence can emerge—but once clear, full steam ahead.

The biggest risk that threatens the survival of a large and complex organization lies in political infighting and collective inaction. That's why committed executives at the very top must be ready to intervene by implementing a new directive when necessary. The "deep dive," as I call it, is when top executives personally intervene at critical junctures, wielding the power to overcome barriers. Deep dives are different from micromanagement in that they rely on knowledge power rather than position power.

The next and final chapter explains how a strategy that blends top-down and bottom-up approaches can remove the final organizational hurdles that may stand in the way of an established company's efforts to reconfigure and rewire itself.

PART III

WHAT NEEDS TO HAPPEN NEXT

7

FROM INSIGHTS TO ORGANIZED ACTIONS

Don't ask managers, "What is your strategy?" Look at what they do! Because people will pretend.

—ANDY GROVE, INTEL'S FORMER CEO AND CHAIRMAN (1936–2016)

A REALLY, REALLY SMALL LAPTOP

THE REFRAIN "IF YOU DON'T KNOW WHERE YOU'RE GOING, ANY road will take you there" captures the importance of managers developing a point of view about the world. But awareness is not the same as commitment, so insights alone never suffice. Because strategy and execution are inextricably linked, unless ideas are translated into everyday actions and operational tactics, a pioneer is still at risk of being displaced by copycats. More often than not, the role of a CEO needs to go beyond strategic visioning and into the substance of strategy implementation, particularly during turbulent times.

Chairman Jonney Shih was not at all happy with the laptop computers his company was making. The year was 2006, four years before Apple launched the first iPad. A practicing Buddhist with a slim frame, sixty-two-year-old Shih had led Taiwan's computer giant, Asus, since 1993. On weekends, employees often found the chairman volunteering at a temple in the rural Taiwanese town of Yuanli, dressed in a polo shirt and khaki pants, among farmers sporting conical straw hats.[1]

But Shih also exhibited a competitive streak, a ferociously driven side that was not exactly Zen-like. Buddhists aren't supposed to think about technology and business while they're meditating, but Shih reportedly often did so.[2] "If you want to be number one," Shih once said of Andy Grove's famous book *Only the Paranoid Survive*, "Is there any difference between being perfectionist and paranoid?"[3]

As I noted in Chapter 4, the personal computer (PC) is a remarkably complicated product, and yet requires one of the simplest assembly processes in modern manufacturing. The components of a laptop include a standard motherboard, a dozen connectors, power supplies, a flat panel display, a keyboard, and a trackpad. Many Taiwanese companies began by producing motherboards in the late 1970s, taking advantage of low labor costs.

In 1989, four engineers jumped ship from Acer, another Taiwanese industry pioneer, and founded Asustek Computer, or Asus. Shih, also a veteran at Acer, left his position as the head of R&D in 1992 and joined Asus, still an upstart at the time, as its CEO.[4] By the mid-2000s, Asus had become the world's largest motherboard maker. The company had also built a large operation in contract manufacturing, which served a long list of international clients, including such big names as Sony, IBM, Dell, and Hewlett Packard (HP). Still, Shih harbored an ambition to strike it big by making Asus a global brand in its own right. "I don't think the Taiwanese got very good training to drive the mentality of innovation," he complained.[5]

In October 2006, Shih started to argue that the traditional laptop had grown too complicated and needed to be radically simplified. A conventional machine needed almost three minutes to boot, demanded massive amounts of memory and storage, and came with a powerful microprocessor. He saw a much simpler, less expensive laptop as the source of the next billion users, new consumers ranging from children to the elderly and from homemakers to teenagers.

The problem was that the launch of such a laptop would be a departure from Asus's traditional offerings. The corporate slogan "Rock-

Solid Quality" had embodied Asus's twenty-year efforts to cultivate quality consciousness and superior technological understanding in its laptop division. It would be exceedingly difficult, if not entirely impossible, for the division to develop a product concept that would be a good fit for a humble segment: consumers who had not bought PCs because they were either too expensive or just too intimidating.

Rather than assigning the task to his underlings, Shih became directly involved in the development of a new line of computers, the Eee PC, better known as the netbook. As chairman, Shih took up the role of project manager all the way down to the operations level. For the first three months, he worked with a small group of engineers on the basic product concept, employing anthropological observations on end-users and shying away from traditional market research, which the mainstream laptop division had relied on heavily.

Because the cost of licensing Microsoft Windows would be prohibitive and would undermine efforts to meet the target price point of $300, Shih's work group sought to design a new user interface (UI) that would work on Linux, a free and open-source operating system. However, incessant internal debates about the basic UI layout quickly ensued, threatening to slow the project to a crawl. It was then that Shih booked his engineers into a hot spring resort in Taipei for two days to free them from all other interruptions. There would be no e-mails, no phone calls, and no meetings with colleagues back at headquarters. Instead, the cross-functional team of software programmers, industrial designers, and hardware engineers focused on designing the UI alone. And for many, the two-day sojourn turned into a six-month foray. "We did not have enough experience, and we made many mistakes that caused delays," recalled the deputy product manager Zing Chen. "We were all thrown into an *obeya* [Japanese for "big room"] to sort out our communications. We ended up staying in the obeya from June to December 2007." That co-location proved to be crucial. Not only did it enhance team dynamics, but it also altered many patterns of interaction. Rapid cross-disciplinary conversation soon became the team's hallmark as the development of the Eee PC continued to unfold.

When it was later known that no vendor could deliver an operating system that met the team's specifications, Shih challenged his staff and told them to embark on a global hunt for a competent partner. "Jonney asked us to look outside for talent, not only within the company, and not only in Asia, but all over the globe. In the end, we found a Canadian company interested in partnering with us to develop the UI," recalled Samson Hu, who later became the general manager of the Eee PC business unit. "We had a hard time locating potential vendors because our tight timing scared everyone away." For the first time, Asus collaborated with a non-Asian software house.

Most dramatic, perhaps, is when Shih decided to approve an initiative to sidestep the corporate assurance department for final product testing, right before the launch of the new netbook. Asus handed out free samples to employees' friends and family under the "Thousand User Testing Initiative." Within weeks, this method uncovered numerous problems that traditional in-house testing procedures would have missed, as these testers operated netbooks vastly differently than the habitual laptop users.

When the Eee PC hit store shelves in Taiwan in October 2007, the initial supply, priced at $340, sold out within thirty minutes. Consumers snatched up as many netbooks as Asus could make, and the company saw its stock price rise by 4.9 percent the following day. A worldwide rollout soon followed the Taiwan debut and the Eee PC was named the most desired gift on Amazon.com during the 2007 holiday selling season. So strong was the demand in the United States that it resulted in the first distribution of other Asus products, including the full range of conventional laptops, by coveted big-box retailers, including Best Buy and Macy's. The Taiwanese computer maker finally entered the home turf of HP and Dell—not by selling anything grandiose but by focusing on a humble netbook.

HOW DOES STRATEGY REALLY WORK?

There is a fine line between genius and megalomania. The storied Silicon Valley is peopled with entrepreneurial CEOs who possess a larger-than-life personality, drive business development firsthand, and endure extreme working hours that hardly seem sustainable. These CEOs often take an obsessive interest in the minutiae of products and insist that other top executives do the same. From Polaroid's Edwin Land to Apple's Steve Jobs, from Amazon's Jeff Bezos to Tesla's Elon Musk, these CEOs have left their personal stamps everywhere on companies and have been admired as much for their ability to create objects of desire as for their obsession with the details of product design.

When Apple introduced the iPod in October 2001, the launch was set to meet the impossibly short schedule Steve Jobs had imposed from the top down. To meet the project deadline, Jon Rubinstein, then head of hardware, had to swiftly assemble an engineering team that focused on integrating standardized third-party components into a small package.[6] These constraints forced the iPod project team to experiment with a new engineering approach that would deliver the required product features not just on time but also at a much lower cost, with virtually no up-front investment in product development. Such were the critical criteria that would make it possible for Apple to profit from an inexpensive device with a much shorter product life cycle and considerably lower margins than the Macintosh computers.

Aside from controlling the project schedule, Jobs remained close during its implementation. Colleagues reported that the CEO would be "horribly offended [if] he couldn't get to the song he wanted in less than three pushes of a button."[7] Importantly, the prime distinction of the iPod lay not only in its elegant industrial design but also in its complementary offering, iTunes. Jobs reportedly insisted that the iTunes user interface be modeled on Palm's HotSync software so that the iPod could transfer songs seamlessly from iTunes.[8]

A year later, while the product team was busy releasing the Windows-compatible iPod, Jobs became the first person to persuade all major record labels to make their music available online. To achieve the ninety-nine-cents-per-song pricing scheme, he personally made product demonstrations to key record executives and leading singers and songwriters. By offering a legitimate online marketplace, Apple promised the music industry a solution to the rampant piracy occurring through services such as Napster. Tellingly, Jobs allowed record labels to retain most of the online revenue, close to 80 percent, from music sales. Rather than using iTunes to generate lucrative profits for Apple, the company positioned it internally as a complementary infrastructure in which it had to invest to further popularize the iPod.

So, how can we understand the managerial behavior of Steve Jobs or Jonney Shih beyond egotistical meddling? Under what circumstances can we view a CEO's intervention as a purposeful act to overcome organizational inertia and promote long-term adaptation? Or, simply put, what is the functional role of a CEO's micromanagement?

❖ ❖ ❖

In 1975, Boston Consulting Group (BCG) presented the British government with a monumental study, "Strategy Alternatives for the British Motorcycle Industry."[9] The 150-page document detailed how Honda had invaded the North American motorcycle industry by using a unique manufacturing strategy that focused on reducing costs, increasing sales, and lowering prices. During the period in question, Honda continued to lower its prices and cut costs until it achieved a dominant position in the motorcycle market that was largely based on volume.

Along with its low-cost, high-volume strategy, Honda incorporated unique design features, launched beguiling marketing campaigns, and established a robust network of retailers and distributors to cater to the needs of recreational motorcycle enthusiasts—the primary target group. In short, Honda's history is a tale of the relentless pursuit of a carefully crafted and flawlessly executed deliberate strategy. There was only one problem with the story BCG reported: it wasn't all true.

In 1959, Honda dispatched thirty-nine-year-old manager Kihachiro Kawashima to scope out the motorbike market in the United States.[10] Following the end of World War II, Honda had successfully established itself as the leading motorbike manufacturer in the Japanese domestic market. At the time, the country was still rebuilding and recovering from poverty, and delivery drivers widely used Honda's small but robust motorbikes in rapidly growing urban zones.

The American motorcycle industry was then selling 50,000 to 60,000 units annually. Entrenched players, such as Harley Davidson, BMW, Triumph, and Moto Guzzi, dominated the sector.[11] Upon his arrival in Los Angeles with two other associates, Kawashima was tasked with exporting three classes of motorcycle, the Super Cub (50 cc), the Benly (125 cc), and the Dream (250 cc and 305 cc). "We had no strategy other than the idea of seeing if we could sell something in the United States," Kawashima would later say.[12]

The venture was frustrating from the start. Customers found that Honda's motorcycles had no discernible benefits, and retailers were reluctant to partner with unknown brands. When Kawashima finally managed to sell hundreds of the larger models through a dozen distributors,[13] the results were nearly disastrous. Engineers in Tokyo had failed to anticipate the wear and tear American riders would impose. Engine failures, worn-out clutches, and oil leaks were common on interstate highways, and the exorbitant expense of air-freighting the warrantied motorcycles between Tokyo and Los Angeles for repair nearly bankrupted Honda.

Around this time, Montgomery Ward and Sears offered to sell Honda's smallest model, the 50-cc Super Cub, in the department store's outdoor power equipment section. Curiously, Honda turned down the opportunity outright. The American team was too fixated on selling the larger motorbikes as had been agreed with the headquarters, even though that strategy was floundering.

One day, the exasperated Kawashima took his Super Cub into the hills to release some tension. He felt much better while dirt-biking, and his two associates began to do the same. People who saw the trio biking in the hills soon started to ask where the executives had acquired their little motorbikes. Out of courtesy, Kawashima imported a number of Super Cubs from Japan especially for their American neighbors. The hobbyists' enthusiasm only grew. Not only would the early adopters of these bikes continue with their activities, but word spread. More people sought out their own little Super Cubs to join the dirt-biking trend and to ride around town. It took a while until Honda's US managers finally realized that they might have stumbled on a whole new market in North

America by chance, that there existed a market for motorbikes built for off-road recreational riding, in which the 50-cc Super Cub fit perfectly.

With growing evidence, the Los Angeles team managed to persuade the Japanese headquarters to alter its original direction. That it would be better off for Honda to stop pursuing the existing market of large bikes, but to refocus on a new market opportunity the company had accidentally created.[14] Of course, these serendipitous events were followed by some truly world-class design engineering and manufacturing execution, which in turn enabled Honda to continually lower prices while improving product quality. As the Super Cubs cost 75 percent less than large Harley Davidson motorcycles, Honda's buyers were casual bikers who showed little interest in larger or more powerful motorcycles.

In retrospect, Honda's original estimation about the US market had been way off the mark. Its initial aspirations upon entry in 1959 had been to capture 10 percent of the market, estimated at 550,000 units per year, with an annual growth of 5 percent. By 1975, the market had grown by 16 percent per year to 5 million annual units—coming largely from an application Honda could not have foreseen, the little Super Cubs in America.

"Their successes, as any Japanese automotive executive will readily agree, did not result from a bold insight by a few big brains at the top. On the contrary, success was achieved by senior managers humble enough not to take their initial strategic positions too seriously," wrote Richard Pascale, now a fellow at Oxford's Saïd Business School. "The Japanese don't use the term 'strategy' to describe a crisp business definition or competitive master plan. They think more in terms of 'strategic accommodation,' or 'adaptive persistence,' underscoring their belief that corporate direction evolves from an incremental adjustment to unfolding events."[15]

OF STRATEGIES, DELIBERATE AND EMERGENT

The Honda example highlights the intertwining of strategy formulation and execution.[16] Under most circumstances, when managers make decisions, they follow a deliberate strategy, building on existing knowledge and prior experience and the guidance of the company's strategic intent. Results are measured by well-defined metrics. Managers are held accountable for their actions. Even among the most innovative companies, energy and efforts are channeled through a system of compensation and rewards. Toyota might measure its success in terms of a constant reduction in product defects, Google by the increasing accuracy of its search results, and Facebook by the growing size of its user base. All these indicators eventually translate into revenue and profit, providing the company with new resources to invest in the next wave of products and services. In such a controlled environment in which the most effective way of working is known, goals should be clearly stated, execution precise.

Still, operating with a deliberate strategy is not without challenges, nor does it deprive managers of the opportunity to exercise creativity. A close examination of Toyota's production system, for instance, reveals that the tools Japanese manufacturers use to achieve world-class production quality are nothing short of innovative. Assembly workers form quality circles to identify the root causes of production problems. They develop small-scale experiments at the local level, without detailed instructions from senior management. When workers identify an effective solution, they rapidly disseminate that knowledge throughout the enterprise. In sum, under the umbrella of just-in-time manufacturing and total quality control, rank-and-file employees are empowered to bring forth their best ideas, which they then validate and scale up to increase impact.

Ed Catmull, the president of Pixar Animation Studios, creator of such blockbusters as *Toy Story*, *Wall-E*, and *Ratatouille*, credited the Japanese quality system with helping "frame [his] approach to managing Pixar going forward."[17] Catmull saw that unshackling the energy of smart creatives everywhere was important, as was empowering them to solve problems across the company. His chosen method was the quality circles the Japanese had pioneered. The pursuit of a deliberate strategy in which knowledge is knowable and continuous experimentation is encouraged is as critical to the success of a car-making giant as it is to the dream factory at Pixar.

However, the story of Honda reminds us also of an alternative set of circumstances in which knowledge was not only incomplete but also unknown. In the words of former US secretary of defense Donald Rumsfeld, these are circumstances in which "we don't know what we don't know." This is when strategy must become emergent.

The Honda executives could not have foreseen an audience in the United States for their little Super Cub, a delivery motorbike designed to navigate the narrow alleys of crowded cities like Tokyo. *Big Americans only drove big motorcycles on broad highways.* Honda's saving grace was that it successfully spotted rather than predicted an emerging trend and then capitalized on it, leading to the explosive growth of a new segment among off-road dirt-biking aficionados. Its success rested entirely upon managers' ability to recognize an unexpected business opportunity instead of relentlessly pursuing a deliberate strategy. Such pivoting is the very definition of an emergent strategy.

The importance of an emergent strategy has been demonstrated in a well-documented study conducted by Professor Amar Bhide, who traced four hundred Harvard Business School graduates who started their own companies.[18] Most of the startups failed, as expected, but Bhide showed that an overwhelming 93 percent of those that succeeded had to abandon their original strategies because they had proved unviable. These entrepreneurs had to use funds raised from the outset but to implement something else. In other words, successful startups almost always have to do something different from what they had promised their investors. Companies that persist in their original strategies do so at their own peril. The problem of false persistence can become particularly pronounced if venture capitalists require a startup to grow too quickly and give it no time to readjust. "Any capital that demands that the early company become very big, very fast, will almost always drive the business off a cliff," Bhide wrote.[19] Those that failed had spent all their money on their original, ill-fated plans. The difference between the successes and the failures was therefore not that the successful startups got it right the first time but that they learned from their mistakes early enough to shift gears. They had just enough money left over to restart after getting it wrong.

That's exactly why famed entrepreneur Eric Ries advocates the "lean startup methodology."[20] He coined the term to describe organizations that maximize the opportunity to learn, gather market insights, and minimize resources spent to achieve market commercialization of a new technology. The biggest danger for innovators is to become fixated on building a perfect machine in the dark when the market has already moved on, leaving entrepreneurs stuck with a product that no one wants. Often better is to build a viable product with the smallest set of features—in industry parlance, a minimal viable product (MVP). An MVP allows managers to complete, as quickly as possible, the build-measure-learn cycle. Speed matters, particularly in the high-tech world. And for established companies seeking to outcompete a startup, they must first behave like a startup. Overwhelming evidence indicates that incumbents who successfully commercialize disruptive innovation must resort to structural separation to manage the strategy process. That is, managers must be given structural autonomy embodied in the form of an independent business unit, when developing a disruptive business model. The mainstream organization of an incumbent can be at times hideously orthodox, exhibiting so much inertia that the best possible approach is to minimize interaction between the old and new business, lest the former smother the latter. An autonomous team doesn't guarantee success, of course, but it is a necessary condition.

YET, THE PROBLEM OF TOTAL DECENTRALIZATION

In academic business research, numerous in-depth field studies have revealed that most strategic initiatives are driven from the bottom up in a company's internal resource allocation process.[21] To resolve discrepancies between current achievements and goals (e.g., production capacity shortages or potential market opportunities), operating managers define the detailed specifics of project proposals.

Regarding the many proposals being championed, general managers at the middle level (division or group executives) provide further impetus to those they perceive to be the most promising. In the process, they commit their credibility and influence. Because they are the last executives with close knowledge of the businesses and its managers, their decisions regarding which initiatives to select or ignore determine what gets funded.

As a consequence, sponsorship and the pattern of execution rather than strategy studies or top management pronouncements dictate what actually happens. Before an initiative receives formal approval at the corporate level, the multilevel process of selection occurs. The definition and selection processes deep in the operating and integrating levels of the company fundamentally determine the strategy realized. The effect of this bottom-up process can be so powerful that lower-level managers should be rightly celebrated as champions of change, while top management can only recognize ex post the fortuitous events that have set the company on a successful course.[22]

As was the case at Honda, the role of top management in strategic change is mostly to be "willing enough to recognize strategically bottom-up initiatives and capitalize on them rather than pass them by."[23] The lever of influence available to top management remains indirect, for instance, manipulating the organizational perception of external threats[24] or establishing structural autonomy in the face of disruption.[25]

Indeed, one of the most admirable traits of Google's structure has been its decentralization. Product groups, from online search to mobile Android, received the unbridled freedom to work independently, and most of Google's products evolved autonomously.[26] The company's legendary perk of 20 percent time (one day a week) enabled employees to work on programs outside their core job, resulting in numerous great products, including Gmail and Google Maps.[27] Founders Eric Schmidt and Larry Page also pushed employees to go in for "moon shots," to create products and services that were ten times better than competitors. "It's natural for people to want to work on things that they know aren't going to fail," said Page. "But incremental improvement is guaranteed to be obsolete over time. Especially in technology, where you know there's going to be non-incremental change."[28] All told, nearly 70 percent of the projects supported Google's core business in some way, 20 percent represented emerging business ideas, and 10 percent were speculative experiments.[29]

The reason Google's myriad experiments never lead to utter chaos is that the firm has a clearly defined strategy: give away products for free, rapidly expand the customer base, drive consumer usage, mine user data, and then sell advertisements. The guide rail serves to distribute strategic responsibilities at all levels of the organization. Corporate strategy becomes *deliberately emergent*; so much so that advertising revenue has been Google's mainstay since the company's foundation. At $60 billion a year, Google is de facto the world's largest advertising company by revenue, dwarfing News Corp ($6.9 billion), Hearst ($4 billion), and Time ($2.9 billion).[30] Only $8 billion of Google's 2015 revenue came from non-advertising activities. Not surprisingly, every time Google has veered from this successful formula, it has gotten itself into trouble.[31]

Back in 2012, Google bought Motorola for $12.5 billion in an attempt to enter the hardware business, but the company ended up fire-selling Motorola to Lenovo at $2.9 billion.[32] Nest, a startup Google bought for $3.2 billion, has basically stuck to its initial product—the learning thermostat. Likewise, the Nexus tablet never took off.[33] Google fiber division similarly shuttered after failing to popularize an ultra-fast Internet service.[34] Even the much-hyped Google Glass, which heralded the arrival of augmented reality, turned out to be a flop.[35] Most tellingly, Google's pioneering autonomous car project has failed to gain traction, only for Uber and Tesla to surpass it.[36] It's as if an invisible hand at Googleplex derails all initiatives that don't fit its advertisement model: "If you can't immediately sell ads on this thing, we'll kill it right away." This is how decentralized innovation can constrain a company, even Google. Whether we call it skunkworks, lean startup, or some other techniques for corporate venturing, if the best that top management can do is to put a few bright people in a dark room, pour in some money, get out of the way, and hope that something wonderful happens, the role of senior leadership is marginal at best. Thankfully, there is another way of managing innovation.

USEFUL INTERVENTION OR WASTEFUL INTERFERENCE?

Some 800 miles north of sunny Silicon Valley is temperate Seattle, where winters are chilly, wet, and mostly cloudy, and where Amazon is headquartered. Like Google, Amazon has a long list of failed projects, including Amazon Destinations (hotel booking), Endless.com (high-end fashion), and WebPay (peer-to-peer payment).[37] "I've made billions of dollars of failures at Amazon.com. Literally," CEO Jeff Bezos recounted.[38] "None of those things are fun, but also they don't matter. What matters is companies that don't continue to experiment or embrace failure eventually get in the position where the only thing they can do is make a Hail Mary bet at the end of their corporate existence. I don't believe in bet-the-company bets." Unlike at Google, Bezos was known to personally set the trajectory for Amazon's myriad experiments. Bezos, insiders like to say, was the ultimate product manager. "I would see him brainstorming wild ideas with the industrial design team, or discussing font sizes and interaction flows with the UI team," recalls a former top-flight designer.[39] Another said, "Jeff had a vision of full integration into every part of the shopping experience."[40]

Since listing its stock publicly in 1997, Amazon has acquired nearly eighty other companies,[41] and, in so doing, it has developed numerous new businesses over the years. The company started by selling books and CDs. Then it offered fashion apparel, video streaming, music streaming, enterprise cloud computing (AWS), e-books, audiobooks, and smart Wi-Fi speakers. Its more recent foray includes retailing high-end produce and fresh groceries, having acquired Whole Foods, and delivering premeasured and ready-to-cook dishes.

Given the varied nature of Amazon's businesses, they often evolve with different resources, unique processes, and profit formulas to deliver a compelling value proposition to end-users. Some sell hardware, others sell services; some are business-to-consumer (B2C) entities, others business-to-business (B2B). None conforms to a single credo. Behind the fantastic growth of the everything store, Bezos acts as the arbiter in chief, the mobilizing hand that has broken all the rules to keep corporate resources fluid.

When Amazon's foray into smartphones came crashing down, Bezos publicly took personal responsibility. The Fire phone, which employed a series of cameras to simulate a 3-D screen, could change its image as the user moved it. This might have been one neat party trick, but could hardly be called a killer app. With all other features designed around Amazon's own services, the phone's biggest selling point was to help consumers shop on Amazon. Adding to consumer skepticism was the small number of third-party apps. One year in, Jeff Bezos had to pull the plug and took a $170 million hit. Some $83 million worth of unsold phones ended up collecting dust. Yet at Lab126, the company's Silicon Valley–based research and development (R&D) group, where the Kindle e-reader was developed, Bezos told employees not to feel bad about the Fire phone fiasco because the company had learned valuable lessons.

That learning was fervently applied to the launch of Amazon Echo, a smart Wi-Fi speaker, a sort of Siri in a tube that listened to and obeyed people's commands, weaving together a search engine and artificial intelligence in the form of a female voice assistant. From the outset, Bezos aggressively pushed his Echo team of one thousand to speed up the certification of third-party apps, called skills. Third-party programmers can easily reuse common skills (e.g., navigate to the next item in a list, pause an action in progress, go back to a previous item, or resume an action) and integrate these basic functions for more advanced features. Opening one's system to third-party developers may sound logically straightforward, but as seen in DARPA in Chapter 4, building a set of easy-to-use tools and motivating people to use them is not a straightforward implementation.

"Google on paper is much better positioned to do something like this than Amazon," said Jan Dawson, the founder of Jackdaw Research.[42] Thanks to its ubiquitous search and an all-powerful algorithm, Google's virtual assistant beats Amazon Echo hands down on answering unstructured and random questions, for example, "What's the average height of a monkey?" Rather than issuing voice commands, Google's users can have a more intuitive and conversational interaction with the voice assistant. Still, Echo has mastered a staggering fifteen thousand skills, including Uber (hail a ride), Fitbit (review health statistics), Mixologist (look up a cocktail recipe), and Domino's (order a pizza), plus applications from other device makers, such as Philips, Samsung, and General Electric.[43] Meanwhile, Google has some 370 voice apps available as of June 30, 2017, and Microsoft, a paltry 65.

With so many third-party apps, neither Google nor Microsoft nor Apple seems likely to break Bezos's stranglehold on the voice-activated home speaker market. At the time of this writing, Amazon's market share in this sector has doubled over the next three competitors combined.[44] "To do this well, we really need to work with developers and third parties so we can provide these actions to our users," conceded Sundar Pichai, Google's chief executive.[45]

Most profoundly, perhaps, Amazon has changed the way back-end operations should be understood. Back in 2012, Amazon started to open its internal computer servers—the backbone of any Internet company—to external clients. Netflix, or Dropbox, or in fact, anyone can pay to use its infrastructure instead of building their own expensive servers. That was the basic idea behind Amazon Web Services. It's a cloud-based solution for the enterprise market, a new way that Bezos found to monetize back-end infrastructure, which is normally seen as a cost center, not a revenue stream. So resolute was Bezos about winning this business that he insisted all services on the platform be built on open APIs, which allowed Amazon's computer servers to communicate easily with external parties over the standard web protocol. On this point, Bezos wrote his instruction in an e-mail that ended with his characteristic signature: "Anyone who doesn't do this will be fired. Thank you; have a nice day!"

Such an authoritarian tactic would seem unthinkable at Google, but it's precisely the kind of intervention that breaks silos in large companies.

WHAT A CEO CANNOT DELEGATE

Famed University of Chicago economist Richard Thaler ran a thought experiment with a large company, asking executives to evaluate an investment scenario:[46] Suppose there existed an investment opportunity in a corporate division that would yield one of two payoffs. After the investment was made, there was a 50 percent chance that it would make a profit of $2 million (an expected gain of $1 million) and a 50 percent chance that it would lose $1 million (an expected loss of half a million). How many of the managers would go for it? Thaler threw in an additional safeguard: the company was large enough to absorb a million-dollar loss. Even when several projects didn't pan out, none would threaten the company's solvency.

Of the twenty-three executives Thaler asked, only three said they would make the investment. The reason for the almost unanimous rejection? If the project was a success, the managers believed they would get a small bonus, but if the project failed, they would probably get fired. They all liked their job, and none of them wanted to risk it. But from the point of view of the CEO, each project was worth an expected profit of half a million, so the logical answer was a no-brainer, that the company should invest in all those opportunities to maximize potential gain. Hence, even with projects that don't require "bet-the-company" resources, the CEO must sometimes absorb career risks that individual midlevel general managers would shun. This is exactly what Jeff Bezos, Jonney Shih, and Steve Jobs have done.

In an increasingly turbulent business environment where companies need to act fast, a purely decentralized innovation model won't suffice. Corporate leaders must lend their positional power to the rank and file who are equipped with market knowledge. This doesn't make the case for mindless micromanagement or corporate interference, but there are times when strategic intervention from the very top can prove critical. Jack Welch, former chairman and CEO of General Electric, understands this intuitively: "One of my favorite perks was picking out an issue and doing what I called a 'deep dive.' It's spotting a challenge where you think you can make a difference . . . then throwing the weight of your position behind it. I've often done this—just about everywhere in the company."

Once you become aware of the "deep dive," it becomes visible everywhere.[47]

THE CEO DEEP DIVE

Situated between Maiden Lane and Water Street near downtown Wall Street is the Community Solutions headquarters—the spin-off of Common Ground we saw from the last chapter. Today, Community Solutions is an entirely independent entity. In fact, in 2011, Rosanne Haggerty left her position as the president of Common Ground after promoting Brenda Rosen, the former director of housing operations and programs, to the position.

Rosanne decided she needed to dedicate her full-time efforts to the development of Community Solutions, which focuses entirely on knowledge dissemination without owning and running its own housing unit—a light asset model, many would say. "To let go of Common Ground was not as difficult a choice in the end as for many years, I thought it might be," Rosanne told me. "We were doing wonderful work [at Common Ground], operating and building housing for those we can help directly. But I was becoming, over many years, more and more concerned about those we are not able to reach through that mechanism, so my excitement at finding an approach to this issue through our innovation work [knowledge dissemination] really made that transition pretty straightforward for me."

Still, hearing that from Rosanne was a shock to me. I couldn't help wonder how many CEOs of corporate America would be willing to throw away their past successes to embrace a future with a clean slate, however promising it might seem. It is human nature to treasure familiarity and cherish legacy. What I've learned further was, before Rosanne left Common Ground for good, there had been deep dives all over the organization before Community Solutions was able to stand on its own.

When Becky Kanis's team first speculated on the importance of targeting the "chronically homeless," it was no more than a hypothesis based on close-up observation of a small sample. There was no proof of the strategy's effectiveness, and no one, except perhaps Rosanne herself, was ready to bet on the idea. Unlike any other routine projects, Rosanne did not delegate the implementation of housing the chronically homeless to a staff member, even though the project concerned only eighteen individuals. Compared to the three housing buildings that Common Ground was operating throughout New York City, servicing eighteen individuals could have seemed a meaningless distraction for a CEO.

But instead, Rosanne hastened the process by changing Common Ground's existing housing policies to cater to those few chronically homeless individuals. She called up Common Ground's long-standing social services partner, the Center for Urban Community Services (CUCS), to enlist its support in assessing applicants. CUCS was far more experienced at handling psychiatric patients, expertise that was especially useful for the new target group. Rosanne then mandated that Common Ground's housing operation become accountable for filling up a certain quota of chronically homeless people.

That directive did not sit well with her staff from the housing operation. "Everyone was skeptical. People were saying things like 'There goes the building. They are going to be terrible tenants. They are going to mess things up. They are going to be crazy!'" Rosanne said with a chuckle. Managers resisted Rosanne's idea on the grounds that these potential tenants would likely miss rent payments, or worse, vandalize the housing facilities—a nightmarish scenario as each housing manager was accountable for the annual budget.

To allay fears and minimize resistance, Rosanne agreed to keep track of the impact as new individuals were steadily accepted into the buildings. Additional resources from CUCS were lined up in case more intensive psychiatric interventions were needed. Rosanne even made a personal commitment to honor any requests for new funding if additional financial needs arose.

After eighteen months, there was almost no negative effect. "Once again, it was one of those situations where what we think might happen did not pan out. We thought these [chronically homeless] people would need many mental health services to help them adjust to the new environment. We were just wrong," explained Rosanne. "People who have lived on the street for years are instinctively adaptive. They have learned how to survive anywhere. The only extra work was for the office manager who needed to help people set up a bank account and manage their money. This is where they need some help," she recalled.

As the previous chapters showed, this singular focus on eighteen individuals proved that housing the chronically homeless would have a transformative effect on a neighborhood. It was no longer just eighteen fewer individuals on the street; homelessness in Times Square actually began to disappear. This precise understanding of why "housing first" was important laid the foundation for the wildly successful 100,000 Homes Campaign. Targeting the most visible homeless individuals and offering them the housing they wanted made it possible to persuade others who had been on the street for shorter periods to accept help.

BUT WHAT IF?

Now let's imagine a parallel universe where Rosanne or, earlier, Jonney Shih did not intervene. Rather, the two leaders simply walked away after their initial splashes and left lower-level managers to tackle the implementation realities.

At Common Ground, the manager in charge would undoubtedly have continued to lobby, haggle, and negotiate with those from the housing operation before any of the chronically homeless could be housed—a situation that could easily have derailed the entire initiative.

At Asus, the manager in charge would undoubtedly have gotten dragged into endless debates regarding myriad corporate policies— using a software supplier outside Asia, selling a laptop at an unacceptably low price point, violating corporate assurance by giving the first products away to end-users for testing. It would have been months, if not years, before the Eee PC could be launched, thereby missing a critical time window.

As one product manager recounted, "There were times when people outside the Eee PC team saw the project as a failure. . . . We also required a lot of technical expertise from the laptop unit, and the resource demands created a lot of tension. But Jonney personally quieted those 'noises.'" Again, playing the counterfactual game is fun, and it can be illuminating—and in case you were wondering, the initial Eee PC taskforce had become a new business unit, which expanded and continued to make consumer electronics other than high-end laptops. At that point, Shih felt he no longer needed to supervise its day-to-day operations and named two executives to oversee further business development. He moved on to dive deep elsewhere in the company.

So, there we have it. When the required innovation becomes disruptive, staffing the team appropriately and giving it autonomy are necessary but insufficient. Every time an organization successfully leaps into a new knowledge base, as we saw in Part 1 at Novartis and P&G, the senior leaders need to go beyond formulating a strategy and should get their hands dirty during its implementation. Corporate leaders need to absorb career risks that individual midlevel general managers normally shun. Success requires an exact combination of knowledge power and positional power. That entrepreneurial spirit and the corresponding behaviors exhibited at the apex of the enterprise remain, perhaps, the critical functions of the CEO role, which cannot be delegated. These are the chief functions of a top executive.

EPILOGUE

HAVING ACHIEVED A SUSTAINABLE COMPETITIVE POSITION IS every executive's envy. It was once thought that vertical integration and control over every stage of the production system would give companies an unparalleled advantage. This is why firms engage in research development, manufacturing, sales, and marketing all under one roof. Size matters, economies of scope reign supreme. This strategy allowed General Motors, General Electric, and IBM to become corporate behemoths by the middle of the last century. Then the rise of Japan, led by Sony, Toyota, Honda, Toshiba, and the like, saw quality control, Six Sigma, and lean manufacturing as the real answer. Next came Dell in the late 1990s, which demonstrated the advantage of outsourcing everything auxiliary along the supply chain and focusing on the firm's core competency to deliver exceptional performance. Yet with every promising innovation in management, the goal of achieving a sustainable advantage seems all the more elusive.

This volume began with the epic race of textile manufacturing in which waves of new companies have successively overtaken industry pioneers, effectively displacing them, but only to fall victim to the next wave. In the 1850s, half of Britain's exports were cotton goods, and by the early twentieth century, British mills manufactured almost half of the world's cotton cloth. In less than two decades, however, companies from the United States overtook their British counterparts. Nevertheless, a wave of new competitors surpassed the US companies that had come to dominate the textile industry. This time, they came from Asia: first Japan, then Hong Kong, followed by Taiwan and South Korea, and finally China, India, and Bangladesh. As competition raged, large, populous mill towns that had once made up manufacturing basins across Britain and the United States were reduced to ghost towns. Industrial buildings were either painfully repurposed or completely abandoned.

The textile industry is no outlier, however. From manufacturers of heavy machinery to home appliances and from makers of automobiles to solar panels and wind turbines, incumbents have constantly been dislodged. If we were to use the S&P 500 as a reference, we would see that a company's average life span on that index dropped from sixty-seven years in the 1920s to fifteen years today and that the average tenure of a CEO in corporate America has shrunk over the past thirty years.[1] We live in a world of accelerated change.

That a competitive advantage is so elusive was exactly the complaint of German drug maker Hoechst more than a century ago against its Swiss copycats, CIBA, Geigy, and Sandoz. The land of counterfeiters, or as the French called Switzerland, *le pays de contre-facteurs*, had yet to establish patent law as late as 1888. Local chemists were free, or even encouraged, to imitate foreign inventions. When antipyrine, the first synthetic fever-reducing drug, was created in the Hoechst laboratory, the world couldn't get enough of it—and the Swiss were selling an imitation as fast as they could make it. Organic chemistry was the hotbed of innovation. Only when Alexander Fleming discovered the antibiotic penicillin did everyone understand that the next blockbuster would come not from chemistry alone but from an entirely new discipline, namely microbiology. Immediately after the Second World War, from Europe to the United States, nascent pharmaceutical firms rushed to set up soil screening programs around the world, looking for exotic fungi, hunting down the pay dirt, in the pursuit of ever more potent antibiotics. Field workers retrieved soil from cemeteries and sent balloons up in the air to collect windblown samples. They ventured down to the bottom of mine shafts, hiked up to mountaintops, and went anywhere in between. The study of microbes took center stage, displacing organic chemistry as the key discipline for scientific discovery. Along with new techniques of deep-tank fermentation and medicine purification, the world saw a precipitous drop in infectious disease. What had once been nasty, brutish, and fatal infections were transformed into curable inconveniences.

Then came the biotechnology revolution in the 1970s. Scientists marveled at the inner workings of chromosomes within the cell nucleus, and in the wake of these discoveries, they became capable of recombining DNA molecules, instructing bacteria to produce insulin for diabetics, and synthesizing many other active ingredients that couldn't be abundantly harvested from nature. Now, with the complete scanning of the human genome and the advance of computational applications, genetic engineering has essentially gone digital. Scientists are uncovering molecular pathways, the biological underpinnings of rare cancers. We have again seen the transition to a new knowledge frontier, a discipline under the rubric of genomics and bioengineering. Today, staying at the forefront of the industry takes extravagantly equipped laboratories, huge budgets, and large teams of investigators. Switzerland's Novartis alone spent close to $10 billion on research and development in 2014, and in that same year, the combined market capitalization of the two giants, Novartis and Roche, was still on the upswing, exceeding $400 billion. From cancer therapy to HIV treatment, Western pioneers continue to lead the global industry in the latest developments. In contrast to the automotive industry, in which global competition has decimated Detroit, turning it into the capital of the American rust belt, the wealth in Basel, where Novartis and Roche are headquartered, seems forever bountiful. Its inhabitants continue to enjoy one of the highest standards of living in Western Europe.

Capital expenditures in the pharmaceutical industry, however, cannot explain why newcomers in emerging countries have yet to overtake Western pioneering incumbents. In fact, capital expenditures, trade secrets, and patent protection were hardly a challenge for the

United States when it overtook Great Britain as the leading exporter of textiles at the turn of the twentieth century. The same can be said for heavy machinery, wind turbines, solar panels, personal computers, mobile phones, and automobiles, where latecomers have irrevocably displaced early pioneers. What the history of pharmaceuticals has shown is that a shift of knowledge disciplines—chemistry, microbiology, and then genomics—opened new paths for willing pioneers to race ahead. Sustainable advantage turns out not to be a utopian position that companies can try to attain. Rather, only by constantly infusing new knowledge and changing the rules of the game can a pioneer create headroom for innovation and thus avoid being overtaken by latecomers. This is the miracle drug that century-old pharmaceutical firms have created to keep themselves evergreen.

Understanding the past is helpful only if doing so informs decision making about the future. We must therefore ask, "How do we spot the next frontier? Where will the rules of competition be rewritten next?" Three leverage points shape the answer: the emergence of ubiquitous connectivity, the inexorable rise of intelligent machines, and the changing role of human work. They will impact most firms over the next few decades and become part of everyday business life. They are the intersections where companies need to rewrite the rules of the game in their own favor.

Just as Steinway's piano craftsmanship was felled by Yamaha's mass production, we now face a new change in the way decisions are made. New competitors are moving away from relying on the judgment calls of a few seasoned managers inside the firm to relying on the wisdom of the crowd. Just as mass production transformed artisanal labor in the industrial revolution, so the wisdom of the crowd is transforming decision making in the digital revolution.

WeChat and DARPA demonstrate that embracing open collaboration must go beyond soliciting volunteers and must also adhere to a set of principles: from parceling a complex problem into smaller pieces, to developing enabling toolkits and putting them into the hands of individuals. When done right, it is indeed possible to have amateurs solve the most intractable technical problems.

Another leverage point is the automation of human intuition. The victory of Google's AlphaGo over a human player of the Chinese board game Go has deep implications for the company's quest to stay ahead of competitors. Big tech giants, such as Google, Facebook, IBM, and Microsoft, have all set up corporate labs dedicated to advanced machine learning. Recruit Holdings—the classified advertisement, publication, and human resources conglomerate from Japan—has also ramped up its artificial intelligence laboratory and made the infrastructure so open that its customers—beauty salons, restaurants, and other small-time entrepreneurs—can directly access its world-class data infrastructure. But here lies the rub: at Recruit, numerous sales forces and support staff continue to play a crucial role in bringing customers onto the machine-learning platform. As a substantial part of office work becomes automated, the new system doesn't make all workers redundant but simply releases the human brain for higher purposes. That ties to our third leverage point, the blending of AI and human expertise by augmenting creativity.

In the midst of predictive analytics and machine learning, the importance of small data cannot be overstated. As our society generates and retains ever more data, human empathy and anthropological observation, paradoxically, will become even more critical. Rosanne at Common Ground, Doug at General Electric, Claudia at P&G all demonstrated that businesses cannot rely on big data alone. Businesses must also make sense of the rich and deep and oftentimes small data, and excel in areas where human creativity outshines machines. The understanding of the human condition, on the driving forces of desire and emotion, is as important to a consumer product company as to an industrial service firm. The importance of small data will only grow in a world deluged by a widening stream of online data.

These three leverage points on future competition—ubiquitous connectivity, the inexorable rise of intelligent machines, and a stronger emphasis on human-centric creativity—demand a committed response from corporate leadership. Commitment is not the same as mere awareness. Insights alone are never sufficient, as strategy and execution are inextricably linked. Unless new ideas are translated into everyday actions and operational tactics, a pioneer is still at risk of being displaced. If there has been one commonality in the failures of leading pioneers, including Steinway, GM, Panasonic, and countless textile mills, to stanch the encroachment of low-cost copycats, it has been the collective resistance to accept cannibalization as an inevitable cost for long-term survival. In contrast, forward-looking incumbents—from Procter & Gamble (P&G) to Novartis, from Apple to Amazon—recognize the need to cannibalize their own products ahead of time. Embracing self-cannibalization is unnatural, which is why CEO interventions, or deep dives, where a top executive personally intervenes, wielding the power to overcome specific barriers, is critical. As Novartis CEO Daniel Vasella said on the verge of launching Gleevec, "Money doesn't matter. Let's just do it." As chairman William Cooper Procter, the last family manager of P&G, said of synthetic detergents, "This may ruin the soap business. But if anybody is going to ruin the soap business it had better be Procter & Gamble."

The human suffering in the rust-belt cities is all too real—unemployment, de-urbanization, high rates of addiction, rising crime rates, shortened life expectancies, and suicide. But if textile manufacturing is a story of woe, a victim of global competition, here's an industry that is equally, if not more, ancient, but can offer us hope: the farming equipment industry. In that industry, one company has done more than merely survive. It has thrived for over a century and a half.

CAN ANYONE LEAP?

In 1836, a thirty-two-year-old blacksmith from Vermont decided to move west. This was the farmer's age, during which the American population was spreading westward and bringing along labor-saving equipment and new farming techniques. But as Americans arrived on the midwestern prairies, they struggled with the new soil. Soil in New England resembled a rich mixture of clays and sands, whereas prairie soil stuck together and formed a gluey texture that grew resistant year after year. Cast-iron plows that would till through eastern soils like a warm knife slices through butter were quickly dulled in the sticky earth of what was then America's northwest.

In Grand Detour, Illinois, a young blacksmith had heard enough grumbling among farmers. He took note at a local hydraulic mill and saw a broken steel blade in the corner. He decided to attach it to an iron moldboard with the idea of making a plow that would scour the land, and then let dirt slide off it. Farmers would no longer need to scrape off the sticky soil from the moldboards every few yards.[2] This self-scouring steel plow was a big hit. "I will not put my name on a product that does not have in it the best that is in me," the resourceful inventor would later say.[3] Known as "an intense and thorough" man, the blacksmith was gruff and undiplomatic just like the rough, ever-expanding, rapidly developing American frontier.[4] His name was John Deere.

Under the watch of his second son, Charles Deere, the family firm mastered selling horse-drawn plows, harrows, wagons, and buggies through "branch houses," a primordial network of independent dealers. Charles would sign up enterprising proprietors to sell not only John Deere's plows but also complementary equipment from other manufacturers, including competitors. The genius of the strategy was, of course, that farmers could buy everything from one salesman, John Deere got a cut from competitors' profits as commission, and no more sole reliance on internal funding to expand the company's sales territory.

The first disruption that confronted John Deere was none other than the gasoline engine. Although John Deere was already the leading manufacturer of plows and implements by the turn of the century, it was all too clear that with the emergence of the automobile, horses would have to give way in the fields as in the cities. The responsibility for figuring out how the company would compete with Ford and General Motors and other automakers fell squarely on the shoulders of the third CEO, William Butterworth, Charles Deere's son-in-law.

For a long while Butterworth had contemplated specializing in plows and supplying automotive companies with high-performance implements. That would have been a conservative strategy, to stick to one's knitting. But it carried an existential risk: animal power was over. If John Deere were to remain relevant in the agricultural business, it would have to get into the tractor business. Just as pharmaceutical companies snapped up biotech startups in the wake of the bioengineering revolution, John Deere boldly acquired a tractor plant named the Waterloo Gasoline Traction Engine Company. The plow maker thus turned into a tractor manufacturer almost overnight. Within the first year of the acquisition, 5,634 Waterloo Boy machines were sold. From metallurgy rooted in plow making, John Deere leapt into mechanical engineering.

Having survived the Great Depression during the 1930s, Charles Deere Wiman, John Deere's great-grandson and the fourth leader of the company, contacted a New York design firm, Henry Dreyfuss and Associates, to "streamline" its tractor design, making it more aesthetically pleasing.[5] A pioneer of industrial design in America, the Dreyfuss group enclosed the steering shaft, added an electric starter and lights, incorporated a grille and a radiator cowl, covered the engine with a metal hood, and narrowed the width for better visibility. All these changes were meant to accentuate the tractor's massiveness and to create the impression that "the vehicle was in the process of pulling, reinforcing the added power."[6]

By the time CEO Bill Hewitt took over, style was no longer reserved for urban luxuries. With a keen flair for product launching, Hewitt put up a public spectacle at Neiman Marcus, a posh department store headquartered in Dallas. He placed a brand-new tractor inside a large gift box in front of the jewelry department. As the velvet ribbon was cut, an excited crowd gathered, and the wrapping was pulled away. A gleaming green and yellow tractor twinkled, and the name "John Deere" greeted the floor. Diamonds decorated the hood and the exhaust pipe.[7] A Texas-style barbecue accompanied the great fanfare in the evening, complete with fireworks. The four-cylinder tractor was as unprecedentedly powerful as it was fashionable.

By the 1960s, John Deere had effectively blended its founding knowledge in metallurgy with mechanical engineering acquired through Waterloo Gasoline and with top-of-the-line industrial design and marketing. As with P&G in Part I, it was the combination of different disciplines of knowledge that explains corporate long-term success. By 1963, John Deere had surpassed International Harvester to become the world's largest producer and seller of farm and industrial tractors and equipment, a position it has never since relinquished. With $26.6 billion in annual sales and more than fifty-six thousand employees, John Deere continues to prevail in the farm machinery industry, with the headquarters located in the company's original hometown in Illinois.

But that's not all. For more than fifteen years, long before Google and Tesla were working on driverless cars, John Deere has pioneered autonomous tractors across America.[8] Like all the examples in Part II, John Deere has leveraged ubiquitous connectivity and artificial intelligence to fend off industry latecomers, including Mumbai-based Mahindra & Mahindra, a $13 billion automobile manufacturing corporation that produces low-cost tractors for rural India. John Deere did not, and could not, stoop to compete on price. So, John Deere made its 7760 cotton stripper a technical marvel by marrying GPS, sensing, and automation. Climbing into the driver's cabin feels a little like stepping into a spaceship: The computer displays surrounding the driver tell what is going on, and as the harvester plows through a field, collecting cotton for instance, belts are activated intermittently, churning the cotton into round bales and then wrapping the bales in protective plastic. The driver simply makes a U-turn at the end of every row and continues harvesting with no interruption.[9] Commodity-crop farming has long since become a highly precise and automated affair in the United States, even on family-owned farms.[10]

Still, automated tractors and harvesters can deliver only so much growth. What farmers ultimately want is to optimize the overall farm productivity, which means connecting farm machineries with the irrigation systems, and soil and nutrient sources with information on weather, crop prices, and commodity futures.[11] That is why the company launched MyJohnDeere, which connects its equipment with other machines, owners, operators, dealers, and agricultural consultants. The software analyzes individual data collected through sensors combined with historical data on everything from weather and soil conditions to crop features. The idea of a platform strategy, as illustrated in Chapters 4 and 5, cannot be overstated. Across industries, profits have gone to platform providers instead of traditional manufacturers. By one estimate, Apple captured 91 percent of global smartphone profits in 2016. Apple's only real competition is of course Google, whose success has been largely brought on by being another thriving platform builder. Samsung makes excellent and sophisticated smartphones but captures little profitability from the market in which it participates.[12] The service industry can exhibit the same deleterious dynamics. In an article that analyses the future of the banking industry, *The Economist* argued the real risk for big banks lies not so much in being displaced by Fintech startups, but simply because their margins are shrinking and their positions are becoming less secure, with a future "as a sort of financial utility—ubiquitous but heavily regulated, unglamorous and marginally profitable."[13] John Deere, rightly, as we also saw with Recruit Holdings, joined ranks to become a platform player in its respective sector.

But realizing that John Deere, like most other companies, comprises talented and devoted but nonetheless ordinary people, the senior leadership has been ambitiously realistic in its efforts. "We do have a few geniuses, but most of us are not," said former CEO Bob Lane, who retired in 2010. And so, in the spirit of open innovation that we saw in Chapter 4, MyJohnDeere opened its doors to third parties in 2013, allowing input suppliers, agriculture retailers, local agronomists, and software companies to develop their own applications. "Adding the post-harvest review of nitrogen plans [for example] will help growers better understand what happened in their field through the season and why," observed Eric Boeck, marketing director of DuPont Pioneer, the agronomic division of chemical giant DuPont, which now pools data with John Deere so that growers can "make more informed decisions about critical crop inputs and equipment optimization." "When growers opt to share their data . . . they open a whole new set of advanced management insight," explained Kevin Very, business solutions manager at John Deere, who saw the benefits of the open partnership. "This means more efficient deployment of equipment and labor."[14]

Perhaps John Deere's strongest commitment in the pursuit of a new knowledge discipline surrounding computer vision and machine learning was the opening of the John Deere Labs in San Francisco. With smartphone-controlled tractors that steer themselves via GPS and intelligent sensors that know precisely how much fertilizer to spray, the inevitable trend is precision farming—combining connected devices with machine learning to make faster and more precise decisions, possibly one day's worth of work, without a farmer's input. Why San Francisco? "We found ourselves renting hotel rooms quite a bit," said the head of the John Deere Labs, Alex Purdy, explaining that his company had long spent a lot of time in the Bay Area, meeting with various partners in the tech sector.[15]

As many former giants of America's industrial heartland fall prey to global competition, John Deere stood out as a shining example. Like Novartis and P&G, John Deere has evolved over more than a century and a half and still stands as the world leader in products related to the land. It turns out that regardless of the industry, it is possible to radically rewrite the rules of the game so as to demand a whole new field of knowledge in support of the change. Any pioneer can indeed avoid being overtaken by copycats—and if a plow maker from Illinois can drive its corporate development the way a pharmaceutical company did in Switzerland, by leaping from one knowledge discipline to another, so can anyone else. We can all thrive, even in a world where everything can be copied.

This book started off as a historical account, a memoir of Western pioneers. Some failed, some survived, others prospered. But it's also a playbook for the future. More importantly, it's a manifesto for how pioneering companies can rethink their businesses, their relationship with customers, and the reasons they exist. Your organization—like all others, large or small—has a set of traditional strengths, important products that helped build the organization into what it is today. Your customers, your local community, your stakeholders all depend on you and count on you to innovate. There is no perfect moment. We have exactly enough time, starting now. Let's leap.

ACKNOWLEDGMENTS

To write a book takes not only the writer's time but also a village of others who have the will to tolerate the writer's particular work habits and the strength to see the project through. Every first-time author is presumed to understand this, and all business school professors, whether they teach in executive education programs or not, know that help from colleagues is always needed.

First and foremost, I need to thank the IMD president, Jean-François Manzoni, who kept reminding me to cut back on my teaching duties while working on this book so that I could carry out all the research and writing that form its foundation. I have been fortunate at IMD to have developed a small group of amazing friends with whom to debate ideas until those ideas got wrestled into the pages of this manuscript. Tom Malnight and Bala Chakravarthy have been my mentors since the first day I joined the school, and they were among the first to shape my thinking back when the book existed merely as a proposal. I have borrowed ideas from and been inspired by many colleagues, including Bill Fischer, Misiek Piskorski, Carlos Cordon, Albrecht Enders, Bettina Buechel, Shlomo Ben-Hur, Goutam Challagalla, Dominique Turpin, Anand Narasimhan, Stefan Michel, Cyril Bouquet, and Naoshi Takatsu. Outside the walls of IMD, I have benefited tremendously from W. Chan Kim, Xavier Castaner, Hila Lifshitz, and Jan Ondrus, who challenged the way I think about innovation. Most importantly, the intellectual backbone of this, my first book, lies directly in my doctoral training, during which Joseph Bower, Clayton Christensen,

Willy Shih, Tom Eisenmann, and Jan Rivkin left an undeniable imprint on the way I understand corporate strategy.

It's often said that business books must go beyond armchair theorizing. I've been able to get up from that armchair and walk into the corporate world because of the generosity of the executives who provided me access to their own organizations or indulged my academic pontification during meals and over drinks. I thank Jørgen Vig Knudstorp, Rosanne Haggerty, Becky Kanis, Paul Howard, Jake Maguire, Jonney Shih, Debby Lee, Eagle Yi, Xi Yang, and Eduardo Andrade for their insights and patience.

A huge thank you must also go to the team at PublicAffairs, in particular to my wise editor, Colleen Lawrie, who made *Leap* stronger, and to my eagle-eyed copyeditor, Iris Bass, who made it tighter than I could have managed alone. Thanks to my publicist, Josie Urwin, marketing director Lindsay Fradkoff, and senior project editor Sandra Beris. In addition, my book agent, Esmond Harmsworth of Aevitas Creative, had more trust in this project—more than I did myself—and shepherded it to light. He helped me focus on what truly mattered at a time when I could easily have been distracted by other projects. And to James Pogue—the resourceful, diligent fact-checker—as well as Beverley Lennox, who proofed the final copy and came to my rescue under tight deadlines and addressed every possible last-minute request. Finally, thanks to Mark Fortier and Lucy Jay-Kennedy for making the final product known to a wider world.

Writing a book is, by definition, a solitary undertaking, but I have never felt alone. My brother, Kenny, who knows me well, has given me much-needed brotherly teasing to ground me in reality whenever my ego soars too high. My mother, Fiona, has shown her unceasing belief that I can achieve beyond what I can see. She and my late father, Jimmy, were the only reason a junior-level banker in Hong Kong with no savings after college would have applied to Harvard Business School in pursuit of a doctoral degree. The most that parents can do is trust their children and encourage them to embark on something they themselves can barely begin to understand. And finally, I thank Brendan, who has sustained me over the past eight years, who turns my gaze to everything that would have eluded me, who teaches me how to be more humane, and continues to grow with me every day.

NOTES

INTRODUCTION

1. Daniel Augustus Tompkins, *Cotton Mill, Commercial Features: A Text-Book for the Use of Textile Schools and Investors* (n.p.: Forgotten Books, 2015), 189.

2. Allen Tullos, *Habits of Industry: White Culture and the Transformation of the Carolina Piedmont* (Chapel Hill: University of North Carolina Press, 1989), 143.

3. "A Standard Time Achieved, Railroads in the 1880s," American-Rails.com, accessed September 8, 2017, http://www.american-rails.com/1880s.html.

4. Piedmont Air-Line System (1882), "Piedmont Air-Line System (advertisement)," J. H. Chataigne, retrieved September 8, 2017.

5. Pietra Rivoli, *The Travels of a T-Shirt in the Global Economy: An Economist Examines the Markets, Power, and Politics of World Trade*, 2nd ed. (Hoboken, NJ: Wiley, 2015), 100.

6. Alexandra Harney, *The China Price: The True Cost of Chinese Competitive Advantage* (New York: Penguin Press, 2009), chap. 1.

7. "Piedmont Manufacturing Company (Designation Withdrawn) | National Historic Landmarks Program," National Parks Service, accessed September 9, 2017, https://www.nps.gov/nhl/find/withdrawn/piedmont.htm.

8. "Oral History," The Greenville Textile Heritage Society, accessed March 11, 2018, http://greenvil le-textile-heritage-society.org/oral-history/.

9. Clayton M. Christensen, "The Rigid Disk Drive Industry: A History of Commercial and Technological Turbulence," *Business History Review* 67, no. 4 (1993): 533–534, doi:10.2307/3116804.

10. "Novartis AG," AnnualReports.com, accessed February 3, 2018, http://www.annualreports.com/Company/novartis-ag.

CHAPTER 1

1. "FDNY vintage fire truck, 1875 - Photos - FDNY Turns 150: Fire Trucks Through the Years," *New York Daily News*, April 25, 2015, accessed February 3, 2018, https://web.archive.org/web/20170608165852/http://www.nydailynews.com/news/fdny-turns-150-fire-trucks-years-gallery-1.2198984?pmSlide=1.2198967.

2. "Steinway & Sons | The Steinway Advantage," accessed February 3, 2018, https://web.archive.org/web/20170611062352/http://www.steinwayshowrooms.com/about-us/the-steinway-advantage; Danne Polk, "Steinway Factory Tour," accessed February 3, 2018, https://web.archive.org/web/20150225093233/http://www.ilovesteinway.com/steinway/articles/steinway_factory_tour.cfm. See also: "Steinway & Sons," www.queensscene.com, accessed March 12, 2018, http://www.queensscene.com/news/2014-08-01/Lifestyle/SteinwaySons.html.

3. Ricky W. Griffin, *Management* (Australia: South-Western Cengage Learning, 2013), 30-31. "Steinway Factory Tour | Steinway Hall Texas," accessed February 3, 2018, https://web.archive.org/web/20160330202353/http://www.steinwaypianos.com/instruments/steinway/factory.

4. Matthew L. Wald, "Piano-Making at Steinway: Brute Force and a Fine Hand," *New York Times*, March 28, 1991, http://www.nytimes.com/1991/03/28/business/piano-making-at-steinway-brute-force-and-a-fine-hand.html.

5. Michael Lenehan, "The Quality of the Instrument," *Atlantic*, August 1982, 46.

6. Joseph M. Hall and M. Eric Johnson, "When Should a Process Be Art, Not Science?" *Harvard Business Review*, March 2009, 59–65.

7. James Barron, *Piano: The Making of a Steinway Concert Grand* (New York: Times Books, 2006), xviii.

8. "Arthur Rubinstein," Steinway & Sons, accessed January 31, 2017, https://www.steinway.com/artists/arthur-rubinstein. A far more complete history of Steinway & Sons can be found in an authoritative narrative by Richard K. Lieberman, *Steinway & Sons* (New Haven, CT: Yale University Press, 1995), 139.

9. "A Sound Investment | Steinway Hall Texas," accessed February 3, 2018, https://web.archive.org/web/20170614055826/http://www.steinwaypianos.com/kb/resources/investment.

10. Elizabeth Weiss, "Why Pianists Care About the Steinway Sale," *Currency* (blog), September 13, 2013, accessed January 31, 2017, http://www.newyorker.com/online/blogs/currency/2013/09/why-pianists-care-about-the-steinway-sale.html.

11. Plowboy, "As Predicted—Steinway's Other Shoe Falls" [re: Steve Cohen], August 14, 2013, http://www.pianoworld.com/forum/ubbthreads.php/topics/2133374.html.

12. "Steinway & Sons | About Steinway Hall," accessed February 3, 2018, https://web.archive.org/web/20170706195110/http://www.steinway

showrooms.com:80/steinway-hall/about; "Steinway Hall: A Place for the Piano in Music, Craft, Commerce and Technology," LaGuardia and Wagner Archives, January 1, 1970, accessed February 3, 2018, http://laguardiawagnerarchives .blogspot.ch/2016/04/steinway-hall-place-for-piano-in-music.html; Richard K. Lieberman, Steinway & Sons (Toronto: CNIB, 1999), 146–152.

13. The Steinway Collection, February 1–23, 1968, box 040241, folder 23, Henry Z. Steinway, LaGuardia and Wagner Archives.

14. "How Yamaha Became Part of the U.S. Landscape," *Music Trades*, July 1, 2010.

15. Adapted from "How Yamaha Became Part of the U.S. Landscape." Much of the data for this part of the analysis came from *The Music Trade*, a highly respected market publication; see "Yamaha's First Century," August 1987, 50–72.

16. Peter Goodman, "Yamaha Threatens the Steinway Grand: The Steinway/Yamaha War," *Entertainment*, January 28, 1988.

17. Ibid.

18. Ibid.

19. *Music Trades,* Vol. 135, Issues 7–12 (Englewood, NJ: Music Trades Corp., 1987), 69, accessed March 15, 2018, https:/ /books.google.com/books ?id= N jAAAAMAAJ&g=robert+p. +bull+%22yamaha%22+ 196 4+pi ano &dg=robert+p.+bul 1+%22Zyamaha%22+1964+piano&hl=en&sa= X&ved =OahUK.EwiL l-X500zZAh Vl04MKHTuFC04Q6AEIKDAA. "On Yamaha's Assembly Line," *New York Times*, February 22, 1981.

20. Two important books have inspired the model I outline here. In *Design of Business,* Roger Martin describes the evolving nature of general knowledge. I believe he was the first to coin the term *knowledge funnel* (see chap. 1, 1–28; Cambridge, MA: Harvard Business Review Press, 2009). In another highly influential book, *The Innovator's Prescription,* Clayton Christensen et al. describe how technology can convert complex intuition into rules-based tasks (see chap. 2, 35–72; New York: McGraw-Hill Education, 2009). The model that I describe here, however, focuses on the outcome of international competition.

21. Siddhartha Mukherjee, *The Emperor of All Maladies: A Biography of Cancer* (New York: Scribner, 2010), 81.

22. David J. Jeremy, *Transatlantic Industrial Revolution: The Diffusion of Textile Technologies Between Britain and America, 1790–1830s* (Cambridge, MA: MIT Press, 1981), 36–37.

23. Robert F. Dalzell, *Enterprising Elite: The Boston Associates and the World They Made* (Cambridge, MA: Harvard University Press, 1987), 5.

24. Charles R. Morris, *The Dawn of Innovation: The First American Industrial Revolution* (New York: PublicAffairs, 2012), 92–93.

25. Mary B. Rose, *Firms, Networks, and Business Values: The British and American Cotton Industries since 1750* (Cambridge, UK: Cambridge University

Press, 2000), 41; quoted in Pietra Rivoli, *The Travels of a T-Shirt in the Global Economy*, 2nd ed. (Hoboken, NJ: John Wiley & Sons, 2009), 96.

26. Tom Nicholas and Matthew Guilford, "Samuel Slater & Francis Cabot Lowell: The Factory System in U.S. Cotton Manufacturing," HBS No. 814-065 (Boston: Harvard Business School Publishing, 2014).

27. Ibid.

28. Dalzell, *Enterprising Elite*, 95–96.

29. Rivoli, *Travels of a T-Shirt*, 97.

30. Henry Z. Steinway private letters, Henry Z. Steinway Archive, February 12, 1993, La Guardia and Wagner Archives.

31. Garvin, David A., "Steinway & Sons," Harvard Business School Case 682–025, September 1981 (rev. September 1986).

32. Carliss Y. Baldwin and Kim B. Clark, "Capital-Budgeting Systems and Capabilities Investments in U.S. Companies After the Second World War," *Business History Review* 68, no. 1 (Spring 1994), http://www.jstor.org/stable /3117016.

33. Cyb Art (website built by), "Steinway History," accessed March 11, 2018. http://steinwayhistory.com/october-1969-in-steinway-piano-history/.

34. Robert Palmieri, *The Piano: An Encyclopedia*, 2nd ed. (New York: Routledge, 2003), 411.

35. "Pianos and Parts Thereof: Report to the President on Investigation No TEA-I-14 Under Section 30l(b)(a) of the Trade Expansion Act of 1962," United States Tariff Commission, December 1969, accessed March 15, 2018, https://www.usitc.gov/publications/tariffaffairs/pub309.pdf

CHAPTER 2

1. Ernst Homburg, Anthony S. Travis, and Harm G. Schröter, eds., *Chemical Industry in Europe*, 18.

2. The Mineralogical Record - Label Archive, accessed January 31, 2018 http://www.minrec.org/labels.asp?colid=765.

3. The Editors of Encyclopaedia Britannica, "Ciba-Geigy AG," Encyclopaedia Britannica, February 19, 2009, accessed January 31, 2018, https://www .britannica.com/topic/Ciba-Geigy-AG.

4. Mark S. Lesney, "Three Paths to Novartis," *Modern Drug Discovery*, March 2004.

5. Ernst Homburg, Anthony S. Travis, and Harm G. Schröter, eds., *The Chemical Industry in Europe, 1850–1914: Industrial Growth, Pollution, and Professionalization* (Dordrecht, Netherlands: Springer Science+Business Media, 1998), 18.

6. Rudy M. Baum, "Chemical Troubles in Toms River: Damning Portrayal of Past Chemical Industry Practices Is Also In-Depth Examination of a Public Health Disaster," *Book Reviews* 91, no. 18 (May 2013): 42–43.

7. Alan Milward and S. B. Saul, *The Economic Development of Continental Europe 1780–1870* (Abingdon, UK: Routledge, 2012), 229.

8. Anna Bálint, *Clariant Clareant: The Beginnings of a Specialty Chemicals Company* (Frankfurt: Campus Verlag, 2012), 28.

9. Walter Dettwiler, *Novartis: How a Leader in Healthcare Was Created Out of Ciba, Geigy and Sandoz* (London: Profile Books, 2014), chap. 1.

10. Anita Friedlin and Kristina Ceca, "From CIBA to BASF: A Brief History of Industrial Basel," *Mozaik*, accessed February 3, 2018, http://www.mozaikzeitung.ch/spip/spip.php?article282.

11. "Switzerland's Industrialization," accessed February 03, 2018, http://history-switzerland.geschichte-schweiz.ch/industrialization-switzerland.html.

12. "History of Sandoz Pharmaceuticals," Herb Museum, accessed February 3, 2018, http://www.herbmuseum.ca/content/history-sandoz-pharmaceuticals.

13. "Company History," Novartis Indonesia, accessed February 3, 2018, https://www.id.novartis.com/about-us/company-history.

14. Markus Hammerle, *The Beginnings of the Basel Chemical Industry in Light of Industrial Medicine and Environmental Protection* (Basel: Schwabe & Co., 1995), 44.

15. Ibid., 41.

16. Robert L. Shook, *Miracle Medicines: Seven Lifesaving Drugs and the People Who Created Them* (New York: Portfolio, 2007), chap. 7.

17. Encyclopaedia Britannica Online, s.v. "Knorr, Ludwig," http://www.britannica.com/EBchecked/topic/1353916/Ludwig-Knorr.

18. Joseph S. Fruton, *Contrasts in Scientific Style: Research Groups in the Chemical and Biochemical Sciences* (Philadelphia: American Philosophical Society, 1990), 211.

19. Kay Brune, "The Discovery and Development of Anti-Inflammatory Drugs," *Arthritis and Rheumatology* 50, no. 8 (August 2004), 2391–2399.

20. P. R. Egan, "Antipyrin as an Analgesic," *Medical Record* 34 (1888), 477–478, cited in Janice Rae McTavish, *Pain and Profits: The History of the Headache and Its Remedies in America* (New Brunswick, NJ: Rutgers University Press, 2004), 80.

21. F. Tuckerman, "Antipyrine in Cephalalgia," *Medical Record* (1888), 180, cited in McTavish, *Pain and Profits*, 80.

22. "Antipyrine a Substitute for Quinine," *New York Times*, January 1, 1886, 6, cited in McTavish, *Pain and Profits*, 74.

23. "Antipyrin," *Druggists Circular* 28 (1884), 185.

24. Parvez Ali et al., "Predictions and Correlations of Structure Activity Relationship of Some Aminoantipyrine Derivatives on the Basis of Theoretical and Experimental Ground," *Medicinal Chemistry Research* 21, no. 2 (December 2010): 157.

25. Dan Fagin, *Toms River: A Story of Science and Salvation* (New York: Bantam, 2013), 11.

26. Popat N. Patil, *Discoveries in Pharmacological Sciences* (Hackensack, NJ: World Scientific, 2012), 672.

27. Dettwiler, *Novartis*, chap. 1.

28. Vladimír Křen and Ladislav Cvak, *Ergot: The Genus Claviceps* (Amsterdam, Netherlands: Harwood Academic Publishers, 1999), 373–378.

29. "First Penicillin Shot: Feb. 12, 1941," *HealthCentral*, February 11, 2013, http://www.healthcentral.com/dailydose/2013/2/11/first_penicillin_shot _feb_12_1941/.

30. Maryn Mckenna, "Imagining the Post Antibiotics Future," *Medium*, November 20, 2013, https://medium.com/@fernnews/imagining-the-post-antibiotics -future-892b57499e77.

31. "Howard Walter Florey and Ernst Boris Chain," *Chemical Heritage Foundation*, last modified September 11, 2015, http://www.chemheritage .org/discover/online-resources/chemistry-in-history/themes/pharmaceuticals /preventing-and-treating-infectious-diseases/florey-and-chain.aspx.

32. "The Discovery and Development of Penicillin," American Chemical Society, 1999, last modified November 5, 2015, https://www.acs.org/content /acs/en/education/whatischemistry/landmarks/flemingpenicillin.htm.

33. Mary Ellen Bowden, Amy Beth Crow, and Tracy Sullivan, *Pharmaceutical Achievers: The Human Face of Pharmaceutical Research* (Philadelphia: Chemical Heritage Foundation, 2005), 89.

34. Joseph G. Lombardino, "A Brief History of Pfizer Central Research," *Bulletin for the History of Chemistry* 25, no. 1 (2000): 11.

35. "Discovery and Development of Penicillin."

36. Alex Planes, "The Birth of Pharmaceuticals and the World's First Billionaire," *Motley Fool*, September 28, 2013, http://www.fool.com/investing /general/2013/09/28/the-birth-of-pharmaceuticals-and-the-worlds-first.aspx.

37. H. F. Stahelin, "The History of Cyclosporin A (Sandimmune®) Revisited: Another Point of View," *Experientia* 52, no. 2 (January 1996): 5–13.

38. Pfizer, Inc., "Pfizer History Text," MrBrklyn, http://www.mrbrklyn.com /resources/pfizer_history.txt.

39. David W. Wolfe, *Tales from the Underground: A Natural History of Subterranean Life* (New York: Basic Books, 2002), 137.

40. "Penicillin: The First Miracle Drug," accessed February 3, 2018, https:// web.archive.org/web/20160321034242/http://herbarium.usu.edu/fungi /funfacts/penicillin.htm.

41. J. F. Borel, Z. L. Kis, and T. Beveridge, "The History of the Discovery and Development of Cyclosporine (Sandimmune®)," in *The Search for Anti-Inflammatory Drugs: Case Histories from Concept to Clinic*, ed. Vincent K. Merluzzi (Basel: Birkhäuser, 1995), 27–28.

42. Donald E. Thomas Jr., *The Lupus Encyclopedia: A Comprehensive Guide for Patients and Families* (Baltimore, MD: Johns Hopkins University Press, 2014), 555.

43. Advameg, "Cyclosporine," *Medical Discoveries*, http://www.discoveries inmedicine.com/Com-En/Cyclosporine.html; Henry T. Tribe, "The Discovery and Development of Cyclosporin," *Mycologist* 12, no. 1 (February 1998): 20.

44. Camille Georges Wermuth, ed., *The Practice of Medicinal Chemistry*, 3rd ed. (Burlington, MA: Academic Press, 2008), 25; D. Colombo and E. Ammirati, "Cyclosporine in Transplantation—A History of Converging Timelines," *Journal of Biological Regulators and Homeostatic Agents* 25, no. 4 (2011): 493.

45. David Hamilton, *A History of Organ Transplantation: Ancient Legends to Modern Practice* (Pittsburgh: University of Pittsburgh Press, 2012), 382.

46. Harriet Upton, "Origin of Drugs in Current Use: The Cyclosporine Story," David Moore's World of Fungi: Where Mycology Starts, 2001, http://www.davidmoore.org.uk/Sec04_01.htm.

47. Karl Heuslera and Alfred Pletscherb, "The Controversial Early History of Cyclosporin," *Swiss Medical Weekly* 131 (2001): 300.

48. Larry Thompson, "Jean-François Borel's Transplanted Dream," *Washington Post*, November 15, 1988, accessed February 3, 2018, https://www.washingtonpost.com/archive/lifestyle/wellness/1988/11/15/jean-francois-borels-transplanted-dream/f3a931b9-e1a1-4724-9f08-a85ec4d3e68f/?utm_term=.9de240694fd1.

49. Ketan T. Savjani, Anuradha K. Gajjar, and Jignasa K. Savjani, "Drug Solubility: Importance and Enhancement Techniques," *ISRN Pharmaceutics*, July 5, 2012, https://www.ncbi.nlm.nih.gov/pmc/articles/PMC3399483/.

50. "Borel, Jean-François (1933–)," Encyclopedia.com, 2003, http://www.encyclopedia.com/doc/1G2-3409800096.html.

51. Nadey S. Hakim, Vassilios E. Papalois, and David E. R. Sutherland, *Transplantation Surgery* (Berlin: Springer, 2013), 17.

52. "Borel, Jean-François (1933–)," Encyclopedia.com.

53. "Gairdner Foundation International Award," Wikipedia, January 24, 2018, accessed February 3, 2018, https://en.wikipedia.org/wiki/Gairdner_Foundation_International_Award.

54. Dettwiler, *Novartis*, chap. 6.

55. "Pfizer's Work on Penicillin for World War II Becomes a National Historic Chemical Landmark," American Chemical Society, accessed September 13, 2017, https://www.acs.org/content/acs/en/pressroom/newsreleases/2008/june/pfizers-work-on-penicillin-for-world-war-ii-becomes-a-national-historic-chemical-landmark.html.

56. Catharine Cooper, "Procter & Gamble: The Early Years," *Cincinnati Magazine* 20, no. 11 (August 1987), 70.

57. "The Art of American Advertising: National Markets," Baker Library Historical Collections, http://www.library.hbs.edu/hc/artadv/national-markets.html.

58. Alfred Lief, *It Floats: The Story of Procter & Gamble* (New York: Rinehart & Company, 1958), 23.

59. Barbara Casson, "It Still Floats," *Cincinnati Magazine* 8, no. 10 (July 1975): 48.

60. Lady Emmeline Stuart-Wortley, *Travels in the United States During 1849 and 1850 (1851)*, as cited in "Cincinnati," Porkopolis, http://www.porkopolis.org/quotations/cincinnati/.

61. Bill Bryson, *One Summer, America 1927* (New York: Anchor, 2014), 235.

62. Ted Genoways, *The Chain: Farm, Factory, and the Fate of Our Food* (New York: Harper Paperbacks, 2015), 26.

63. Writers' Project of the Works Progress Administration, *They Built a City: 150 Years of Industrial Cincinnati* (Cincinnati: Cincinnati Post, [1938] 2015), 112.

64. Oscar Schisgall, *Eyes on Tomorrow: The Evolution of Procter & Gamble* (n.p.: J. G. Ferguson Publishing Company, 1981), 25.

65. Casson, "It Still Floats," 50.

66. Paul du Gay, ed., *Production of Culture/Cultures of Production* (London: Sage Publications Ltd., 1998), 277.

67. Vince Staten, *Did Trojans Use Trojans?: A Trip Inside the Corner Drugstore* (New York: Simon & Schuster, 2010), 90.

68. Allan A. Kennedy "The End of Shareholder Value," *Cincinnati Magazine*, July 1975, 50.

69. Staten, *Did Trojans Use Trojans?*, 91.

70. Pink Mint Publications, *Elvis Was a Truck Driver and Other Useless Facts!* (Morrisville, NC: Lulu Enterprises, 2007), 89.

71. Kennedy, "End of Shareholder Value," 50.

72. Schisgall, *Eyes on Tomorrow*, 33.

73. Joan M. Marter, ed., *The Grove Encyclopedia of American Art*, vol. 1 (New York: Oxford University Press, 2011), 467.

74. Robert Jay, *The Trade Card in Nineteenth-Century America* (Columbia: University of Missouri Press, 1987), 25.

75. Pamela Walker Laird, *Advertising Progress: American Business and the Rise of Consumer Marketing* (Baltimore: John Hopkins University Press, 1998), 87; as cited in "The Art of American Advertising: Advertising Products," Baker Library Historical Collections, accessed February 3, 2018, http://www.library.hbs.edu/hc/artadv/advertising-products.html.

76. "High Art on Cardboard," *New York Times*, December 3, 1882, 4.

77. Davis Dyer, Frederick Dalzell, and Rowena Olegario, *Rising Tide: Lessons from 165 Years of Brand Building at Procter & Gamble* (Boston: Harvard Business School Press, 2004), 35.

78. Bob Batchelor and Danielle Sarver Coombs, eds., *We Are What We Sell: How Advertising Shapes American Life . . . and Always Has* (Santa Barbara, CA: Praeger, 2014), 201.

79. Graham Spence Hudson, *The Design & Printing of Ephemera in Britain & America, 1720–1920* (London: British Library, 2008), 97.

80. Procter & Gamble, "Ivory Advertisement," *Journal of the American Medical Association* 6, no. 7 (1886): xv; as cited in Batchelor and Coombs, eds., *We Are What We Sell*, 202.

81. *Saturday Evening Post*, October 25, 1919, 2, as cited in Batchelor and Coombs, eds., *We Are What We Sell*, 203.

82. Ibid., 35.

83. Dyer, Dalzell, and Olegario, *Rising Tide*, 31.

84. Lief, *It Floats*, 81; "Harley T. Procter (1847–1920)," Advertising Hall of Fame, accessed September 14, 2017, http://advertisinghall.org/members /member_bio.php?memid=766.

85. "Hastings Lush French," *Genealogy Bug*, accessed February 4, 2018, http://www.genealogybug.net/oh_biographies/french_h_l.shtml.

86. Schisgall, *Eyes on Tomorrow*, 34.

87. Dyer, Dalzell, and Olegario, *Rising Tide*, 39.

88. David Segal, "The Great Unwatched," *New York Times*, May 3, 2014, https://www.nytimes.com/2014/05/04/business/the-great-unwatched.html.

89. Walter D. Scott, "The Psychology of Advertising," *Atlantic Monthly* 93, no. 555 (1904): 36.

90. Christopher H. Sterling, *Encyclopedia of Journalism* (Thousand Oaks, CA: Sage, 2009), 20.

91. D. G. Brian Jones and Mark Tadajewski, *The Routledge Companion to Marketing History* (Abingdon, UK: Routledge, 2016), 71.

92. "Ad Man Albert Lasker Pumped Up Demand for California, or Sunkist, Oranges," *Washington Post*, November 14, 2010, http://www.washington post.com/wp-dyn/content/article/2010/11/13/AR2010111305878.html; Robin Lewis and Michael Dart, *The New Rules of Retail: Competing in the World's Toughest Marketplace* (New York: Palgrave Macmillan, 2014), 43.

93. Jim Cox, *The Great Radio Soap Operas* (Jefferson, NC: McFarland, 2011), 115.

94. Batchelor and Coombs, eds., *We Are What We Sell*, 77–78.

95. Anthony J. Mayo and Nitin Nohria, *In Their Time: The Greatest Business Leaders of the Twentieth Century* (Boston: Harvard Business School Press, 2007), 197.

96. Alexander Coolidge, "Ivorydale: Model for More P&G Closings?" Cincinnati.com, last modified June 9, 2014, http://www.cincinnati.com/story /money/2014/06/07/ivorydale-model-pg-closings/10162025/.

97. "A Company History," Procter & Gamble, https://www.pg.com /translations/history_pdf/english_history.pdf.

98. "The Creed of Speed," *Economist*, December 2015, 23.

99. Jerker Denrell, "Vicarious Learning, Under-sampling of Failure, and the Myths of Management," *Organization Science* 14 (2003): 227–243.

100. That companies must leap to new knowledge disciplines in order to create new markets for growth is a conclusion consistent with a growing body of management research, most notably by W. Chan Kim and Renee Mauborgne at INSEAD whose *Blue Ocean Strategy* (2005) and *Blue Ocean Shift* (2017) have influenced and shaped the thinking of generations of practitioners and academics, including my own.

CHAPTER 3

1. Andrew Solomon, *Far from the Tree: Parents, Children and the Search for Identity* (New York: Scribner, 2012), 254.

2. Ashutosh Jogalekar, "Why Drugs Are Expensive: It's the Science, Stupid," *Scientific American*, January 6, 2014, https://blogs.scientificamerican.com/the-curious-wavefunction/why-drugs-are-expensive-ite28099s-the-science-stupid/.

3. Walter Dettwiler, *Novartis: How a Leader in Healthcare Was Created out of Ciba, Geigy and Sandoz* (London: Profile Books, 2014), chap. 8.

4. Günter K. Stahl and Mark E. Mendenhall, eds., *Mergers and Acquisitions: Managing Culture and Human Resources* (Redwood City, CA: Stanford University Press, 2005), 379–380.

5. Daniel Vasella, *Magic Cancer Bullet: How a Tiny Orange Pill is Rewriting Medical History* (New York: HarperCollins, 2003), 32–33.

6. Rik Kirkland, "Leading in the 21st Century: An Interview with Daniel Vasella," McKinsey & Company, September 2012, http://www.mckinsey.com/global-themes/leadership/an-interview-with-daniel-vasella.

7. Bill George, *Discover Your True North* (Hoboken, NJ: John Wiley & Sons, 2015), 58.

8. Bill George, Peter Sims, Andrew N. McLean, and Diana Mayer, "Discovering Your Authentic Leadership," *Harvard Business Review*, February 2007, https://hbr.org/2007/02/discovering-your-authentic-leadership.

9. Ananya Mandal, "Hodgkin's Lymphoma History," News-Medical.net, last modified August 19, 2014, http://www.news-medical.net/health/Hodgkins-Lymphoma-History.aspx.

10. Vasella, *Magic Cancer Bullet*, 34–36.

11. Robert L. Shook, *Miracle Medicines: Seven Lifesaving Drugs and the People Who Created Them* (New York: Portfolio, 2007), chap. 8.

12. Siddhartha Mukherjee, *The Emperor of All Maladies: A Biography of Cancer* (New York: Scribner, 2010), 432; Shook, *Miracle Medicines*, chap. 8.

13. Neil Izenberg and Steven A. Dowshen, *Human Diseases and Disorders: Infectious Diseases* (New York: Scribner/Thomson/Gale, 2002), 30.

14. Shook, *Miracle Medicines*, chap. 8.

15. Andrew S. Grove, *Only the Paranoid Survive* (New York: Doubleday, 1999), 146.

16. Robert A. Burgelman, "Fading Memories: A Process Theory of Strategic Business Exit in Dynamic Environments," *Administrative Science Quarterly* 39, no. 1 (1994): 24, doi:10.2307/2393493.

17. Gordon M. Cragg, David G. I. Kingston, and David J. Newman, eds., *Anticancer Agents from Natural Products*, 2nd ed. (Boca Raton, FL: CRC Press, 2011), 565.

18. Mayo Clinic Staff, "Leukemia Symptoms," Mayo Clinic, January 28, 2016, http://www.mayoclinic.org/diseases-conditions/leukemia/basics/symptoms/con-20024914.

19. Shook, *Miracle Medicines*, chap 8.

20. Ibid.; Nicholas Wade, "Powerful Anti-Cancer Drug Emerges from Basic Biology," *New York Times*, May 7, 2001, accessed January 18, 2018, http://www.nytimes.com/2001/05/08/science/powerful-anti-cancer-drug-emerges-from-basic-biology.html.

21. Ibid.

22. Wade, "Powerful Anti-Cancer Drug."

23. Mukherjee, *Emperor of All Maladies,* 436.

24. Vasella, *Magic Cancer Bullet*, 16.

25. US Department of Health and Human Services, "Remarks by HHS Secretary Tommy G. Thompson: Press Conference Announcing Approval of Gleevec for Leukemia Treatment," HHS.Gov Archive, May 10, 2001, http://archive.hhs.gov/news/press/2001pres/20010510.html.

26. Rob Mitchum, "Cancer Drug Gleevec Wins Lasker Award," *ScienceLife*, September 14, 2009, http://sciencelife.uchospitals.edu/2009/09/14/cancer-drug-gleevec-wins-lasker-award/.

27. Mukherjee, *Emperor of All Maladies*, 438–440.

28. Tariq I. Mughal, *Chronic Myeloid Leukemia: A Handbook for Hematologists and Oncologists* (Boca Raton, FL: CRC Press, 2013), 30–31.

29. Andrew Pollack, "Cancer Physicians Attack High Drug Costs," *New York Times*, April 25, 2013.

30. Joan O. Hamilton, "Biotech's First Superstar: Genentech Is Becoming a Major-Leaguer—and Wall Street Loves It," *Business Week*, April 14, 1986, 68.

31. Andrew Pollack, "Roche Agrees to Buy Genentech for $46.8 Billion," *New York Times*, March 12, 2009, accessed February 3, 2018, http://www.nytimes.com/2009/03/13/business/worldbusiness/13drugs.html?mtrref=www.google.ch&gwh=75ED1CAF2D042A3546663BBF0F5D3706&gwt=pay.

32. Gary Hamel and C. K. Prahalad, "Strategic Intent," *Harvard Business Review*, July/August 2005, https://hbr.org/2005/07/strategic-intent.

33. Andrew Pollack, "F.D.A. Gives Early Approval to Drug for Rare Leukemia, *New York Times*, December 14, 2012, http://www.nytimes.com/2012

/12/15/business/fda-gives-early-approval-to-leukemia-drug-iclusig.html; Dave Levitan, "Nilotinib Effective for Imatinib-Resistant CML," Cancer Network, July 21, 2012, http://www.cancernetwork.com/chronic-myeloid-leukemia /nilotinib-effective-imatinib-resistant-cml.

34. Susan Gubar, "Living with Cancer: The New Medicine," *New York Times*, June 26, 2014, http://well.blogs.nytimes.com/2014/06/26/living-with -cancer-the-new-medicine/?_r=0.

35. Jeremy Rifkin, *Zero Marginal Cost Society: The Internet of Things, the Collaborative Commons, and the Eclipse of Capitalism* (New York: St. Martin's Press, 2014), 379.

36. "Procter & Gamble," Fortune.com, accessed February 3, 2018, http:// beta.fortune.com/fortune500/procter-gamble-34.

37. Alfred Lief, "Harley Procter's Floating Soap (Aug, 1953)" *Modern Mechanix*, July 14, 2008, http://blog.modernmechanix.com/harley-procters -floating-soap/.

38. Robert A. Duncan, "P&G Develops Synthetic Detergents: A Short History," typewritten manuscript, September 5, 1958, P&G Archives, 1.

39. The laboratory visited was that of I. G. Farben, the chemical giant that would later become notorious for engaging in war crimes under the Nazi regime.

40. Duncan, "P&G Develops Synthetic Detergents," 3.

41. Davis Dyer, Frederick Dalzell, and Rowena Olegario, *Rising Tide: Lessons from 165 Years of Brand Building at Procter & Gamble* (Boston: Harvard Business School Press, 2004), 70; Duncan, "P&G Develops Synthetic Detergents," 5.

42. Oscar Schisgall, *Eyes on Tomorrow: The Evolution of Procter & Gamble* (n.p.: J. G. Ferguson Publishing Company, 1981), 42; Advertising Age Editors, *Procter & Gamble: How P & G Became America's Leading Marketer* (n.p.: Passport Books, 1990), 11.

43. American Chemical Society, "Development of Tide Laundry Detergent Receives Historical Recognition," *EurekAlert!*, October 11, 2016, http:// www.eurekalert.org/pub_releases/2006-10/acs-dot101106.php.

44. "Laundry Detergent," MadeHow.com, http://www.madehow.com /Volume-1/Laundry-Detergent.html.

45. "Birth of an Icon: TIDE," *P&G*, November 2, 2012, http://news.pg .com/blog/heritage/birth-icon-tide.

46. G. Thomas Halberstadt, interview, April 7, 1984, P&G Archives, cited in National Historic Chemical Landmarks program of the American Chemical Society, "Development of Tide Synthetic Detergent: National Historic Chemical Landmark," American Chemical Society, October 25, 2006, http://www.acs.org/content/acs/en/education/whatischemistry/landmarks /tidedetergent.html.

47. Ibid.

48. Ibid.

49. Ibid.

50. American Chemical Society, "Development of Tide Synthetic Detergent."

51. Dyer, Dalzell, and Olegario, *Rising Tide*, 73.

52. National Historic Chemical Landmarks program of the American Chemical Society, "Development of Tide Synthetic Detergent."

53. G. Thomas Halberstadt, interview, April 7, 1984, P&G Archives; Dyer, Dalzell, and Olegario, *Rising Tide*, 74; Dan Hurley, "Changing the Tide," *Cincy Magazine*, December 2013/January 2014, http://www.cincymagazine.com/Main/Articles/Changing_the_Tide_3939.aspx.

54. The description is reconstructed from multiple sources, including the Halberstadt interview, April 7, 1984, P&G Archives; and Dyer, Dalzell, and Olegario, *Rising Tide*, 74–75.

55. "Discover Great Innovations in Fashion and Lifestyle," Tide.com, http://www.tide.com/en-US/article/unofficial-history-laundry.jspx.

56. Advertising Age Editors, *How Procter and Gamble*, 23.

57. Alfred Lief, *It Floats: The Story of Procter & Gamble* (New York: Rinehart & Company, 1958), 254.

58. Dyer, Dalzell, and Olegario, *Rising Tide*, 81.

59. G. Thomas Halberstadt, interview, April 7–9, 1984, P&G Archives, 34.

60. Lief, *It Floats*, 253.

61. Howard Yu and Thomas Malnight, "The Best Companies Aren't Afraid to Replace Their Most Profitable Products," *Harvard Business Review*, July 14, 2016, https://hbr.org/2016/07/the-best-companies-arent-afraid-to-replace-their-most-profitable-products.

62. See Rita Gunther McGrath, *The End of Competitive Advantage* (Boston: Harvard Business School Press), 2013. Professor McGrath's work on this topic, in my opinion, constitutes the fundamental paradigm upon which much subsequent research is being built.

63. Ron Adner, "From Walkman to iPod: What Music Tech Teaches Us About Innovation," *Atlantic*, March 5, 2012, https://www.theatlantic.com/business/archive/2012/03/from-walkman-to-ipod-what-music-tech-teaches-us-about-innovation/253158/.

64. One starting point is for managers to "reconstruct market boundaries" described by INSEAD's W. Chan Kim and Renee Mauborgne in *Blue Ocean Shift* (2017), Ch. 10, in which managers are shown six ways to challenge an industry's "self-imposed boundaries." Tills' powerful framework is built upon decades of work, first published in 2005 in *Blue Ocean Strategy*, an international bestseller.

CHAPTER 4

1. Alexander Osterwalder, "The Business Model Ontology: A Proposition in a Design Science Approach" (PhD thesis, HEC, 2004), http://www.hec.unil.ch/aosterwa/PhD/Osterwalder_PhD_BM_Ontology.pdf.

2. Alexander Osterwalder, interview by Howard Yu, December 3, 2015.

3. Paul Hobcraft, "Business Model Generation," *Innovation Management*, September 23, 2010, accessed April 23, 2017, http://www.innovationmanage ment.se/2010/09/23/business-model-generation/.

4. Alex Osterwalder, accessed April 23, 2017, http://alexosterwalder.com/.

5. "The 10 Most Influential Business Thinkers in the World," *Thinkers 50*, November 11, 2015, accessed June 30, 2017, http://thinkers50.com/media /media-coverage/the-10-most-influential-business-thinkers-in-the-world/; "Alexander Osterwalder and Yves Pigneur," *Thinkers 50*, February 1, 2017, accessed June 30, 2017, http://thinkers50.com/biographies/alexander -osterwalder-yves-pigneur.

6. Alex Osterwalder, "How to Self-Publish a Book," Agocluytens, accessed April 23, 2017, http://agocluytens.com/how-to-self-publish-a-book-alexander -osterwalder/. An earlier version of this case study has been published as a back-ground note "Who is Alex Osterwalder?" at IMD based on a private interview with Alexander Osterwalder and public sources. Yu, Howard H., "How a Best-Selling Author Crowdsourced and Broke Every Rule in the Book," IMD, October 28, 2016, accessed March 13, 2018, https://www1.imd.org/publications/articles/ how-a-best-selling-author-crowdsourced-and-brokeevery-rule-in-the-book/.

7. "50 Years of Moore's Law," *Intel*, accessed April 23, 2017, http://www .intel.com/content/www/us/en/silicon-innovations/moores-law-technology.html.

8. Barry Ritholtz, "When Do Scientists Believe Computers Will Surpass the Human Brain?" *The Big Picture*, August 3, 2015, accessed June 30, 2017, http:// ritholtz.com/2015/08/when-do-scientists-believe-computers-will-surpass-the -human-brain/.

9. "Your Smartphone Is Millions of Times More Powerful Than All of NASA's Combined Computing in 1969," *ZME Science*, May 17, 2017, accessed June 30, 2017, http://www.zmescience.com/research/technology/smartphone -power-compared-to-apollo-432/.

10. Daniel J. Levitin, *The Organized Mind: Thinking Straight in the Age of Information Overload* (New York: Dutton, 2016), 381.

11. Berin Szoka, Matthew Starr, and Jon Henke, "Don't Blame Big Cable. It's Local Governments That Choke Broadband Competition," *Wired*, July 16, 2013, accessed September 25, 2017, https://www.wired.com/2013/07/we -need-to-stop-focusing-on-just-cable-companies-and-blame-local-government -for-dismal-broadband-competition/.

12. Steven Cherry, "Edholm's Law of Bandwidth," *IEEE Spectrum*, July 1, 2004, http://spectrum.ieee.org/telecom/wireless/edholms-law-of-bandwidth.

13. Andrew McAfee and Erik Brynjolfsson, *Machine Platform Crowd: Harnessing Our Digital Future* (New York: W. W. Norton & Company, 2017), 98.

14. Ingrid Lunden, "If WhatsApp Is Worth $19B, Then WeChat's Worth 'at Least $60B' Says CLSA," *TC*, March 11, 2014, http://techcrunch.com/2014 /03/11/if-whatsapp-is-worth-19b-then-wechats-worth-at-least-60b-says -clsa.

15. Tencent shares closed at a record high of 248.40 Hong Kong dollars (just under $32). "China's Tencent Is Now Worth $300 Billion," CNNMoney, accessed June 30, 2017, http://money.cnn.com/2017/05/03/investing/china -tencent-300-billion-company/index.html.

16. Tim Higgins and Anna Steele, "Tesla Gets Backing of Chinese Internet Giant Tencent," *Wall Street Journal*, last modified March 29, 2017, https:// www.wsj.com/articles/chinas-tencent-buys-5-stake-in-tesla-1490702095.

17. Jordan Novet, "China's WeChat Captures Almost 30 Percent of the Country's Mobile App Usage: Meeker Report," CNBC, May 31, 2017, accessed July 2, 2017, http://www.cnbc.com/2017/05/31/wechat-captures-about -30-percent-of-chinas-mobile-app-usage-meeker-report.html.

18. "Number of Monthly Active WhatsApp Users Worldwide from April 2013 to January 2017," *Statista*, accessed April 23, 2017, https://www.statista .com/statistics/260819/number-of-monthly-active-whatsapp-users/.

19. Josh Constine, "Facebook Now Has 2 Billion Monthly Users . . . and Responsibility," *TechCrunch*, June 27, 2017, accessed June 30, 2017, https:// techcrunch.com/2017/06/27/facebook-2-billion-users/.

20. "2017 WeChat User Report Is Out!—China Channel," *WeChat Based Solutions & Services*, accessed June 30, 2017, http://chinachannel.co/1017 -wechat-report-users/.

21. David Cohen, "How Much Time Will the Average Person Spend on Social Media During Their Life? (Infographic)," *Adweek*, accessed June 30, 2017, http://www.adweek.com/digital/mediakix-time-spent-social-media -infographic/; Brad Stone and Lulu Yilun Chen, "Tencent Dominates in China. The Next Challenge Is the Rest of the World," Bloomberg.com, June 28, 2017, accessed July 2, 2017, https://www.bloomberg.com/news/features/2017-06-28 /tencent-rules-china-the-problem-is-the-rest-of-the-world. *As for WeChat:* An earlier version of this case study has been published as Shih, Willy, Howard Yu, and Feng Liu, "WeChat: A Global Platform?" Harvard Business School Case 615–049, June 2015 (Rev. August 2017).

22. Beth Carter, "High Tech, Low Life Peeks Through China's Great Firewall," *Wired*, April 27, 2012, https://www.wired.com/2012/04/high-tech-low -life/.

23. He Huifeng, "WeChat Red Envelopes Help Drive Online Payments Use in China," *South China Morning Post*, February 15, 2016, http://www. scmp.com/tech/article/1913340/wechat-red-envelopes-help-drive -online-payments-use-china.

24. Juro Osawa, "China Mobile-Payment Battle Becomes a Free-for-All," *Wall Street Journal*, last modified May 22, 2016, http://www.wsj.com/articles/china -mobile-payment-battle-becomes-a-free-for-all-1463945404; Paul Smith, "The Top Four Mistakes That Make Business Leaders Awful Storytellers," *Fast Company*, November 5, 2016, https://www.fastcompany.com/3065209/work-smart /the-top-four-mistakes-that-make-business-leaders-awful-storytellers.

25. Paul Mozur, "In Urban China, Cash Is Rapidly Becoming Obsolete," *New York Times*, July 16, 2017, accessed September 26, 2017, https://www.nytimes.com/2017/07/16/business/china-cash-smartphone-payments.html?mcubz=0.

26. James H. David, "Social Interaction and Performance," in *Group Performance* (Reading, PA: Addison-Wesley, 1969).

27. Tony Perry and Julian Barnes, "U.S. Rethinks a Marine Corps Specialty: Storming Beaches," *LA Times*, June 21, 2010, http://articles.latimes.com/2010/jun/21/nation/la-na-marines-future-20100621.

28. Christopher Drew, "Pentagon Is Poised to Cancel Marine Landing Craft," *New York Times*, January 5, 2011, http://www.nytimes.com/2011/01/06/business/06marine.html?_r=0.

29. Edward Bowman and Bruce M. Kogut, eds., *Redesigning the Firm* (Oxford: Oxford University Press, 1995), 246.

30. L. J. Colfer and C. Y. Baldwin, "The Mirroring Hypothesis: Theory, Evidence and Exceptions" (Harvard Business School, Tech. Rep. Finance Working Paper No. 16-124, May 2016).

31. Spencer Ackerman, "Build a Swimming Tank for DARPA and Make a Million Dollars," *Wired*, October 2, 2010, http://www.wired.com/2012/10/fang/.

32. DARPAtv, "FANG Challenge: Design a Next-Generation Military Ground Vehicle," YouTube video, 3:26, September 27, 2012, https://www.youtube.com/watch?v=TMa1657gYIE.

33. Christopher Drew, "Pentagon Is Poised to Cancel Marine Landing Craft," *New York Times*, January 5, 2011, http://www.nytimes.com/2011/01/06/business/06marine.html?_r=0; Ackerman, "Build a Swimming Tank for DARPA."

34. Michael Belfiore, "You Will Design DARPA's Next Amphibious Vehicle," *Popular Mechanics*, October 3, 2012, http://www.popularmechanics.com/military/research/a8151/you-will-design-darpas-next-amphibious-vehicle-13336284/.

35. Kyle Maxey, "DARPA FANG Challenge—$1M to the Winners," Engineering.com, April 22, 2013, http://www.engineering.com/DesignerEdge/DesignerEdgeArticles/ArticleID/5624/DARPA-FANG-Challenge—1M-to-the-winners.aspx.

36. "Test and Evaluation of AVM Tools for DARPA FANG Challenge," *NASA JPL*, accessed April 23, 2017, https://www-robotics.jpl.nasa.gov/tasks/showTask.cfm?TaskID=255&tdaID=700059.

37. Lane Boyd, "DARPA Pushes for an Engineering Internet," *Computer Graphics World* 21, no. 9 (1998).

38. "DARPA Challenges Combat Vehicle Designers: Do It Quicker," *Aviation Week*, November 5, 2012, http://aviationweek.com/awin/darpa-challenges-combat-vehicle-designers-do-it-quicker.

39. Allison Barrie, "Could You Design the Next Marine Amphibious Assault Vehicle?" *Fox News*, April 25, 2013, http://www.foxnews.com/tech/2013/04/25 /could-design-next-marine-amphibious-assault-vehicle/.

40. Beth Stackpole, "Dispersed Team Nabs \$1 Million Prize in DARPA FANG Challenge," *DE*, May 3, 2013, http://www.deskeng.com/virtual_desktop /?p=7101.

41. Sean Gallagher, "Tankcraft: Building a DARPA Tank Online for Fun and Profit," *Ars Technica*, April 24, 2013, http://arstechnica.com/information -technology/2013/04/tankcraft-building-a-darpa-tank-online-for-fun-and -profit/.

42. Graeme McMillan, "The Family That Stays Together, Designs Award-Winning Military Vehicles Together," *Digital Trends*, April 25, 2013, http:// www.digitaltrends.com/cool-tech/the-family-that-stays-together-designs -award-winning-tanks-together/.

43. Ibid.

44. Stephen Lacey, "How Crowdsourcing Could Save the Department of Energy," *GTM*, February 27, 2013, accessed September 29, 2017, https:// www.greentechmedia.com/articles/read/how-crowdsourcing-could-save-the -department-of-energy#gs.FQgDUb8; Robert M. Bauer, and Thomas Gegenhuber, "Crowdsourcing: Global Search and the Twisted Roles of Consumers and Producers," *Organization* 22, no. 5 (2015): 661–681, doi:10.1177 /1350508415585030.

45. McMillan, "Family That Stays Together."

46. "DARPA Challenges Combat Vehicle Designers."

47. Oliver Weck, *Fast Adaptable Next-Generation Ground Vehicle Challenge, Phase 1 (FANG—1) Post-Challenge Analysis*, September 21, 2013, http:// web.mit.edu/deweck/Public/AVM/FANG-1percent20Post-Analysispercent 20Technical percent20Report percent20(de percent20Weck).pdf.

48. Anita McGahan, "Unlocking the Big Promise of Big Data," *Rotman Management Magazine*, Fall 2013.

49. Sandi Doughton, "After 10 Years, Few Payoffs from Gates' 'Grand Challenges,'" *Seattle Times*, December 22, 2014, accessed September 27, 2017, http://www.seattletimes.com/seattle-news/after-10-years-few-payoffs-from -gatesrsquo-lsquogrand-challengesrsquo/.

50. Maxey, "DARPA FANG Challenge."

51. David Szondy, "DARPA Announces Winner in FANG Challenge," *New Atlas*, April 24, 2013, http://newatlas.com/darpa-fang-winner/27213/.

52. I would like to thank Professor Hila Lifshitz-Assaf at the New York University Stern School of Business, who first explained to me the importance of decontextualization for successful collaboration in the open. For her excellent research, please refer to Karim Lakhani, Hila Lifshitz-Assaf, and Michael Tushman, "Open Innovation and Organizational Boundaries: Task Decomposition, Knowledge Distribution, and the Locus of Innovation," in *Handbook*

of Economic Organization: Integrating Economic and Organizational Theory, ed. Anna Grandori (Northampton, MA: Elgar, 2014), 355–382.

53. L. Argote, B. McEvily, and R. Reagans, "Managing Knowledge in Organizations: An Integrative Framework and Review of Emerging Themes," *Management Science* 49, no. 4 (2003): 571–582.

54. "Gennady Korotkevich Wins Google Code Jam Fourth Time in a Row," Новости Университета ИТМО, accessed January 31, 2018, http://news.ifmo.ru/en/university_live/achievements/news/6871/.

55. Joseph Byrum, "How Agribusinesses Can Ensure Success with Open Innovation," AgFunder News, November 14, 2016, https://agfundernews.com/tips-agribusinesses-succeed-open-innovation.html.

56. Ibid.

57. Discussion with multiple Syngenta managers on March 1, 2016, at a strategy workshop in Lausanne, Switzerland.

58. Lizzie Widdicombe, "The Programmer's Price," *New Yorker*, November 24, 2014, http://www.newyorker.com/magazine/2014/11/24/programmers-price; Frederick Brooks, *The Mythical Man-Month: Essays on Software Engineering* (Boston: Addison-Wesley, 1995), chap. 3.

59. An earlier version of this argument has been published as a supplementary reading, "Why Do People Do Great Things Without Getting Paid?" IMD Case IMD-7-1537, 2013. A great source on this topic can be found in *The Power of Habit: Why We Do What We Do in Life and Business* (New York: Random House, 2012) by Charles Duhigg, Ch. 5.

60. See Charles Duhigg, *The Power of Habit*. For more details, please refer to Duhigg's book for a succinct explanation of the series of fascinating experiments conducted by Professor Mark Muraven at SUNY Albany.

61. The concept of social bragging rights is articulated in Jonah Berger, *Contagious: Why Things Catch On* (New York: Simon & Schuster, 2013), chap. 1.

62. For a review of this line of inquiry on human willpower by Mark Muraven and his colleagues, see Andrew C. Watson, *Learning Begins—The Science of Working Memory and Attention/or the Class* (Rowman & Littlefield, 2017), 123–128

63. Yue Wang, "How Chinese Super App WeChat Plans to Lock Out Foreign App Stores in China," *Forbes*, January 9, 2017, https://www.forbes.com/sites/ywang/2017/01/09/chinese-super-app-wechat-launches-new-plan-to-rival-app-stores-in-china/#156830965748; Yi Shu Ng, "WeChat Beats Google to Release Apps That Don't Need to be Downloaded or Installed," *Mashable*, January 10, 2017, http://mashable.com/2017/01/10/wechat-mini-programs/#fKWl6IRhosqE; Jon Russell, "China's Tencent Takes on the App Store with Launch of 'Mini Programs' for WeChat," *TC*, January 9, 2017, https://techcrunch.com/2017/01/09/wechat-mini-programs/.

64. Sarah Perez, "Nearly 1 in 4 People Abandon Mobile Apps After Only One Use," *TC*, May 31, 2016, https://techcrunch.com/2016/05/31/nearly-1-in -4-people-abandon-mobile-apps-after-only-one-use/.

65. Wang, "How Chinese Super App WeChat Plans."

66. Sijia Jiang, "With New Mini-Apps, WeChat Seeks Even More China Clicks," *Reuters*, May 28, 2017, http://www.reuters.com/article/us -tencent-wechat-china-idUSKCN18E38Z.

CHAPTER 5

1. "What AlphaGo Means to the Future of Management," *MIT Sloan Management Review*, accessed May 28, 2017, http://sloanreview.mit.edu /article/tech-savvy-what-alphago-means-to-the-future-of-management/.

2. Alan Levinovitz, "The Mystery of Go, the Ancient Game That Computers Still Can't Win," *Wired*, May 12, 2014, https://www.wired.com/2014/05/the -world-of-computer-go/.

3. Cho Mu-Hyun, "AlphaGo Match 'a Win for Humanity': Eric Schmidt," *ZDNet*, March 8, 2016, http://www.zdnet.com/article/alphago-match-a-win -for-humanity-eric-schmidt/.

4. Brad Stone, *The Everything Store: Jeff Bezos and the Age of Amazon* (New York: Back Bay Books, 2014), 134.

5. Seth Fiegerman, "Man vs. Algorithm: When Media Companies Need a Human Touch," *Mashable*, October 30, 2013, accessed September 30, 2017, http://mashable.com/2013/10/30/new-media-technology/#H4yVxcTntkq7.

6. "The Valentines!" *Stranger*, February 7, 2002, accessed September 30, 2017, http://www.thestranger.com/seattle/the-valentines/Content?oid=9976.

7. Molly Driscoll, "'The Everything Store': 5 Behind-the-Scenes Stories About Amazon," *Christian Science Monitor*, November 4, 2013, http://www .csmonitor.com/Books/2013/1104/The-Everything-Store-5-behind-the-scenes -stories-about-Amazon/Less-space-for-creativity.

8. "History of the World Jeopardy Review Game Answer Key," accessed May 28, 2017, https://www.superteachertools.us/jeopardyx/answerkey.php ?game=1408637225.

9. An earlier version of this case study has been published as "IBM Watson (A): Will a Computer Replace Your Oncologist One Day?" IMD Case IMD-3-2402, 2013. Stephen Baker, *Final Jeopardy: The Story of Watson, the Computer That Will Transform Our World* (Boston: Mariner Books, 2012), 3.

10. Paul Cerrato, "IBM Watson Finally Graduates Medical School," *InformationWeek*, accessed May 28, 2017, http://www.informationweek .com/healthcare/clinical-information-systems/ibm-watson-finally-graduates -medical-school/d/d-id/1106982.

11. "Memorial Sloan-Kettering Cancer Center, IBM to Collaborate in Applying Watson Technology to Help Oncologists," IBM News Room, March 22,

2012, https://web.archive.org/web/20141222165826/http://www-03.ibm.com/press/us/en/pressrelease/37235.wss; "The Science Behind Watson," IBM Watson, accessed May 28, 2017, https://web.archive.org/web/20130524075245/http://www-03.ibm.com/innovation/us/watson/the_jeopardy_challenge.shtml.

12. IBM, "Perspectives on Watson: Healthcare," YouTube video, 2:16, February 8, 2011, https://www.youtube.com/watch?v=vwDdyxj6S0U.

13. Ken Jennings, "Watson Jeopardy! Computer: Ken Jennings Describes What It's Like to Play Against a Machine," *Slate Magazine*, February 16, 2011, http://www.slate.com/articles/arts/culturebox/2011/02/my_puny_human_brain.2.html.

14. Brian Christian, "Mind vs. Machine," *Atlantic*, February 19, 2014, https://www.theatlantic.com/magazine/archive/2011/03/mind-vs-machine/308386/.

15. Natasha Geiling, "The Women Who Mapped the Universe and Still Couldn't Get Any Respect," *Smithsonian*, September 18, 2013, http://www.smithsonianmag.com/history/the-women-who-mapped-the-universe-and-still-couldnt-get-any-respect-9287444/.

16. A. M. Turing, "Computing Machinery and Intelligence," *Mind* (1950): 433–460, doi:10.1093/mind/LIX.236.433.

17. IBM, "IBM Healthcare," YouTube video, February 21, 2013, https://www.youtube.com/watch?v=D07VJz0uGM4.

18. Baker, *Final Jeopardy*.

19. IBM, "IBM Watson: Watson After Jeopardy!" YouTube video, 4:36, February 11, 2011, accessed October 2, 2017, http://www.youtube.com/watch?v=dQmuETLeQcg&rel=0.

20. Deepak and Sanjiv Chopra, *Brotherhood: Dharma, Destiny, and the American Dream* (New York: New Harvest, 2013), 187.

21. Malcolm Gladwell, *Blink: The Power of Thinking Without Thinking* (Boston: Little, Brown, 2007), 9.

22. Gary Klein, a psychologist, originally reported this story, which a number of authors have since popularized. For additional accounts, please refer to http://www.fastcompany.com/40456/whats-your-intuition; Daniel Kahneman, *Thinking, Fast and Slow* (New York: Farrar, Straus and Giroux, 2011); Gladwell, *Blink: The Power of Thinking Without Thinking*.

23. "Simon Property Group Fights to Reinvent the Shopping Mall," *Fortune*, accessed October 1, 2017, http://fortune.com/simon-mall-landlord-real-estate/.

24. "Simon Property Group Inc.," AnnualReports.com, accessed October 1, 2017, http://www.annualreports.com/Company/simon-property-group-inc.

25. "China's Dalian Wanda 2015 Revenue up 19 Pct as Diversification Takes Hold," Reuters, January 10, 2016, accessed October 1, 2017, http://www.reuters.com/article/wanda-group-results/chinas-dalian-wanda-2015-revenue-up-19-pct-as-diversification-takes-hold-idUSL3N14V1DU20160111.

26. "Dalian Wanda to Open Nearly 900 Malls by 2025, Focus on Lower-Tier Cities," Reuters, April 20, 2015, accessed October 1, 2017, http://www.reuters.com/article/dalian-wanda/dalian-wanda-to-open-nearly-900-malls-by-2025-focus-on-lower-tier-cities-idUSL4N0XH2MM20150420.

27. Zhu Lingqing, "Top 12 Chinese Firms Debuted in 2016 Fortune Global 500," ChinaDaily.com, accessed October 2, 2017, http://wap.chinadaily.com.cn/2016-07/22/content_26203491.htm.

28. Wang's Dalian Wanda Group is one of China's biggest conglomerates. Sherisse Pham, "China's Wang Jianlin Battles Talk of Trouble at Dalian Wanda," CNNMoney, accessed October 2, 2017, http://money.cnn.com/2017/07/20/investing/wanda-wang-jianlin-battles-rumors/index.html.

29. Barbara Goldberg, "Trump's Net Worth Dwindled to $3.5 Billion, Forbes Says," Reuters, March 20, 2017, accessed October 2, 2017, https://www.reuters.com/article/us-usa-trump-forbes-idUSKBN16R250.

30. Daniel J. Levitin, *The Organized Mind: Thinking Straight in the Age of Information Overload* (New York: Dutton, 2016), chap. 6.

31. Nicholas Bakalar, "No Extra Benefits Are Seen in Stents for Coronary Artery Disease," *New York Times*, February 27, 2012, accessed November 18, 2017, http://www.nytimes.com/2012/02/28/health/stents-show-no-extra-benefits-for-coronary-artery-disease.html.

32. Brian Christian, "The A/B Test: Inside the Technology That's Changing the Rules of Business," *Wired*, April 25, 2012, accessed October 15, 2017, https://www.wired.com/2012/04/ff_abtesting/.

33. Jerry Avorn, "Healing the Overwhelmed Physician," *New York Times*, June 11, 2013, http://www.nytimes.com/2013/06/12/opinion/healing-the-overwhelmed-physician.html.

34. "Watson Is Helping Doctors Fight Cancer," IBM Watson, accessed May 28, 2017, http://m.ibm.com/http/www-03.ibm.com/innovation/us/watson/watson_in_healthcare.shtml.

35. "Big Data Technology for Evidence-Based Cancer Treatment," *Experfy Insights*, August 28, 2015, accessed July 3, 2017, https://www.experfy.com/blog/big-data-technology-evidence-based-cancer-treatment.

36. David Kerr, "Learning Machines: Watson Could Bring Cancer Expertise to the Masses," *Huffington Post*, March 29, 2012, http://www.huffingtonpost.com/david-kerr/learning-machines-watson-_b_1388429.html.

37. Cerrato, "IBM Watson Finally Graduates Medical School."

38. "Memorial Sloan Kettering Cancer Center, IBM to Collaborate in Applying," Memorial Sloan Kettering, March 22, 2012, https://www.mskcc.org/press-releases/mskcc-ibm-collaborate-applying-watson-technology-help-oncologists.

39. Memorial Sloan Kettering, "Memorial Sloan-Kettering's Expertise Combined with the Power of IBM Watson Is Poised to Help Doctors," YouTube video, 2:45, January 8, 2014, https://www.youtube.com/watch?v=nNHni1Jm4p4.

40. Cerrato, "IBM Watson Finally Graduates Medical School."

41. Jon Gertner, "IBM's Watson Is Learning Its Way to Saving Lives," *Fast Company*, October 16, 2012, http://www.fastcompany.com/3001739/ibms -watson-learning-its-way-saving-lives.

42. Sy Mukherjee, "Digital Health Care Revolution," Fortune.com, April 20, 2017, http://fortune.com/2017/04/20/digital-health-revolution/.

43. Ian Steadman, "IBM's Watson Is Better at Diagnosing Cancer Than Human Doctors," *Wired UK*, May 23, 2016, http://www.wired.co.uk/article /ibm-watson-medical-doctor.

44. Jacob M. Schlesinger, "New Recruit IPO, New Era for Japan?" *Wall Street Journal*, September 11, 2014, https://blogs.wsj.com/japanrealtime/2014 /09/12/new-recruit-ipo-new-era-for-japan/.

45. Susan Carpenter, *Japan's Nuclear Crisis: The Routes to Responsibility* (Basingstoke, UK: Palgrave Macmillan, 2014), 130.

46. *Recruit's AI lab:* An earlier version of this case study has been published as "Recruit Japan: Harnessing Data to Create Value," IMD Case IMD-7-1815, 2016. Iwao Hoshii, *Japan's Pseudo-democracy* (Sandgate, UK: Japan Library, 1993), 175.

47. This network effect is sometimes referred to as Metcalfe's law, after Xerox's PARC researcher Bob Metcalfe, who posited that the value of a network is proportional to the square of the number of users.

48. Richard Teitelbaum, "Snapchat Parent's IPO Filing Omits Monthly Data," *Wall Street Journal*, February 8, 2017, https://www.wsj.com/articles /snapchat-parents-ipo-filing-omits-monthly-data-1486580926.

49. Nicholas Jackson and Alexis C. Madrigal, "The Rise and Fall of MySpace," *Atlantic*, January 12, 2011, https://www.theatlantic.com/te/archive /2011/01/the-rise-and-fall-of-myspace/69444/.

50. Stuart Dredge, "MySpace—What Went Wrong: 'The Site Was a Massive Spaghetti-Ball Mess,'" *Guardian*, March 6, 2015, https://www.theguardian.com /technology/2015/mar/06/myspace-what-went-wrong-sean-percival-spotify.

51. Amy Lee, "Myspace Collapse: How the Social Network Fell Apart," *Huffington Post*, June 30, 2011, http://www.huffingtonpost.com/2011/06/30 /how-myspace-fell-apart_n_887853.html.

52. Christopher Mims, "Did Whites Flee the 'Digital Ghetto' of MySpace?" *MIT Technology Review*, October 22, 2012, https://www.technologyreview .com/s/419843/did-whites-flee-the-digital-ghetto-of-myspace/.

53. "GE's Jeff Immelt on Digitizing in the Industrial Space," McKinsey & Company, accessed May 28, 2017, http://www.mckinsey.com/business -functions/organization/our-insights/ges-jeff-immelt-on-digitizing-in-the -industrial-space.

54. KurzweilAI, "Watson Provides Cancer Treatment Options to Doctors in Seconds," accessed May 28, 2017, http://www.kurzweilai.net/watson-provides -cancer-treatment-options-to-doctors-in-seconds.

55. Bruce Upbin, "IBM's Watson Gets Its First Piece of Business in Health-care," *Forbes*, February 15, 2013, https://www.forbes.com/sites/bruceupbin/2013/02/08/ibms-watson-gets-its-first-piece-of-business-in-healthcare/.

56. "IBM Watson Hard at Work: New Breakthroughs Transform Quality Care for Patients," Memorial Sloan Kettering, February 8, 2013, https://www.mskcc.org/press-releases/ibm-watson-hard-work-new-breakthroughs-transform-quality-care-patients.

57. Kerr, "Learning Machines."

58. David H. Freedman, "What Will It Take for IBM's Watson Technology to Stop Being a Dud in Health Care?" *MIT Technology Review*, June 27, 2017, accessed June 29, 2017, https://www.technologyreview.com/s/607965/a-reality-check-for-ibms-ai-ambitions/.

59. Christof Koch, "How the Computer Beat the Go Master," *Scientific American*, March 18, 2016, http://www.scientificamerican.com/article/how-the-computer-beat-the-go-master/.

60. Cade Metz, "In Two Moves, AlphaGo and Lee Sedol Redefined the Future," *Wired*, March 16, 2016, https://www.wired.com/2016/03/two-moves-alphago-lee-sedol-redefined-future/.

61. Measured in calculations performed per second per thousand dollars of hardware, computer performance has increased since 1960 from one ten-thousandth of a calculation per second (one every three hours) to 10 billion calculations per second. See Edward O. Wilson, *Half-Earth: Our Planet's Fight for Life* (New York: Liveright Publishing Corporation, 2017), 199.

62. Sam Byford, "Why Google's Go Win Is Such a Big Deal," *Verge*, March 9, 2016, http://www.theverge.com/2016/3/9/11185030/google-deepmind-alphago-go-artificial-intelligence-impact.

63. Metz, "In Two Moves."

64. Pui-wing Tam, "Daily Report: AlphaGo Shows How Far Artificial Intelligence Has Come," *New York Times*, May 23, 2017, https://www.nytimes.com/2017/05/23/technology/alphago-shows-how-far-artificial-intelligence-has-come.html; Cade Metz, "AlphaGo's Designers Explore New AI After Winning Big in China," *Wired*, May 27, 2017, https://www.wired.com/2017/05/win-china-alphagos-designers-explore-new-ai/.

65. David Runciman, "Diary: AI," *London Review of Books*, January 25, 2018, accessed February 9, 2018, https://www.lrb.co.uk/v40/n02/david-runciman/diary.

66. Paul Mozur, "Google's AlphaGo Defeats Chinese Go Master in Win for A.I.," *New York Times*, May 23, 2017, https://www.nytimes.com/2017/05/23/business/google-deepmind-alphago-go-champion-defeat.html.

67. "AI May Be 'More Dangerous Than Nukes,' Musk Warns," CNBC, August 4, 2014, http://www.cnbc.com/2014/08/04/ai-potentially-more-dangerous-than-nukes-musk-warns.html.

68. Greg Kumparak, "Elon Musk Compares Building Artificial Intelligence to 'Summoning the Demon,'" *TechCrunch*, October 26, 2014, https://tech crunch.com/2014/10/26/elon-musk-compares-building-artificial-intelligence -to-summoning-the-demon/.

69. Stacey Higginbotham, "Elon Musk, Reid Hoffman and Amazon Donate $1 Billion for AI Research," Fortune.com, December 12, 2015, http:// fortune.com/2015/12/11/open-ai/.

70. "Steve Wozniak: The Future of AI Is 'Scary and Very Bad for People,'" *Yahoo! Tech*, March 23, 2015, https://www.yahoo.com/tech/steve-wozniak -future-ai-scary-154700881.html.

71. Rory Cellan-Jones, "Stephen Hawking Warns Artificial Intelligence Could End Mankind," *BBC News*, December 2, 2014, http://www.bbc.com /news/technology-30290540.

72. Andrew Nusca, "This Man Is Leading an AI Revolution in Silicon Valley—and He's Just Getting Started," November 16, 2017, accessed November 26, 2017, http://fortune.com/2017/11/16/nvidia-ceo-jensen-huang/.

73. "Predix—The Premier Industrial Internet Platform," *GE Digital*, May 15, 2017, https://www.ge.com/digital/predix?utm_expid=109794401-13 .6V0rEbO8RzmRu71-IsKIUQ.0.

74. "Internet of Everything," Cisco, accessed May 28, 2017, http:// ioeassessment.cisco.com/.

75. The importance of cloud computing to the success of Airbnb has been documented excellently in Leigh Gallagher, *The Airbnb Story* (London: Virgin Books, 2017), 45.

76. Joseph Treaster, "Buffett Holds Court at Berkshire Weekend," *New York Times*, April 30, 2000, http://www.nytimes.com/2000/05/01/business /buffett-holds-court-at-berkshire-weekend.html.

77. Daniel Howley, "Warren Buffett: AI Is Good for Society but 'Enormously Disruptive,'" *Yahoo! Finance*, May 6, 2017, https://finance.yahoo.com /news/warren-buffett-ai-good-society-enormously-disruptive-203957098.html.

CHAPTER 6

1. Theodore Levitt, "Marketing Myopia," *Harvard Business Review*, March 20, 2017, https://hbr.org/2004/07/marketing-myopia.

2. "An Interview with Steve Jobs," *Nova*, October 10, 2011, http://video. pbs.org/video/2151510911/.

3. Steve Lohr, *Data-Ism: The Revolution Transforming Decision Making, Consumer Behavior, and Almost Everything Else* (New York: Harper Business, 2015), 65.

4. An earlier version of this case study has been published as "Finding Community Solutions from Common Ground: A New Business Model to End Homelessness," IMD Case IMD-3-2289, 2012. Pam Fessler, "Ending Homelessness: A Model That Just Might Work," *NPR*, March 7, 2011, http://

www.npr.org/2011/03/07/134002013/ending-homelessness-a-model-that-just-might-work.

5. Alastair Gordon, "Higher Ground," *WSJ Magazine RSS*, accessed June 6, 2017, https://web.archive.org/web/20120608011853/http://magazine.wsj.com/hunter/donate/higher-ground/.

6. Dennis Hevesi, "On the New Bowery, Down and Out Mix with Up and Coming," *New York Times*, April 13, 2002, http://www.nytimes.com/2002/04/14/realestate/on-the-new-bowery-down-and-out-mix-with-up-and-coming.html?pagewanted=3.

7. Gordon, "Higher Ground."

8. Brad Edmondson, *Ice Cream Social: The Struggle for the Soul of Ben & Jerry's* (San Francisco: Berrett-Koehler, 2014), 76–77, 136.

9. Malcolm Gladwell, "Million-Dollar Murray," *New Yorker*, June 7, 2017, http://www.newyorker.com/magazine/2006/02/13/million-dollar-murray.

10. "Linking Housing and Health Care Works for Chronically Homeless Persons," *HUD USER*, accessed June 15, 2017, https://www.huduser.gov/portal/periodicals/em/summer12/highlight3.html.

11. TEDx Talks, "How to Solve a Social Problem: Rosanne Haggerty at TEDxAmherstCollege," YouTube video, 18:31, December 19, 2013, https://www.youtube.com/watch?v=DVylRwmYmJE.

12. Fessler, "Ending Homelessness."

13. Becky Kanis, "Facing into the Truth," National Archives and Records Administration, accessed June 9, 2017, https://obamawhitehouse.archives.gov/blog/2013/03/21/facing-truth.

14. Carl Benedikt Frey and Michael A. Osborne, "The Future of Employment: How Susceptible Are Jobs to Computerisation?" *Technological Forecasting and Social Change* 114 (2017): 254–280, doi:10.1016/j.techfore.2016.08.019.

15. Edward O. Wilson, *Half-Earth: Our Planet's Fight for Life* (New York: Liveright Publishing Corporation, 2017), 199–200.

16. Gordon, "Higher Ground."

17. Brenda Ann Kenneally, "Why It's So Hard to Stop Being Homeless in New York," *Daily Intelligencer*, accessed October 8, 2017, http://nymag.com/daily/intelligencer/2017/03/nyc-homelessness-crisis.html.

18. "Turning the Tide on Homelessness in New York City," City of New York, accessed October 8, 2017, http://www1.nyc.gov/assets/dhs/downloads/pdf/turning-the-tide-on-homelessness.pdf.

19. Alana Semuels, "How to End Homelessness in New York City," *Atlantic*, January 4, 2016, accessed October 8, 2017, https://www.theatlantic.com/business/archive/2016/01/homelessness-new-york-city/422289/.

20. Ellen Lupton, *Beautiful Users: Designing for People* (New York: Princeton Architectural Press, 2014), 21.

21. Tom Kelley and David Kelley, "Kids Were Terrified of Getting MRIs. Then One Man Figured Out a Better Way," *Slate Magazine*, October 18, 2013,

http://www.slate.com/blogs/the_eye/2013/10/18/creative_confidence_a_new_book_from_ideo_s_tom_and_david_kelley.html.

22. "From Terrifying to Terrific: The Creative Journey of the Adventure Series," *GE Healthcare: The Pulse*, January 29, 2014, http://newsroom.gehealthcare.com/from-terrifying-to-terrific-creative-journey-of-the-adventure-series/.

23. An excellent recount of Doug Dietz's story can be found in an authoritative exposition of design thinking by Tom Kelley and David Kelley, *Creative Confidence Unleashing the Creative Potential Within Us All* (New York: HarperCollins, 2015). Kelley and Kelley, "Kids Were Terrified of Getting MRIs."

24. "Doug Dietz: Transforming Healthcare for Children and Their Families," PenneyLaneOnline.com, January 24, 2013, http://www.penneylaneonline.com/2013/01/22/doug-dietz-transforming-healthcare-for-children-and-their-families/.

25. "'Adventure Series' Rooms Help Distract Nervous Youngsters at Children's Hospital," May 28, 2012, *Pittsburgh Post-Gazette*, accessed June 11, 2017, http://www.post-gazette.com/news/health/2012/05/28/Adventure-Series-rooms-help-distract-nervous-youngsters-at-Children-s-Hospital/stories/201205280159.

26. "From Terrifying to Terrific," *GE Healthcare: The Pulse*.

27. "Changing Experiences Through Empathy—The Adventure Series," This Is Design Thinking! July 6, 2015, http://thisisdesignthinking.net/2014/12/changing-experiences-through-empathy-ge-healthcares-adventure-series/.

28. Kelley and Kelley, "Kids Were Terrified of Getting MRIs." If readers are interested in learning more about Doug Dietz's experience, they may see Tom and David Kelley's *Creative Confidence: Unleashing the Creative Potential Within Us All* (New York: Crown Business, 2013) and Robert I. Sutton and Huggy Rao's *Scaling Up Excellence: Getting to More Without Settling for Less* (New York: Crown Business, 2014). I depended heavily on these two excellent references to summarize Doug's personal discovery.

29. Martin Lindström, *Small Data: The Tiny Clues That Uncover Huge Trends* (New York: Picador, 2017).

30. Jeffrey Guhin, "History (and Logic) Explains Why Neil deGrasse Tyson's Proposed Rational Nation Is a Terrible Idea," *Slate Magazine*, July 5, 2016, http://www.slate.com/articles/health_and_science/science/2016/07/neil_degrasse_tyson_wants_a_nation_ruled_by_evidence_but_evidence_explains.html.

31. David Leonhardt, "Procter & Gamble Shake-Up Follows Poor Profit Outlook," *New York Times*, June 9, 2000, http://www.nytimes.com/2000/06/09/business/procter-gamble-shake-up-followspoor- profit-outlook.html.

32. Nikhil Deogun and Robert Langreth, "Procter & Gamble Abandons Talks with Warner-Lambert and AHP," *Wall Street Journal*, January 25, 2000, http://www.wsj.com/articles/SB94873352953885170.

33. "P&G Warning Hurts Dow," CNNMoney, March 7, 2000, http:// money.cnn.com/2000/03/07/companies/procter/.

34. "P&G CEO Quits amid Woes," CNNMoney, June 8, 2000, http:// money.cnn.com/2000/06/08/companies/procter/.

35. Leonhardt, "Procter & Gamble Shake-Up." *"Proctoids"*: Numerous public sources can be found that document P&G's turnaround under the leadership of CEO A. G. Lafley. Of all the available sources, I find Roger L. Martin's *The Design of Business: Why Design Thinking Is the Next Competitive Advantage* (Boston: Harvard Business Press, 2009) most illustrative. Martin's writing has been a main source of reference for this part of the case study.

36. Dana Canedy, "A Consumer Products Giant Will Most Likely Stay With What It Knows," *New York Times*, January 25, 2000, http://www. nytimes.com/2000/01/25/business/a-consumer-products-giant-will-most-likely -stay-with-what-it-knows.html.

37. Warren Berger, *CAD Monkeys, Dinosaur Babies, and T-Shaped People: Inside the World of Design Thinking and How It Can Spark Creativity and Innovation* (New York: Penguin Books, 2010), chap. 6.5.

38. Kamil Michlewski, *Design Attitude* (Farnham, UK: Ashgate, 2015).

39. Jennifer Reingold, "Claudia Kotchka Glides from the Design World to the Business World and Back with Ease. Now She Has to Teach 110,000 Employees at Procter Gamble to Do the Same Thing," *Fast Company*, June 2005 http://www.fastcompany.com/53060/interpreter.

40. Roger L. Martin, *The Design of Business: Why Design Thinking Is the Next Competitive Advantage* (Boston: Harvard Business Press, 2009), 83.

41. Ibid., 87.

42. Warren Berger, *Glimmer: How Design Can Transform Your Life, and Maybe Even the World* (New York: Penguin Press, 2009), 172.

43. Martin, *Design of Business*, 86.

44. Reingold, "Claudia Kotchka Glides."

45. Sutton and Rao, *Scaling Up Excellence*, 20.

46. Dorothy Kalins, "Going Home with the Customers," *Newsweek*, May 22, 2005, http://www.newsweek.com/going-home-customers-119233.

47. Martin, *Design of Business*.

48. Harvard Business Review, "Innovation at Procter & Gamble," YouTube video, 14:27, June 23, 2008, http://www.youtube.com/watch?v=xvIUSxXrffc.

49. Ibid.

50. Dev Patnaik, "Forget Design Thinking and Try Hybrid Thinking," *Fast Company*, August 25, 2009, http://www.fastcompany.com/1338960/forget -design-thinking-and-try-hybrid-thinking.

51. Sutton and Rao, *Scaling Up Excellence*, 5.

52. "Automation and Anxiety," *Economist*, June 25, 2016, accessed February 3, 2018, https://www.economist.com/news/special-report/21700758-will -smarter-machines-cause-mass-unemployment-automation-and-anxiety.

53. David Autor, "Polanyi's Paradox and the Shape of Employment Growth," *National Bureau of Economic Research*, 2014, doi:10.3386/w20485.

54. Mercatus Center, "Atul Gawande on Priorities, Big and Small," *Medium*, July 19, 2017, accessed October 9, 2017, https://medium.com/conversations -with-tyler/atul-gawande-checklist-books-tyler-cowen-d8268b8dfe53.

55. Andrew McAfee and Erik Brynjolfsson, *Machine Platform Crowd: Harnessing Our Digital Future* (New York: W. W. Norton & Company, 2017), 78.

56. Siddhartha Mukherjee, "A.I. Versus M.D.," *New Yorker*, June 19, 2017, accessed October 9, 2017, https://www.newyorker.com/magazine/2017/04/03 /ai-versus-md.

57. Clayton M. Christensen and Michael E. Raynor, *The Innovator's Solution: Creating and Sustaining Successful Growth* (Boston: Harvard Business Review Press, 2013), 58.

58. "Weekly Adviser: Horror at Credit Scoring Is Not Just Foot-Dragging," *American Banker*, November 2, 1999, accessed October 15, 2017, https:// www.americanbanker.com/news/weekly-adviser-horror-at-credit-scoring -is-not-just-foot-dragging.

59. Norm Augustine, "The Education Our Economy Needs," *Wall Street Journal*, September 21, 2011, https://www.wsj.com/articles/SB1000142405 3111904265504576568351324914730?mg=prod   percent2Faccounts-wsj #articleTabs percent3Darticle.

60. William Taylor, *Simply Brilliant: How Great Organizations Do Ordinary Things in Extraordinary Ways* (London: Portfolio Penguin, 2016), 83.

61. Christian Madsbjerg, *Sensemaking: The Power of the Humanities in the Age of the Algorithm* (New York: Hachette Books, 2017); Cathy O'Neill, *Weapons of Math Destruction: How Big Data Increases in Equality and Threatens Democracy* (Great Britain: Penguin Books, 2017), Afterword.

62. Ethem Alpaydin, *Machine Learning: The New AI* (Cambridge, MA: MIT Press, 2016), 58, 162.

63. Larry Greenemeier, "20 Years After Deep Blue: How AI Has Advanced Since Conquering Chess," *Scientific American*, accessed October 9, 2017, https://www.scientificamerican.com/article/20-years-after-deep-blue-how-ai -has-advanced-since-conquering-chess/.

64. "Just like Airbnb," *Economist* January 6, 2015, accessed February 3, 2018, http://www.economist.com/blogs/democracyinamerica/2015/01/data -and-homelessness.

65. James Bessen, "The Automation Paradox," *Atlantic*, January 19, 2016, accessed July 15, 2017, https://www.theatlantic.com/business/archive/2016 /01/automation-paradox/424437/.

66. James Bessen, "Scarce Skills, Not Scarce Jobs," *Atlantic*, April 27, 2015, accessed July 15, 2017, https://www.theatlantic.com/business/archive /2015/04/scarce-skills-not-scarce-jobs/390789/.

67. Christopher Mims, "Automation Can Actually Create More Jobs," *Wall Street Journal*, December 11, 2016, accessed November 19, 2017, https://www.wsj.com/articles/automation-can-actually-create-more-jobs-1481480200.

68. Vanessa Fuhrmans, "How the Robot Revolution Could Create 21 Million Jobs," *Wall Street Journal*, November 15, 2017, accessed November 19, 2017, https://www.wsj.com/articles/how-the-robot-revolution-could-create-21-million-jobs-1510758001; Mims, "Without Humans."

69. A. G. Lafley, "A Liberal Education: Preparation for Career Success," *Huffington Post*, December 6, 2011, http://www.huffingtonpost.com/ag-lafley/a-liberal-education-prepa_b_1132511.html.

CHAPTER 7

1. Elizabeth Woyke, "Environmental Balance," *Forbes*, September 13, 2011, http://www.forbes.com/global/2011/0926/feature-environmental-balance-shih-revamp-taiwan-farms-woyke.html.

2. Michael V. Copeland, "The Man Behind the Netbook Craze," *Fortune*, November 20, 2009, http://fortune.com/2009/11/20/the-man-behind-the-netbook-craze/.

3. Andrew S. Grove, *Only the Paranoid Survive* (New York: Doubleday, 1999); Willy C. Shih, Ho Howard Yu, and Hung-Chang Chiu, "Transforming ASUSTeK: Breaking from the Past," Harvard Business School Case 610-041, January 2010 (revised March 2010).

4. *Many Taiwanese companies:* An earlier version of this case study has been published as two case studies: Willy C. Shih, Ho Howard Yu, and Hung-Chang Chiu, "Transforming ASUSTeK: Breaking from the Past." Harvard Business School Case 610-041, January 2010 (Rev. March 2010) and Willy C. Shih, Chintay Shih, Hung-Chang Chiu, Yi-Ching Hsieh, and Ho Howard Yu, "ASUSTeK Computer Inc. Eee PC (A)." Harvard Business School Case 609-011, July 2008 (Rev September 2009). It was Professor Willy Shih at Harvard Business School who spurred me to investigate the Taiwanese PC industry. The findings were published as "Taiwan's PC Industry, 1976-2010: The Evolution of Organizational Capabilities," by Howard H. Yu and Willy C. Shih, *Business History Review*, Vol. 88, Issue 02, June 2014, pp. 329–357. Richard Lai, "The Past, Present and Future of ASUS, According to Its Chairman," Engadget, July 14, 2016, accessed February 3, 2018, https://www.engadget.com/2015/08/16/asus-chairman-jonney-shih-interview/.

5. Keith Bradsher, "In Taiwan, Lamenting a Lost Lead," *New York Times*, May 12, 2013, http://www.nytimes.com/2013/05/13/business/global/taiwan-tries-to-regain-its-lead-in-consumer-electronics.html.

6. Jeffrey S. Young and William L. Simon, *iCon: Steve Jobs, the Greatest Second Act in the History of Business* (Hoboken, NJ: Wiley, 2006).

7. Leander Kahney, "Inside Look at Birth of the iPod," *Wired*, July 21, 2004, https://www.wired.com/2004/07/inside-look-at-birth-of-the-ipod/.

8. Leander Kahney, *Inside Steve's Brain* (London: Atlantic Books, 2012); Steven Levy, *The Perfect Thing* (London: Ebury, 2007).

9. Department of Trade and Industry, "Strategy Alternatives for the British Motorcycle Industry," gov.uk, accessed July 10, 2017, https://www.gov.uk/government/publications/strategy-alternatives-for-the-british-motorcycle-industry.

10. American Honda 50th Anniversary Timeline, accessed July 8, 2017, http://hondanews.com/releases/american-honda-50th-anniversary-timeline?l=en-US&mode=print.

11. "Establishing American Honda Motor Co. / 1959," Honda Worldwide, accessed July 8, 2017, http://world.honda.com/history/challenge/1959 establishingamericanhonda/page03.html.

12. Adam Richardson, "Lessons from Honda's Early Adaptive Strategy," *Harvard Business Review*, July 23, 2014, https://hbr.org/2011/02/lessons-from-hondas-early-adap.

13. Richard T. Pascale, *Perspectives on Strategy* (Palo Alto, CA: Graduate School of Business, Stanford University, 1982), 55.

14. Clayton M. Christensen, *The Innovator's Dilemma: When New Technologies Cause Great Firms to Fail* (Boston: Harvard Business Review Press, 2016), 150–153.

15. Richardson, "Lessons from Honda's Early Adaptive Strategy."

16. Henry Mintzberg and James A. Waters, "Of Strategies, Deliberate and Emergent," *Strategic Management Journal* 6, no. 3 (1985): 257–272, doi:10.1002/smj.4250060306.

17. Edwin Catmull and Amy Wallace, *Creativity, Inc. Overcoming the Unseen Forces That Stand in the Way of True Inspiration* (New York: Random House, 2015).

18. Amar Bhide, "Bootstrap Finance: The Art of Start-ups," *Harvard Business Review*, August 22, 2014, https://hbr.org/1992/11/bootstrap-finance-the-art-of-start-ups.

19. Justin D. Martin, "How to Predict Whether a New Media Venture Will Fail," *Quartz*, December 10, 2012, https://qz.com/35481/how-to-predict-whether-a-new-media-venture-will-fail/.

20. "The Lean Startup," The Lean Startup: The Movement That Is Transforming How New Products Are Built and Launched, accessed July 9, 2017, http://theleanstartup.com/.

21. J. L. Bower and C. G. Gilbert, eds., *From Resource Allocation to Strategy* (Oxford, New York: Oxford University Press, 2005).

22. R. A. Burgelman, "Intraorganizational Ecology of Strategy Making and Organizational Adaptation: Theory and Filed Research," *Organization Science* 2, no. 3 (1991): 239–262.

23. T. Noda and J. L. Bower, "Strategy Making as Iterated Processes of Resource Allocation," *Strategic Management Journal* 17, no. 7 (1996): 159–192.

24. C. G. Gilbert, "Unbundling the Structure of Inertia: Resource Versus Routine Rigidity," *Academy of Management Journal* 48, no. 5 (2005): 741–763.

25. Christensen, *Innovator's Dilemma*.

26. Fortune Editors, "Is Google Suffering from Microsoft Syndrome?" Fortune.com, July 31, 2014, http://fortune.com/2011/08/04/is-google-suffering-from-microsoft-syndrome/.

27. Jessica E. Lessin, "Apple Gives In to Employee Perks," *Wall Street Journal*, November 12, 2012, https://www.wsj.com/articles/SB10001424127887324073504578115071154910456.

28. Steven Levy, "Google's Larry Page on Why Moon Shots Matter," *Wired*, January 17, 2013, accessed October 16, 2017, https://www.wired.com/2013/01/ff-qa-larry-page/.

29. "Google Inc. (NASDAQ:GOOG), 3M Company (NYSE:MMM)—Google: An Ecosystem of Entrepreneurs," Benzinga, accessed October 16, 2017, https://www.benzinga.com/general/10/09/498671/google-an-ecosystem-of-entrepreneurs.

30. Lara O'Reilly, "The 30 Biggest Media Companies in the World," *Business Insider*, May 31, 2016, http://www.businessinsider.com/the-30-biggest-media-owners-in-the-world-2016-5/#20-hearst-corporation-4-billion-in-media-revenue-11.

31. Eric Rosenberg, "The Business of Google (GOOG)," *Investopedia*, August 5, 2016, http://www.investopedia.com/articles/investing/020515/business-google.asp.

32. Zach Epstein, "Google Bought Motorola for $12.5B, Sold It for $2.9B, and Called the Deal 'a Success,'" *BGR*, February 13, 2014, http://bgr.com/2014/02/13/google-motorola-sale-interview-lenovo/.

33. Charlie Sorrel, "Google to Stop Selling Nexus One," *Wired*, June 4, 2017, https://www.wired.com/2010/07/google-to-stop-selling-nexus-one/.

34. Klint Finley, "Google Fiber Sheds Workers as It Looks to a Wireless Future," *Wired*, June 3, 2017, accessed October 16, 2017, https://www.wired.com/2017/02/google-fiber-restructure/.

35. Andrew Cave, "Why Google Glass Flopped," *Forbes*, February 15, 2015, https://www.forbes.com/sites/andrewcave/2015/01/20/a-failure-of-leadership-or-design-why-google-glass-flopped/.

36. Doug Gross, "Google: Self-Driving Cars Are Mastering City Streets," CNN, April 28, 2014, http://www.cnn.com/2014/04/28/tech/innovation/google-self-driving-car/; Max Chafkin, "Uber's First Self-Driving Fleet Arrives in Pittsburgh This Month," Bloomberg.com, August 18, 2016, https://www.bloomberg.com/news/features/2016-08-18/uber-s-first-self-driving-fleet-arrives-in-pittsburgh-this-month-is06r7on; Neal E. Boudette, "Tesla Upgrades Autopilot in Cars on the Road," *New York Times*, September 23, 2016, https://www.nytimes.com/2016/09/24/business/tesla-upgrades-autopilot-in-cars-on-the-road.html.

37. Eugene Kim, "Jeff Bezos Says Amazon Is Not Afraid to Fail—These 9 Failures Show He's Not Kidding," *Business Insider*, October 21, 2015, http://www.businessinsider.com/amazons-biggest-flops-2015-10/#in-2012-amazon-shut-down-endlesscom-a-high-end-fashion-commerce-site-and-moved-it-under-amazoncomfashion-it-still-owns-other-non-amazon-branded-fashion-sites-like-zappos-and-shopbop-7.

38. Issie Lapowsky, "Jeff Bezos Defends the Fire Phone's Flop and Amazon's Dismal Earnings," *Wired*, June 2, 2017, https://www.wired.com/2014/12/jeff-bezos-ignition-conference/.

39. Austin Carr, "The Real Story Behind Jeff Bezos's Fire Phone Debacle and What It Means for Amazon's Future," *Fast Company*, July 8, 2017, https://www.fastcompany.com/3039887/under-fire.

40. Joshua Brustein and Spencer Soper, "The Real Story of How Amazon Built the Echo," Bloomberg.com, April 18, 2016, https://www.bloomberg.com/features/2016-amazon-echo/.

41. James F. Peltz and Makeda Easter, "Amazon Shakes up the Grocery Business with Its $13.7-Billion Deal to Buy Whole Foods," *Los Angeles Times*, June 16, 2017, http://www.latimes.com/business/la-fi-amazon-whole-foods-20170616-story.html.

42. Tim Higgins and Nathan Olivarez-Giles, "Google Details New Pixel Smartphones, Amazon Echo Rival," *Wall Street Journal*, October 5, 2016, https://www.wsj.com/articles/google-to-detail-amazon-echo-fighter-called-home-new-phones-1475592365.

43. Sarah Perez, "Amazon's Alexa Passes 15,000 Skills, up from 10,000 in February," *TechCrunch*, July 3, 2017, https://techcrunch.com/2017/07/03/amazons-alexa-passes-15000-skills-up-from-10000-in-february/.

44. Mike Sullivan and Eugene Kim, "What Apple's HomePod Is Up Against," *Information*, June 20, 2017, https://www.theinformation.com/what-apples-homepod-is-up-against.

45. Brian X. Chen, "Google Home vs. Amazon Echo. Let the Battle Begin," *New York Times*, May 18, 2016, https://www.nytimes.com/2016/05/19/technology/personaltech/google-home-a-smart-speaker-with-a-search-giant-for-a-brain.html?_r=0.

46. Richard H. Thaler, *Misbehaving: The Making of Behavioral Economics* (New York: W. W. Norton, 2016).

47. The concept of a "deep dive" was first published as a working paper while I was a doctoral student at Harvard Business School. Yu, Howard H., and Joseph L. Bower. "Taking a 'Deep Dive: What Only a Top Leader Can Do." Harvard Business School Working Paper, No. 09-109, April 2009 (Rev. February 2010, May 2010.) The study then won the Best Paper Award in the Israel Strategy Conference 2010. See Yu, Howard H., "Leopards Sometimes Change Their Spots: How Firms Manage a Shift between Strategic Archetypes" (September 9, 2010). Israel Strategy Conference, 2010. Available at

SSRN: https://ssrn.com/abstract=1733430. I owe much of this discovery to my dissertation committee chair Joseph Bower.

EPILOGUE

1. Kim Gittleson, "Can a Company Live Forever?" *BBC News*, January 19, 2012, http://www.bbc.com/news/business-16611040.

2. Neil Dahlstrom and Jeremy Dahlstrom, *The John Deere Story: A Biography of Plowmakers John & Charles Deere* (DeKalb: Northern Illinois University Press, 2007), 12–14.

3. Margaret Hall, *John Deere* (Chicago: Heinemann Library, 2004), 30.

4. David Magee, *The John Deere Way: Performance That Endures* (Hoboken, NJ: John Wiley, 2005), 6.

5. Randy Leffingwell, *Classic Farm Tractors: History of the Farm Tractor* (New York: Crestline, 2010), 82.

6. Magee, *The John Deere Way*, 57.

7. Ronald K. Leonard and Richard Teal, *John Deere Snowmobiles: Development, Production, Competition and Evolution, 1971–1983* (Jefferson, NC: McFarland & Company, 2014), 15.

8. Andrea Peterson, "Google Didn't Lead the Self-Driving Vehicle Revolution. John Deere Did," *Washington Post*, June 22, 2015, https://www.washingtonpost.com/news/the-switch/wp/2015/06/22/google-didnt-lead-the-self-driving-vehicle-revolution-john-deere-did/?utm_term=.402c93254201.

9. Pietra Rivoli, *The Travels of a T-Shirt in the Global Economy* (Hoboken, NJ: Wiley, 2009), 41.

10. USDA ERS, "Glossary," accessed July 14, 2017, https://www.ers.usda.gov/topics/farm-economy/farm-household-well-being/glossary.aspx#familyfarm.

11. Michael E. Porter and James E. Heppelmann, "How Smart, Connected Products Are Transforming Competition," *Harvard Business Review*, March 17, 2017, https://hbr.org/2014/11/how-smart-connected-products-are-transforming-competition.

12. Andrew McAfee and Erik Brynjolfsson, *Machine Platform Crowd: Harnessing Our Digital Future* (New York: W. W. Norton, 2017), 204.

13. "Why Fintech Won't Kill Banks," *Economist*, June 16, 2015, accessed October 20, 2017, https://www.economist.com/blogs/economist-explains/2015/06/economist-explains-12.

14. DuPont Pioneer and John Deere, "DuPont Pioneer and John Deere Help Growers to See More Green," Pioneer Hi-Bred News Releases, May 24, 2016, https://www.pioneer.com/home/site/about/news-media/news-releases/template.CONTENT/guid.0642711A-FCCC-A4F0-21A6-AF150D49ED01.

15. Ina Fried, "John Deere Quietly Opens Tech Office in San Francisco," *Axios*, June 26, 2017, https://www.axios.com/john-deere-quietly-opens-a-lab-in-san-francisco-2448240040.html.

INDEX

HOWARD YU is the LEGO professor of management and innovation in the prestigious IMD business school in Switzerland as well as the director of its signature program, the three-week Advanced Management Program (AMP), an executive education course. In 2015, Yu was selected by Poets&Quants as one of "The World's Top 40 Business Professors Under 40," and in 2018 he appeared on the Thinkers50 Radar list of thirty management thinkers "most likely to shape the future of how organizations are managed and led." He has delivered customized training programs for leading organizations including Mars, Maersk, Daimler, and Electrolux. His articles have appeared in *Forbes, Forture, Harvard Business Review, The Financial Times,* and *The New York Times.* Yu received his doctoral degree from Harvard Business School. Prior to his beginning his doctorate, he worked in the banking industry in Hong Kong.

PublicAffairs is a publishing house founded in 1997. It is a tribute to the standards, values, and flair of three persons who have served as mentors to countless reporters, writers, editors, and book people of all kinds, including me.

I. F. STONE, proprietor of *I. F. Stone's Weekly*, combined a commitment to the First Amendment with entrepreneurial zeal and reporting skill and became one of the great independent journalists in American history. At the age of eighty, Izzy published *The Trial of Socrates*, which was a national bestseller. He wrote the book after he taught himself ancient Greek.

BENJAMIN C. BRADLEE was for nearly thirty years the charismatic editorial leader of *The Washington Post*. It was Ben who gave the *Post* the range and courage to pursue such historic issues as Watergate. He supported his reporters with a tenacity that made them fearless and it is no accident that so many became authors of influential, best-selling books.

ROBERT L. BERNSTEIN, the chief executive of Random House for more than a quarter century, guided one of the nation's premier publishing houses. Bob was personally responsible for many books of political dissent and argument that challenged tyranny around the globe. He is also the founder and longtime chair of Human Rights Watch, one of the most respected human rights organizations in the world.

·   ·   ·

For fifty years, the banner of Public Affairs Press was carried by its owner Morris B. Schnapper, who published Gandhi, Nasser, Toynbee, Truman, and about 1,500 other authors. In 1983, Schnapper was described by *The Washington Post* as "a redoubtable gadfly." His legacy will endure in the books to come.

Peter Osnos, *Founder*